The Many Lives of Syeda X

Praise for the Book

'A trenchant and invaluable people's history of the bottom of the pyramid in the world's most populous nation' – ***Financial Times***

'In the climate currently pervading India under Modi's decade-long rule, Dixit's book is a brave and damning indictment of Hindutva fascism that shines a crucial spotlight on the ordinary lives that continue to suffer its horrifying impact. It is also an unapologetically feminist celebration of their daily existence' – ***Jacobin***

'One might imagine that it doesn't get harder than being poor and uneducated, a Muslim and a woman in today's India. This unique biography of a brave and tenacious woman worker in the unorganized sector shows how the state, through its fitful acts of heavy-handed regulation, makes it much worse. She tries many things and masters them, but just when it looks like her economic life has turned a corner, the state steps in to fix some problem that it should not have permitted to arise in the first place, and her job and hope are gone. An important and eye-opening work' – ***Abhijit V. Banerjee***

'This remarkable book blends fine-grained reportage with moving evocations of time and place. Through the struggles of a single family Neha Dixit deftly traces the tumultuous and conflict-ridden history of our country over the past three decades. The focus always remains on Syeda, her husband and her children, yet through their lives we come to acquire a deeper understanding of religious majoritarianism, the darker side of India's much trumpeted 'growth story', and the corruption and criminalization of the state. This is a deeply impressive debut by a gifted and extremely courageous writer' – ***Ramachandra Guha***

'This is the heart-wrenching reality of modern India, the unvarnished truth through the eyes of a melancholic woman and the people around her. They are the nameless poor whose monotonous existence is both a blessing and an irritant for us. Syeda's life is a mirror held to us. She is Mother India, wailing for a healing touch and some compassion. Neha Dixit has found an unusual protagonist to tell us the unvarnished, ugly truth about us' – *Josy Joseph*

'Neha Dixit is a resolute, courageous and empathetic writer. In this powerful and bracing book, she puts the spotlight on one ordinary Indian. In a spare but effective, matter-of-fact style that lets the story speak for itself, she rescues the lives of ordinary Indians from invisibility. But she also rescues them from time-worn tropes of condescension, pity and resilience, and restores dignity to their agency. The story of this life, grappling with the weight of fate and society will leave you defenceless and gutted' – *Pratap Bhanu Mehta*

'Neha Dixit is a fiercely ethical and committed journalist and a writer of integrity and passion. She brings all these qualities to this searing story about an anonymous woman whose life over three decades she has traced, through cataclysmic events in the history of India that is also the history of this working-class Muslim woman's life' – *Nivedita Menon*

The Many Lives of Syeda X

A People's History of Invisible India

Neha Dixit

First published in the UK in 2025 by
Footnote Press
An imprint of Bonnier Books UK
5th Floor, HYLO, 105 Bunhill Row,
London, EC1Y 8LZ

www.footnotepress.com

First published in India in 2024 by Juggernaut Books

First printing
1 3 5 7 9 10 8 6 4 2

Copyright © 2025 Neha Dixit

The right of Neha Dixit to be identified as the author of this work has been asserted in accordance with the Copyright, Designs and Patents Act 1998.

All rights reserved. No part of this publication may be reproduced, stored in a retrieval system, or transmitted in any form or by any means without the written permission of the publisher, nor be otherwise circulated in any form of binding or cover other than that in which it is published and without a similar condition being imposed on the subsequent purchaser.

A CIP catalogue record for this book is available from the British Library.

ISBN (hardback): 9781804442272
ISBN (ebook): 9781804442289

Printed and bound in Great Britain
by Clays Ltd, Elcograf S.p.A.

The authorised representative in the EEA is
Bonnier Books UK (Ireland) Limited.
Registered office address: Floor 3, Block 3, Miesian Plaza,
Dublin 2, D02 Y754, Ireland
compliance@bonnierbooks.ie

For my father, Alok Dixit, who I miss. My tasalli, *my solace. Who proudly carried my business card instead of his own, even when he disagreed with my choice of work.*

For the women who left home.

For those in jail for protecting our freedom.

Contents

Introduction ix

1. Zari 1
2. Raisin 40
3. Gajak 66
4. Doorknob 95
5. Almond 135
6. Soft Toy 172
7. Incense Stick 205
8. Tricolour 230
9. Wedding Card 257

Author's Note 297
Acknowledgements 301
Index 304

Introduction

Twelve years ago, I started working as an independent journalist. Prior to that I had been working at a media house, a significant stake of which was bought by a big corporation. The editorial team of the media house was briefed soon after. The executive editor told us that from then on our target viewership would be the 'urban rich'. The prototype of that 'urban rich' viewer was a thirty-five-year-old male techie in Bengaluru. The programming of the content, the headlines, the bulletin, the graphics, everything, would be according to his preferences. When he would come home from work, we were told, he should want to watch this TV news channel. So, we had to stop doing 'back-of-beyond', and 'bleeding-heart' stories about farmer suicides, human trafficking or clinical trials on the poor. Instead, investigative journalists like me would have to do groundbreaking exposes on, for instance, rich kids racing fast cars in south Delhi.

After this forty-minute briefing, I asked a question, 'Is there a she?' Because the executive editor had gone on about how 'he should like this', 'he should not switch the channel', 'he does not want to see this'. To this, the editor declared, in front of all the editorial staff, that 'scientific research suggests women do not watch television news. So there is no she.' To this a producer replied, 'But we have so many women anchors'. The editor responded, 'They are also for the liking of the male techie.'

I had zero skills or interest in reporting on the rich. Soon after I quit that job.

Within a few months of that career move, the anti-rape movement in December 2012, which started in Delhi and spread all across the country after the brutal gang rape of a young woman, forced a changing of gears on the general perception of gender-based violence. The public protests not only brought significant changes in the laws on sexual violence in 2013, but a new law on sexual harassment of women in the workplace was also passed the same year. Most importantly, though, newsrooms could no longer dismiss a story on sexual violence.

In the following years, I reported extensively on sexual violence in rural and urban areas, organized and unorganized sectors, during periods of communal violence and within domestic spaces. While patriarchy was the obvious reason, the questions that persisted for me were also about the class, caste, religion and geographical locations of these women.

I met a Dalit woman who had been sentenced to imprisonment for perjury because she withdrew her testimony against her dominant-caste rapists. In the Hindu caste order, Dalit community falls at the bottom and has been subjected to centuries of socio-economic marginalisation and the practice of untouchability. She had to do that because the dominant caste held a council that decided none of the Dalit people in the village would be employed in their farms until she withdrew the case.

I met Muslim women from the Shamli–Muzaffarnagar area who were farm labourers and had been raped by farm owners during the riots that took place there in 2013. Some of these women had to return to the very same farms later for employment.

I also met Dalit women who had been raped when they had gone out in the morning to relieve themselves in the fields near their homes. The entire world reported that Indian women were raped because they have no toilets, but I found out that they were raped because the Dalit community had asked for their share of public land from the dominant caste.

I met a tribal woman who could not get an abortion after she was raped because she could not afford to take leave from the mining quarry she worked at. Later, she struggled to raise the child.

I met a woman who had been raped by her father and brother repeatedly for nine years but managed to report it only when she found a job at a call centre, and with it some measure of financial independence.

By now mainstream newsrooms had started competing on who broke a rape story first, but the debate did not transcend a narrow focus on policing and laws for the protection and safety of women.

The women I had reported about were not just victims or survivors. They were people who were battling sexual violence, but at the same time dealing with questions of poverty, displacement, unemployment, lack of basic amenities, migration, casteism, sectarianism and globalization.

Since 2014, when Bhartiya Janata Party (BJP), a Hindu supremacist political party that believes in the political ideology of Hindutva, came to power, another kind of flattening and erasure of women has been under way. Like all dogma, Hindutva, political Hinduism, also views women only as mothers, sisters, wives and daughters. It has a low opinion of women and underestimates their intelligence.

Demand all the toilets, cooking gas and education you want, but if you are a Hindu woman who has chosen a life partner who is Muslim, you have unwittingly been lured into an Islamist conspiracy by men in fancy denims and sunglasses, with seductive bikes and phones because women are not considered capable of making choices for themselves. If you are a Muslim woman, you are part of a conspiracy to produce countless children to target the Hindu majority. If you are a Dalit or Adivasi woman, you only belong to the margins.

My book was born out of a lack of an intersectional gender lens in the mainstream media. To put it simply, I wanted to report on women as legitimate and equal citizens of the world, who have the same concerns as any other human being. Sexual violence may be part of their story but it is not the whole story. It is an extra 'thing' they have to handle but it is not the only thing. I wanted to tell the full story.

❧

Delhi, the national capital, has forever been explored through the eyes of its rulers – either via the charms of the Mughals or the power corridors of New Delhi – but hardly through the eyes of the roughly 35,000 poor migrants who come to the city every day, never to return.

It is not only an administrative city but also one of the largest wholesale centres in northern India and one of the single biggest centres for small-scale industries in the country. Migrant women keep these industries functional.

I wanted to report on these women and all the things they deal with in life – along with the sexual violence, which is ubiquitous.

By the end of 2014, I started meeting working-class women in Delhi to find out what their average day was like. Through the help of the Bigul Mazdoor Dasta, an organization that focuses on workers' rights, I met some women who were part of an almond workers' strike in 2009 in north east Delhi. The strike stood out to me.

It was one of the biggest and longest strikes by unorganized workers in Delhi where women refused to carry on the work of shelling and cleaning almonds until they were promised better pay, among other things. The strike brought the international almond processing supply chain to a halt, increasing almond rates globally by almost 40 per cent.

Unlike a conventional trade union where mobilization happens in the same workplace, these women did not have fixed wages or fixed workplaces and yet managed to unionize.

But many of them would not even admit – or recognize – that they worked. 'This is just to buy daily milk and groceries.' This was a standard response because women, who are so used to doing unpaid work, would not consider themselves as workers. They were home-based workers, who were indirectly employed, sometimes by some of the largest companies in the world. They were paid piece-based, not time-based, wages. For example, the almond workers were paid Rs 50 for cleaning a 23 kilo bag for twelve to sixteen hours.

Almost 82 per cent of working women in India are concentrated in the informal sector. After agricultural work, home-based work is the single largest working sector for women. Yet they are not considered workers by the state or the conventional male-dominated trade unions. They are not allowed to admit they worked because of family honour. 'Women from "good families" do not work,' is the refrain. Most importantly, the money they make is so abysmal that despite working twelve to sixteen hours every day, according to estimates, their monthly income is one-fifth of the legal minimum wage in Delhi. It just didn't make sense for them to call themselves 'workers'. This in spite of the fact that many of the women I met were the primary breadwinners of their families.

One such woman I met was Syeda X. This book is her story. What emerges is a picture of a life lived under constant corrosive tension, similar to the lives of many faceless Indian women. She moved to Delhi from Banaras in 1995 with her husband and three children in the aftermath of riots triggered by the demolition of the Babri mosque in north India. In Delhi, she moved from Chandni Chowk to Sabhapur to Karawal Nagar. She settled into the life of a poor migrant, juggling multiple jobs a day – from trimming the loose threads of jeans to cooking savouries, and from shelling almonds to making tea strainers, doorknobs, pressure cookers and photo frames, among many other things. Various Supreme Court orders on polluting industries forced her, from time to time, to move further and further away from the centre, to the margins of the city. She has had over fifty jobs in almost thirty years, earning paltry wages in the process. And if she ever took time off, to nurse an illness or to attend to her children, her job would be lost to another faceless migrant fighting to take her place.

In these years, she encountered various people: from a rickshaw driver who ends up tragically dead in a terrorist blast to a slumlord who grew 'too big for his boots' and is shot by rival landlords. From a doctor who gets arrested for pre-natal sex determination to *gau rakshak*s, vigilantes who ostensibly guard against cow slaughter. From corrupt policemen who delight in beating young Muslim men to a cheerful band of home-based women workers who look out for each other. The aspirations of her young children, and the existential crisis of her husband, a skilled weaver who is forced to do menial jobs as a migrant worker and keeps failing to meet the standards of masculinity, underscore her struggles.

In the end, things come to a grotesque full circle for Syeda. Her life is upturned for the umpteenth time as the Delhi riots of 2020 cause another cataclysmic displacement. But displacement, tragedy and hardship are things she is used to – being poor and Muslim and a woman.

❧

It is tempting to see Syeda first and foremost as a Muslim. But she set the record straight: 'I don't get up daily to think about how to defeat the Hindu supremacists. I think about how my family and I will survive this day.'

Many middle-class urban Indians may not know what the life of an ordinary working-class Indian looks and feels like. Officially, there has been no update in the poverty estimates in India since 2011. India has the highest number of poor children in the world. One-quarter of the world's undernourished live in India.

Inequality is at a historic high, worse than in the colonial era. The top 1 per cent owns 40.1 per cent of India's wealth compared to the 6.4 per cent owned by the bottom 50 per cent.

While looking at the last thirty years of India through Syeda's eyes and life, some incessant thoughts have stayed with me.

The most important and sometimes the only asset the poor have is their body. When there are no permanent jobs and rising inflation, what do the poor eat? When I started work on the book, many ate potato curry day in and day out. In the last nine years, I have seen many switch to boiled potatoes and salt because they could no longer afford edible oil. Occasionally a few drops of oil are added to the children's meals. And when there is no functional, affordable public healthcare, can their bodies survive on this meal and then deal with a pandemic like COVID-19?

The poor are often blamed for India's rising population because that supposedly leads to a resource crunch. But the state of basic resources like land, water, food, public spaces, and civic amenities like sanitation available to them are abysmal compared to those available to the rich. The poor consume subhuman quantities of our resources while the per capita consumption by the Indian rich would rival those in the first world countries.

In this backdrop, retelling Syeda's story is futile if restricted only to violent, sectarian, Hindu-versus-Muslim events. Nor can it be summed up through the economic story alone: numbers, wages, public goods and so forth. Stories like hers, a blend of themes of gender, communal bigotry and poverty cannot be told in parts.

If the conversation on pluralism does not marry caste, class and gender intersections, it will only remain the discourse of the elite.

Syeda's story may not be neat, but it tells us how the most vulnerable have negotiated with global markets and the rising socio-economic strife in the country in the last thirty years. In their individual capacity, they try to triumph but there is no systemic support or political will to make their life better.

It shows the macro changes in India through a microlens. Syeda's life is a portal to a harsh, often brutal, world hidden away from elite Indians. It is the story of untold millions and an account of urban life in New India.

1
Zari

The year India got independence, most Banarasi saree weavers made at least one tricolour saree.

Rashid was seven years old.

One day, his father, Mohd Kasbe, whom everyone called Abbaji, was readying a saree for the idol for Durga Puja, the annual Hindu festival celebrating the Hindu goddess Durga.

It had the three colours of the new flag of independent India.

'We are Muslims. Why are we weaving a saree for a Hindu goddess?' Rashid asked Abbaji.

'A saree is not Hindu or Muslim,' Abbaji told Rashid. 'It is a Banaras tradition for Muslim weavers to prepare a saree for the annual Hindu celebration.'

'Is Banaras a Hindu city?' Rashid asked Abbaji.

Abbaji replied, 'Only since the Angrez started calling it that. Banaras is a *masaaldan*, a spice box.'

Angrez. The British.

'It is hard for those who have only seen one skin colour, one religion, one climate, to understand how many spices coexist in a dish, each enhancing the flavour in their own way,' Abbaji said.

Banaras, some say, is the oldest city in the world. It has several complex identities. Banaras is the old name for Varanasi district in the north Indian state of Uttar Pradesh (UP).

Abbaji told Rashid that Banaras was the city of Hindus who believed you could attain salvation by dying there. It was also that of Muslims who formed a quarter of the city's population. It belonged to

Sufi saints like Kabir, who had been a weaver himself and advocated syncretism, and Sant Ravidas, who challenged the oppressive Hindu caste order. It belonged to Sikhs, whose holy book, the Guru Granth Sahib, includes the teachings of both Kabir and Ravidas – collected by Guru Nanak, their first guru, who visited the city in 1506. It belonged to Buddhists because the Buddha delivered his first sermon here after gaining enlightenment, to Jains because Sant Parshvanath, one of their prominent saints, was born and taught here. It belonged to everyone.

The British only understood binary identities. And so it was easier to project Banaras as a place contested between Hindus and Muslims, where Hindus won.

The proportion of Muslims in Banaras's population is high compared to the national average. Most of them are weavers. The Banarasi weaving community comprises Momin Ansaris, a working-class artisanal community of Muslim weavers who were earlier called 'Julahas' in a derogatory way, and a few lower-caste Hindus; the main textile traders are Hindu upper-caste Banias.

Like most Banarasi weavers, Abbaji believed that Hindu–Muslim relations mirror the intricately woven Banarasi saree.

Tana–bana.

Warp and weft.

Time and space.

⁂

Weaving in Bararas largely runs on family labour; everyone has to pitch in.

After turning ten, boys would sit on the loom, a male prerogative in the weaving community. Girls continued to do preparatory work, designated for women.

By his teenage years, Rashid had not displayed any promise in weaving. He would often escape to listen to Bismillah Khan, on the pretext of helping Kamlesh Chacha, their neighbour, who created and sold garments for Hindu deities in the Balaji temple premises.

Ustad Bismillah Khan, a shehnai player, would often play at the aarti there, when light is offered with songs to Hindu gods. The shehnai is a reeded wooden wind instrument.

Bismillah Khan was known to have brought it to the world stage.

Though a Muslim, Bismillah Khan grew up practising the shehnai in this temple. He is considered the true embodiment of Banarasipan, the composite culture of Banaras.

Rashid's love for music germinated here and later flowered at the annual Banaras fairs. The fairs were held around the time of major festivals and brought in a large number of visitors, traders and performers from across the country.

That's where Rashid acquired *nautanki ki lat*, as everyone would say. An addiction for *nautanki*.

⁓

Bismillah Khan introduced Rashid to music. *Nautanki*s made him realize that he couldn't live without music.

Nautanki originated in the early twentieth century. A travelling popular theatre that incorporated dialogues and singing, it derived its themes from Indian mythology, folk tales and contemporary social issues. It was the most popular source of entertainment in small towns and villages in north India and was a mandatory feature at the annual fairs that were held at various religious sites – Sufi dargahs, Hindu and Sikh temples – and farmers' markets. The fairs were visited by people of all religions, castes and classes.

Nautanki songs were influenced by folk lyrics and were sung by the masses. The song-and-dance sequences with dialogues had an instant connection with the public. The productions were exciting, soul-stirring and much sought after. They even broke new ground by depicting wild, romantic, sassy, raunchy exchanges between gods and goddesses. The latest heroine would often play a cop, a dancer, a goddess, a queen and a village girl, all in the same production.

Precolonial India was less conservative about sex and sexuality. During the British period, public singing and dancing came to acquire a stigma. Women performers were seen as prostitutes and the male troupe members as facilitators of immorality and sleaze. Cross-gender acting and cross-dressing, once common, were now frowned upon. And so was *nautanki*.

By the 1950s, Muslim weavers, traditionally seen as less rigid and more syncretic, and later known as Momin Ansaris, became increasingly Islamized. The Momin Ansari community had opposed both the formation of the Muslim League, which was seen as a separate political party for Muslims, and the partition of India in 1947. Now, offering namaz five times a day, shunning music, and greater segregation among men and women were becoming increasingly common among the Momin Ansaris.

༺ ༻

Abbaji was under tremendous peer pressure to conform to these orthodox ways of life in order to remain in favour, in business and in circulation in the larger weaving community. Rashid's waywardness could have affected their socio-economic position. The trusted antidote to fix him was quickly administered. Sometime in 1959 he was married off to his second cousin Mehreen.

Mehreen was considered a bit slow and so less marriageable. Her father compensated for this by giving Rashid's family a larger dowry than usual – a loom, a gold chain, a pair of gold earrings and Rs 5,000 – a bounty that only traders – and not weavers – of Banarasi sarees could usually afford.

Dowry is not an Islamic custom but it became a common practice across religions and castes in the Indian subcontinent. Abbaji decided to ditch the religious mandate in this case.

Rashid was deeply unhappy. Of course, as was the norm, no one asked him how he felt, what he thought. Parents arranged marriages without the approval of their children, who would often have their first interaction with their partner on their wedding night. Rashid found Mehreen to be quite insipid after his experiences in the world of art and music.

Initially, he made an effort with her. He was around nineteen and she was fifteen. But the gap between his youthful passion and her childish naivety seemed too wide.

He had picked up sewing by observing Kamlesh Chacha, the neighbour who stitched garments for Hindu deities. Once Rashid stitched a *lehenga choli* for Mehreen with the same cuts and flare that the *nautanki* heroines wore. An excited Mehreen went around showing it to all her aunts, who were scandalized and shamed Rashid: 'Now he wants to turn his wife into a *nautankiwali* too!'

Six months into the marriage, Rashid ran away, taking with him a dozen freshly woven Banarasi brocade sarees, and could not be traced for several years.

Nadi nare na jao shyam paiyan padun . . .

Don't go near the river, Shyam!
I beg of you.

– Gulab Bai's famous *dadra* sung since the 1930s

Rashid met Gulab Bai at a fair in a Sufi shrine in Mau, a town in UP, to sell her the sarees he had run away with.

In 1955, Gulab Bai, reputed to be the first woman to join the *nautanki*, an all-male space till the 1930s, started her own company, the Great Gulab Theatre Company.

In 1960, after doing odd jobs in the *nautanki* for some time, Rashid started working as the *nautanki* tailor. But he missed Banaras. He had even written a few letters to Abbaji but received no response.

In 1964, Abbaji succumbed to tuberculosis, a common disease among weavers. Years of ingesting fibre has fatal consequences for the lungs. That was when Rashid came home for the first time in five years.

Mehreen, with her childlike face and two long twin braids, was still considered 'slow'. But she was the most efficient worker. When others would cut threads and finish four sarees in a day, she would sometimes manage six.

She was happy to receive Rashid and did not judge him like their other worldly-wise family members did. This comforted him and he renewed his family ties.

Monsoons were not good for *nautanki* companies but they started to bring joy to Mehreen. For those four months, known as *chaumasa*, the *nautanki* could not travel from one place to another because of the rains. This was also a period when weaving work came to a standstill because the yarn could not be dyed, dried or spread out to mount on the spool to weave sarees.

Rashid kept coming back to visit her around this time every year. One after the other, three *barsaati mendhaks* were born.

Rain frogs.

The last rain frog was Syeda, their only daughter after two sons, in 1973.

On 11 May 1973, the Hindi film Zanjeer, starring Amitabh Bachchan, was released. It popularized the angry young man prototype in Indian movies.

Rashid had already married an actor in the *nautanki* and started another family in Kanpur when Syeda was born. Many *nautanki* team members had two families, one in the company and the other in their hometown. Mehreen did not probe too much into this. She didn't want Rashid's annual visits to stop.

By the time Syeda was born, cinema had become the preferred and more respectable form of entertainment over *nautanki*. Gulab Bai's company was struggling financially. To cut costs, the cook, the tailor, the accountant and the other support staff all started doubling up as performers.

Syeda has a faint memory of Rashid in her growing-up years. He told them that he played the role of *vidhushak*, a fool who makes people laugh, during the interval when the set was changed for the next act. With the popularity of *Mera Naam Joker*, a movie set in a circus that released in 1970, this role began to be known as 'the joker'.

Syeda remembers Rashid saying animatedly that painting the face in red, white, blue and yellow did not make people laugh; just several facial expressions and witty humour were enough. She often wondered if Rashid was the reason why she couldn't imagine her life without cinema.

Over the years, Rashid's paternal family had become poorer and also more ritualistic and judgemental. He could no longer relate to them. He grew more distant and started visiting less often, only once every other year. One day in 1982, his first family heard he had died in a road accident while driving a *nautanki* truck. They never heard from his second family.

Syeda was nine then.

⁓

Ek do teen,
Chaar paanch chhe saat aath nau,
Dus gyarah, barah terah,
Tera karun din gin gin ke intezaar,
Aaja piya aayi bahaar!

One two three,
Four five six seven eight nine,
Ten eleven, twelve thirteen
I count every day as I wait for you,
Come O beloved, spring is here!

– Song from the movie *Tezaab* (1988)

At one point, every nook and cranny in Banaras had a cinema hall. And those narrow lanes were flooded by a sea of cinemagoers each time a blockbuster film was released. People from the neighbouring towns and cities from all over Purvanchal – eastern UP – ditched work and stood in queues all day to buy movie tickets.

Syeda loved films.

Since watching *Tezaab* with her brothers at Deepak Talkies, her ardent hope was that her potential husband had a similar interest in films and, if not, would at least not stop her from seeing a 'picture' once in a while.

Mohini, the protagonist in *Tezaab* played by Madhuri Dixit, was forced by her father to dance to make money. Like the young Gulab Bai. And that is why Mohini's father did not want her to get married.

Making money means you don't need to get married. Syeda was being married off because, after Mehreen's death in 1987, no one wanted to take over 'responsibility' for her.

Mehreen died within a few hours of catching a fever, before she could be taken to the doctor. No one ever found out the exact cause of her death. She was gone, just like that. After years of doing unpaid labour for her brothers-in-law and uncles and living on their generosity. After years of being called slow and a simpleton, with only spurts of affection here and there to survive on. After years of living with an absent husband and three children whom she treated as grown-up friends, not children, and with whom she would get into fistfights and bawling matches.

Syeda always thought Mehreen was not the mother she needed. Mehreen would turn to Syeda for advice, burdening her with emotional responsibility instead of guiding her and nurturing her. It was Syeda who had to mother her, take care of her, protect her, and cook for her and the entire family. Her two elder brothers had deftly slipped into the roles decided for them under the tutelage of Abbaji and Akbar, Mehreen's father, who was a master weaver himself. Their future was secure.

Saleema, her grandmother, had already declared that her last wish was to see Syeda in 'her own house'. It is considered okay to keep repeating to an Indian girl all her childhood that her parents' house is not hers. Her husband's home is supposed to be hers – except that it hardly ever is.

It has also been a common Indian practice to coax people into getting married to meet the last wishes of the ageing elders in the family. Except that it is never the last *last* wish.

For the first three decades of Indian independence, the handloom sector, as part of cottage industry, was supported as a space for employment generation and to uplift the weaving communities. Handlooms exclusively produced traditional products like border sarees, dhotis and bedsheets.

Syeda's growing-up years were considered a golden period for Banarasi sarees. But the new textile policy of 1985 changed everything. Only eleven items were reserved for handlooms to produce, down from twenty-two.

The new policy favoured exports. It gave more incentives to set up a power loom and replicate handloom products at a cheaper cost and in less time. Many handloom weavers were unprepared for this kind of quick mechanization and market competition.

୧୨

Around the same time, in 1988, Akmal moved with his two older brothers and their families to Lohta, a village on the outskirts of Banaras city. Located about 20 kilometres from Banaras, Lohta was emerging as an important weaving and trading centre. The family had moved from the township of Chandauli, then in Varanasi district, an hour away from Lohta.

Akmal's family were weavers who specialized in high-end work and produced a variety of export-quality sarees. With the demand for specialized handloom work shrinking, such products could now only be sold and distributed by traders in Madanpura who continued to have an assured market. Madanpura was still in the heart of Banaras.

Madanpura Rewari Talab, a locality in the southern part of Banaras, housed the rich, elite Muslim master weavers who produced superior quality silk sarees and traders who bought sarees from other weavers. The poorer weavers were concentrated in the north of the city – in Sareyan, Jalalipura and Jaitpura – and in the centre in Lallapura and Bazardiha, where Syeda's family lived.

Most of these neighbourhoods were overflowing with people, with barely any space to live and to set up the looms. Multiple property divisions among families had also shrunk the areas.

Many weavers from all over had started migrating to Lohta in search of better rates and wages, for more space, and for direct contact with traders. Compared to the older settlements it had bigger houses at a distance from each other, more open spaces, and a certain abandon. 'It had the vibe of a new, fresh neighbourhood,' remembers Syeda.

Akmal, a slim, tall, muscular young man with droopy eyes and protruding cheekbones, was a skilled weaver. He had turned eighteen just that year.

He preferred to dye the threads himself for special pieces and could finish them within a week while others took at least three weeks. For his age, his skill was a rarity. But it came with a caveat: Akmal reserved his commitment for exclusive sarees with designs he liked. This happened only once or twice in two months. But since these kinds of sarees sold for very high prices, his brothers tolerated his slacking on other days of the month. It was for this reason they convinced him to move with them to Lohta instead of staying back with their parents in Chandauli.

It was a family of ten. Akmal's two brothers and their wives and their five children, and Akmal himself, lived on the same premises but each nuclear unit had a separate kitchen. Unlike other weaver families, they still shared the same looms.

The warping was done by the patriarch, the eldest brother, Rameez. The second brother, Alam, prepared the weft threads. Akmal sometimes punched design cards or dyed the yarn and at other times took the finished sarees to the traders.

Ever since they had moved to Lohta, four or five mausoleums of Sufi saints known as 'dargahs' had become popular hang-out places in the area. Because they were Sufi shrines, people from all religions came to them.

'When you leave your hometown and village for a new place and you have no one to watch over you, watch out for you, a dargah makes you feel that you are not alone. Someone is listening, someone is there for you,' Akmal often said. Like therapy. Once a week, there were Sufi *qawwali* performances and aspiring singers would learn from the trained singers. These dargahs were the anchors for the struggling migrants.

One day, Akmal was loitering at the Ahmad Shah mausoleum. As usual, he was staring into thin air, lost in his thoughts.

'This Rameez from Chandauli. Where is his house?' asked someone. It was Kashif, Syeda's elder brother.

The question did not register with Akmal.

Kashif shook Akmal's shoulder and asked again.

Akmal said, 'Rameez? Oh, he's my brother. What do you want with him?'

Kashif sized him up. 'Are you Akmal?'

Akmal nodded. Kashif thought of him as someone with a young, fit body but a very old face.

Akmal guided him to his house.

A local *maulvi* in Bazardiha, whose pastime was to recommend matches for young people, had tipped off Kashif about Akmal and his brothers. Kashif was very clear that he did not want Syeda to be married within their extended family, which was a common practice among the Muslim weavers of Banaras. He himself had had to marry his second cousin. Her family lived in the vicinity and he found them breathing down his neck all the time.

Why are you asking her to make rice instead of roti?

Why do you not buy her new silver anklets?

You work all day and yet you have so little money.

He did not want one more source of suffocation. 'Some distance between families is good,' he told Syeda. 'People who are afar are respected more. Because you don't know every small detail about their lives. Less scope to judge.'

Rameez and Kashif spoke at length. Weaving largely operates on family labour. Getting outside labour means paying for it. You didn't need to pay the women of the family. Also, Akmal's family had only one loom that the three brothers were sharing. Having another loom would make a significant difference to the family income.

Syeda was trained in weaving preparatory work and Kashif was willing to give a loom as part of her dowry. They could afford that much to get rid of the 'responsibility'.

Akmal did not participate in this conversation. It was perfectly common for an elder brother to arrange the marriage of his younger sibling with someone he hadn't met. He acquiesced because all young men his age were doing the same thing: getting married, wearing new clothes and discussing their brides.

When Syeda heard about her impending marriage, she didn't resist much either. Choosing a groom of your choice was unheard of. She had already studied till Class 8, a special privilege accorded to her by her grandmother. No one was willing to let her study further, or get a job.

'I was bored,' she confesses. Cooking, cleaning, cutting saree threads, listening to the constant fights of her sisters-in-law and her grandmother, taking care of her nieces and nephews – and then hearing that her family house was not 'her' home! Marriage, she thought, was the only ticket available to her to break away, to get some authority and the possibility of some agency in her life.

One day, she had been up on the terrace of their house and happened to look at her brother's friend who had come to meet him in the courtyard. His sister-in-law told everyone that Syeda cast the 'wrong eye' on men. Her grandmother beat her up for that.

So she went up to the terrace again, to cry her heart out. 'When I stood there, all the houses around me were full of my distant cousins and relatives who were staring at me. I wanted to run away from Bazardiha,' she recalls. What hurt her was that not one woman walked up to her to comfort her. Even though all of them had been unfairly accused of being 'wayward' at some point or another in their lives. 'Almost like another woman's oppression was their gratification' – in a system where women had no power.

In 1988, the voting age was lowered from twenty-one years to eighteen.

Syeda and Akmal got married 'sometime in December 1988, a few days before Christmas'. In the *waleema*, the wedding reception, guests were served biryani, poori subzi and rasgulla.

Syeda, small, petite, with shoulder-length braided hair, and an expressive face, dazzled in a Banarasi *sharara*, a pair of loose pleated trousers worn by South Asian women. She was packed off to Akmal's house with five new salwar kameezes, two gold bangles, one gold chain, one pair of gold earrings, Rs 5,000 and a loom. The same dowry as Mehreen.

She liked that the small compound of Akmal's house had many flowerpots.

On their first night together, when Akmal entered their room, he told Syeda, 'Let me tell you in advance, don't ask me for money every day.'

This was the first time they had met. Akmal's friends had told him to establish who was the boss in the marriage on the wedding night itself.

'*Aaja piya aayi bahaar.*' Come O beloved, spring is here! These were the words in the song from *Tezaab* that she loved. And *this* was what Syeda's *piya* had to say when he met her for the first time? *What an introduction to romance*, she thought.

Syeda, the rebellious fifteen-year-old teenager that she was, decided she was not going to talk to him. 'If he wants to be Amitabh Bachchan, he can, but not in front of me.'

Akmal, tall and dark, with slightly long hair, had fashioned himself after Amitabh Bachchan, the angry young man of the movies.

The next few days, as she was getting to know the family, they both exchanged glances now and then. When Akmal would come to sleep next to her on the same bed at night, he tried initiating conversation: 'It is very cold today.'

Syeda would reply with a 'hmmm' and nothing more. Almost a month passed.

Her new sisters-in-law were gentle but distant. They had a lot to do every day: sizing and curing yarn, reeling bobbins, filling spools, cooking, cleaning, rearing children, fetching water and washing up. They had no time for her or anyone else.

Syeda didn't mind that. She was relieved there was no one to tell her what to do or stop her from doing what she wanted to.

Syeda was tasked with cutting the threads and finishing the sarees, folding and packing them, and keeping accounts. That was because she was the only literate member of the family. It took her less than half a day to do all this work.

She was happy she had to cook for only two people now, with all the brothers having separate kitchens. She could decide if she wanted to cook baingan ka bharta or potato and pea curry, chicken curry or dal. It was liberating to have the choice to eat what you wanted and not have the menu dictated by the family elders. Akmal would quietly eat what was cooked and sometimes even asked for a second serving, perhaps to indicate that he liked the food.

He had a radio at home and she listened to Hindi film songs throughout the day. After Rashid ran away to work in the *nautanki*, music and radio had been banned at Abbaji's house.

In her free time, Syeda would try her hand at weaving on the loom, which she had learnt by watching her uncles and brothers.

In the first month of marriage, Akmal once left Rs 500 on her pillow. It was most of what he had made that month after selling a beautiful neon-green Banarasi piece. The saree was so stunning that Syeda's heart had skipped a beat. Her self-imposed restriction on talking to him was wearing off.

Then one winter evening, Akmal got piping hot gajar ka halwa for everyone. The family was just about comfortable financially. They had a regular income. But sweets were still bought only on special occasions. The children were elated. As the family proceeded with the mini celebration, Syeda sat in silence on the side.

Akmal served her a plate of halwa. She stared at him blankly instead of accepting the plate.

He smiled and said, 'Take it, na. Next time, I will cook it for you. I cook well.'

His sisters-in-law smiled at each other and turned their gaze on Syeda.

'You cook too?' asked Syeda with an embarrassed half-smile, as she accepted the plate.

Akmal smiled and looked away.

The halwa warmed up Syeda and Akmal's relationship. They started talking about food, cinema – thankfully, Akmal was interested in films too – and waterfalls. Syeda had seen the banks of Banaras, and the boats that ferried people to the small islands in the middle of the Ganga. But now Akmal described to her the waterfalls of the Chandraprabha river.

Syeda had grown up in a semi-urban set-up with looms and spools, rickshaws, tempos and scooters passing through the narrow lanes of Bazardiha carrying raw and finished materials. She had heard about jungles, the trees, the silence and the mystery in them, but had never seen a forest. As for animals, she had only seen cows, buffaloes, pigs, goats, dogs and cats, and the terrifying bulls found all over Banaras because they are considered the vehicle of the Hindu god Shiva, the Vishwanath Baba of Banaras.

She had never seen a body of water except for the Ganga. Chandraprabha means the glow of the moon. The river was a tributary of the Karamnasha river. It flows through a dense forest in Chandauli, where Akmal and his brothers used to live before moving to Lohta, and has many unexplored caves, as well as leopards, porcupines, wild boars, bears, pythons and crocodiles.

Akmal described a porcupine as a big fat rat with lots of thorns, and a python as a serpent that could swallow a cow and not move for days. He drew them on the mud floor with a pebble, for her to visualize. Syeda did not sweep the floor for days, looking at them for hours and trying to imagine them in the flesh. Akmal said that the waterfall looked like several litres of milk were being thrown from a mountain, turning brown as it hits the bottom. He told her that in the sarees he wove, he tried to replicate the white dots from the fall that splatter on the ground.

Akmal was not much of a talker, though when he did speak he wanted the kind of attention a seer commands. He never directly expressed love but she could feel that he cared.

She had not seen anyone show romantic love in her life. Her parents, her brothers and their wives, and her grandparents. It was all about duty and what one was supposed to do and not do. Two people were put together and they lived their lives with no conversation or expression of this kind of love ever.

She had only heard of love in films, in ways that no one expressed in real life. To her, love was care, something she was starved of, like most women.

Akmal ate a lot of chilli in his food, but she did not. Whenever he cooked, he took out a portion of cooked food for her before adding chilli or spices for himself.

Who had ever thought of doing these small things for her? In the last few years before she got married, by the time everyone had finished eating, there would only be roti and pickle left for her. And she never bothered to cook more for herself.

One day Syeda asked Akmal for some money to buy a new kerosene stove. He left home in a huff and sat at the dargah the whole day and night.

His erratic spells of anger were something that she was getting used to. He just didn't like to have any discussion about money or earning it.

'You told me that you didn't want me to ask for money every day. I didn't. But at least sometimes, I'll need it,' she said to him when he returned.

'Then do something yourself too. I will give you money whenever I earn it but not always,' he told her.

But that is what he was, she gradually realized. Gentle, kind and caring but not a very conventional man who took responsibility for the family, the primary breadwinner.

Manmauji. Whimsical.

A bit like her father?

Something women are not allowed to be.

But life was far more flavourful than before. Akmal's family was younger. They were migrants and so the rigid Momin Ansari identity had still not overtaken their lives, as had happened with most other Banarasi weavers. She was not expected to wear the burqa or follow many rituals except the daily namaz.

And since Syeda was expected to cook only for the two of them and clean her part of the house, there was a lot more time to take a nap, or do other work like applying beads or *gota*, a type of appliqué craft using gold and silver ribbons, on clothes, taking up amateur *aari* work, an embroidery style that uses hooked needles to create intricate designs, or even making a quilt for fun and for extra income, which she started using for everyday expenses like groceries.

༄

Within a year of marriage, Shazeb was born in November 1989. Syeda, just sixteen, could not feel her body for almost a month. She was weak and her legs trembled as she walked. Doctors said she was anaemic. She was sent off to her brother's house where her *dadi*, grandmother, took care of her for the first time. Syeda realized that the only way to get any respect in India as a woman was to get married and become a mother.

Dadi fed her laddoos, massaged her and her child every day, and banned her from doing any housework. Her sisters-in-law didn't like that.

'I was asked to cook for ten people within a week of my delivery even when I was just fourteen. And she is being treated like *Mallika Victoria*,' one of them grumbled.

Queen Victoria.

Dadi replied, 'Yes, because she is my granddaughter and you are my granddaughter-in-law. You should have gone to your *maika* if you wanted to be taken care of.'

Maika. Mother's house. The only place where married women are allowed to take a break or to be cared for. A bonus earned only when you get married. As a single woman you are not even treated as a complete person. The only way to demand care forcefully as a woman is to wait till you are a mother-in-law.

Akmal had woven two exclusive pieces in November and December 1989 and made some good money. After giving his brothers a share, he handed over all the money to Syeda.

They celebrated her return from her *maika* by watching *Maine Pyar Kiya*, a family Bollywood drama where class difference separates lovers. The film popularized the actor Salman Khan who portrayed a spoilt brat, a macho hero with a golden heart. The radio played songs from *Maine Pyar Kiya* for months.

At the time, the thriving Hindi industry featured many Muslim actors, most of whom had had to take a Hindu screen name for a wider appeal. Yusuf Khan became Dilip Kumar, and Mumtaz Jehan became Madhubala. In the late 1980s and 1990s, three Khans made their debut: Salman, Shah Rukh and Aamir. They not only kept their Muslim names but went on to become superstars for decades – perhaps a marker of how India was changing.

Their second son was born a year after Shazeb, in November 1990.

As an infant, he would throw his fists in the air. 'Like Salman Khan packing punches,' Akmal said. And so the boy was named Salman. Dadi once again stepped in to heal her. Her sisters-in-law held Dadi's favouritism for Syeda against her for life.

❧

Hindu kahe mohe Ram pyara,
Turk kahe Rehmana
Aapas me dou lad lad muye,
Marm na kou jana . . .

Hindus say their Ram is supreme,
Muslims have firm faith in their Rehman.
Many have lost their lives in fighting in the name of God.
But no one was able to know who the real God actually is.

– Kabir, fourteenth-century weaver and Sufi saint from Banaras

'Have you heard? Akmal has two sons now. His family is complete. Did he feed you laddoos or not?' Govind asked Purushottam.

Govind Aggarwal was a trader of Banarasi sarees in Godowlia, a prominent commercial centre in Banaras. Purushottam Yadav was a weaver from Lohta.

'Arre, not yet. The "*Hum do, humare do*" rule is only for Hindus. For them it is "*Hum paanch aur humare pachees,*"' replied Purushottam. We five, our twenty five.

'*Hum do, humare do*' – 'We two, our two' – is a popular slogan of India's family-planning programme that encourages Indians to follow a two-child norm and have a small family.

'But you also have six kids, when will you stop?' Govind responded with a smirk.

Akmal was sitting on the stairs of Govind's shop with this conversation happening in front of him. He regularly sold sarees to Govind. He carried on smoking his *beedi* and did not react.

Close to 65 per cent of the new settlers in Lohta were Momin Ansaris. The rest were Hindus, mostly Scheduled Caste, also known as Dalits from the Maurya community or Other Backward-Class Yadavs (OCBs). The Scheduled Castes are the most disadvantaged socio-economic groups in India. A step above them in this hierarchy are Other Backward Classes (OBC). It is a collective term to classify communities that are socially or educationally disadvantaged.

Many of the non-Muslims like Purushottam were new entrants into weaving, shifting from dairying and similar professions. After working as daily wagers with master weavers for a few years, some of them bought their own looms.

India has several Personal laws that govern a person's family matters including marriage, divorce and inheritance on the basis of religion and community. Under Muslim Personal law, Muslim men are allowed to have four wives but with stringent conditions: this includes that the man treats all of the wives equally and fulfils their rights and needs.

In the decade of the 1980s, several right-wing Hindu supremacist groups had popularized the narrative '*Hindu khatre mein hain.*'

Hindus are in danger.

According to the 1981 census, over 82 per cent of the Indian population was Hindu, 11 per cent Muslim, over 2 per cent Christian, and less than 2 per cent Sikh.

Despite the large Hindu population of India, the Hindu supremacists kept fuelling paranoia by propagating the myth that

Muslims were trying to capture political power in India through a population explosion.

❧

In the 1980s, the Rashtriya Swayamsevak Sangh (RSS), a Hindu supremacist organization that believes in political Hinduism – also known as Hindutva – and aims to establish a Hindu state in India, gained prominence. It has several arms and affiliates that are collectively called the Sangh Parivar. It includes the Vishwa Hindu Parishad (VHP), the RSS outfit exclusively devoted to consolidating Hindu society.

The Sangh Parivar identified three north Indian towns in UP – Ayodhya, Mathura and Kashi (Banaras) – as project sites to politicize the Hindu religion.

Ayodhya is believed to be the birthplace of the Hindu god Ram; Mathura is believed to be the birthplace of the Hindu god Krishna, and Banaras, also known as Kashi, is believed to have been created by the Hindu god Shiva. All three cities had Muslim mosques that were rumoured to have been built on the site of Hindu temples razed by Muslim kings over the last several centuries.

In 1980, the RSS also relaunched its political arm: the Bharatiya Janata Party (BJP).

Within a decade of its formation, the party had increased its seat tally in the Indian Parliament from 2 in 1984 to 85 in the general elections of 1989 in the name of 'restoring the honour of the Hindu religion'. L.K. Advani, a Sindhi leader, was appointed the party president. He often spoke of the 'anti-Hindu' violence in Pakistan that displaced him during the Partition of India in 1947 and the 'Muslim appeasement' in secular India. Advani played a big role in using religion as bait for votes.

The BJP escalated the Ram Janmabhoomi campaign to 'reclaim' the disputed birthplace of Hindu god Ram in Ayodhya. They believed that the Mughal emperor Babar had destroyed the temple that existed at the birthplace of Ram and constructed the Babri mosque there in the sixteenth century.

India was in political turbulence in the late 1980s and early 1990s. In Kashmir, several militant groups started demanding a separate Kashmir nation, in lieu of the plebiscite that India had promised before the UN Security Council in 1948. To curb this, the armed forces entered the state in large numbers. After several violent exchanges, a large section of Kashmiri Pandits, a minority Hindu community in Kashmir, fled the Muslim-majority Kashmir.

This exodus was fodder for Hindu fanaticism. It gave the Sangh Parivar a chance to demonize the Muslim minority in the rest of India and reiterate the narrative of 'Hindus are in danger': the one Purushottam had repeated in front of Akmal that day.

Everything started acquiring a religious taint.

Within a few months of coming to power, in August 1990, the V.P. Singh government implemented reservations for Other Backward Classes (OBCs) throughout the country based on the recommendations of the Mandal Commission report. It reserved 27 per cent of all vacancies in Indian government-run institutions for candidates from 'socially and educationally backward classes' identified by the commission. While many welcomed it as a corrective measure to end the dominance of upper castes in public services, there was a backlash from them across the country.

The RSS, both ideologically and in terms of representation, is dominated by upper-caste men, particularly Brahmins, the top category in the Hindu caste hierarchy, who have enjoyed privileges while dominating, oppressing and discriminating against other castes. They viewed the implementation of the Mandal Commission report as an attempt to take away their privileges and to 'divide' Hindu society. Their axis of mobilization was religion instead of caste.

The Sangh used this opportunity. They projected the demand for the construction of the Ram temple at the disputed site in Ayodhya as a way to restore the pride and honour of the Hindus – but most importantly as a device to unify Hindu votes.

Within a month of V.P. Singh's reservation announcement, on 25 September 1990, Advani launched a rath yatra, a campaign to raise the issue of the Ram temple across the country. He travelled in a van fitted to look like the chariot of Lord Ram. It was a five-week-long progress through north and west India covering 10,000 kilometres, starting from Somnath in Gujarat and ending in Ayodhya in Uttar Pradesh. This yatra was characterized by bigoted and anti-Muslim speeches across the country.

Eventually, a series of riots broke out in UP. Hindu mobs attacked Muslim localities. The VP government of the National Front supported by the BJP fell, as the BJP withdrew support.

Riots translated into votes. The BJP's vote tally went up in the general and assembly elections that followed in 1991. It managed to form a government in UP for the first time, with Kalyan Singh, from the OBC community, becoming chief minister in June 1991. The party's tally in Parliament also jumped from 85 in 1989 to 120 in the 1991 general elections.

It is believed that Banaras has had a weaving industry for over 1,000 years. When Abbaji said that Hindu–Muslim relations are the warp and weft of the Banarasi saree, he meant that one cannot survive without the other. Traditionally, the weavers were Muslims and the traders were Hindus. Both depended on each other. Banaras's Hindus and Muslims were cordial with each other but distance was maintained in the social sphere.

Muslim friends were given tea and coffee in different cups and they were supposed to dine separately when invited to a wedding. Hindus would accept only water in Muslim houses, and that only sometimes. Inter-marrying was unthinkable. Stereotypes about each other were propagated. Yet, there was coexistence and acceptance.

The weaver Purushottam's jibe was the very first one Akmal heard that invoked his Muslim identity as an abuse. Govind had already defended him – by pointing out jokingly that Purushottam himself had more than two children while Akmal had only two – and so he ignored it.

But it was only the beginning.

There were practically no communal riots in Banaras from 1947 to 1966 but from 1966 to 1990 there were about eleven of them.

In the 1991 general elections, the BJP increased its seats in Lok Sabha from 85 in the previous term to 120. The Congress party still formed the government at the Centre. During the elections, Banaras remained communally polarized. There was curfew at several places, 9 people died and over 500 were arrested, and there was loss of property for Hindus and Muslims.

While the Hindi belt was turning to Shah Rukh and Salman, Kashif, Syeda's brother, was still an Amitabh Bachchan loyalist. Promotions for his new film, *Akayla*, endlessly talked about a wonder car, Rampyari, the first of its kind in Hindi cinema.

On 8 November 1991, he had gone to the Sushil Cinema in Godowlia for the evening showing of the movie. Syeda was cooking when Akmal came with the news that Kashif had barely survived a murderous attack by a mob.

Godowlia is a commercial centre and predominantly a Hindu area. Since Advani's rath yatra, the air was rife with distrust among Hindus and Muslims. An idol was desecrated in Allahabad, a shrine was demolished in Chandauli, a Muslim mob kidnapped a Hindu man, a Hindu area was barred to Muslims – rumours of all kinds, never confirmed, kept fuelling suspicion.

That day, a rumour was floating that the Muslims in the Muslim-majority area of Madanpura had stopped a Kali idol procession, broken the idol and held some Hindus hostage.

In response, in the middle of the film, several Muslim men were dragged out of the cinema hall. The Muslims were identified mostly by their caps and beards. Abbaji, conforming with the new Momin Ansari identity, had mandated beards for the men of the family and so Kashif carried the physical markers of his religion too.

The cinema hall manager acted in time. He locked Kashif and several other men in a secure closet to save their lives.

But other Muslims were stabbed and burned to death in the presence of the police.

'Till then we had known hunger, grief, sorrow, and frustration, like everyone else. But this was the first time we experienced terror. Because of our religion,' Syeda recalls.

Curfew was imposed in the area. But several Hindu supremacists still kept making rounds of the area, chanting anti-Muslim slogans. Five days later, on 13 November, there were reports of a Muslim mob killing eight passers-by in retaliation in Madanpura. There were similar reports from all over the city. Of skirmishes, small disagreements, blowing up into communal fights.

After this, an indefinite curfew was clamped down on the city that would last, in some areas, for forty-five days. While many political leaders were denied permission to visit the affected locality, the only one allowed in was S. C. Dixit, a former director general of police who was the vice president of the VHP. In addition to the Ram Janmabhoomi issue, Dixit had also raised the Gyanvapi mosque question in the 1991 general election campaign.

The Gyanvapi mosque was less than 50 metres from the Kashi Vishwanath temple in Banaras. It was also on the hit list of the Sangh Parivar. At the end of the eighteenth century, the present Kashi Vishwanath temple was built at its current site next to the Gyanvapi mosque. It was believed that the earlier Kashi Vishwanath temple was demolished on the orders of Mughal emperor Aurangzeb in 1669. The Sangh Parivar believed that the Gyanvapi mosque was built at the same site using material from the demolished temple. There is no documentary evidence or record that corroborates the Sangh Parivar's theory.

To appeal to Hindu voters, Dixit had vociferously raised the demand to 'liberate' the Hindu Kashi Vishwanath temple from the presence of the Muslim Gyanvapi mosque. This got him elected as member of Parliament (MP) from Varanasi in the 1991 general elections held from May to June that year.

After the Madanpura riots, several newspapers reported that Dixit held meetings with the police officers of Banaras and instructed them on what to do. Before his visit, the police were conspicuous by their absence from the riot-affected areas for a full five days.

During the curfew, the common people were cooperating to survive. When an old Muslim woman died and her family needed *zam-zam*, holy water, a Hindu woman with a curfew pass got it from another Muslim's house. Another Hindu woman arranged flowers from her house for the funeral.

The police, the Provincial Armed Constabulary (PAC) and the Central Reserve Police Force (CRPF) were given a free hand to conduct *talaashi*, intense house-to-house search operations, in Bazardiha, Madanpura and other Muslim-dominated areas. Almost 2,000 Muslim houses were searched and several inhabitants were beaten up over 14–16 November 1991 in various parts of Banaras. The police looted cash and jewellery, and destroyed looms under the pretext of searching for hidden arms and weapons.

Many civil society members questioned the sectarian conduct of the police.

'After that, *talaashi* became a part of life for us,' remembers Syeda.

Madanpura has secret tunnels that are connected to Pakistan.
They can only be detected by military equipment.

Such statements were regularly repeated by newspapers and BJP members in their speeches. They started referring to Muslim-majority areas like Lohta and Madanpura as 'mini Pakistan'.

This was when Akmal's brothers started thinking of leaving Lohta and returning to Chandauli.

Dr Anees Ansari, a prominent leader who was part of several peace committees that were responsible for maintaining communal harmony in the past, was arrested in the Madanpura riots. He died in police custody a day later. His family was one of the biggest saree-trader families in the city. Similarly, thirty members of Mayor Mohammad Swaleh Ansari's family were arrested. He was also a rich saree dealer.

The targeting of prominent Muslim leaders was bringing down the morale of the Muslim weavers.

Akmal recalls his brother saying, 'When *paisewalas* [moneyed] and *gaddidar* [trader] Muslims are not being spared, who are we?'

Many also believed that the underlying cause of the Madanpura riots was the economic competition between emerging Muslim entrepreneurs and established Hindu traders of Banarasi sarees who had traditionally monopolized the trade.

In these riots, a total of 326 Muslims and 328 Hindus were arrested. These included children as young as ten and people as old as ninety. While the Muslims were charged with various crimes, the Hindus were largely let off.

The riots affected the Banarasi weaving community across religions and castes. Academic research indicates that since this was seriously affecting business, Hindu traders finally approached Advani, requesting him to stop the riots while assuring him they would give a hefty donation to the BJP.

'By then, the warp and the weft had already been unravelled,' recalls the trader Govind.

Paon Saryu mein abhi Ram ne dhoye bhi na the,
Ki nazar aaye wahan khoon ke gehre dhabbe . . .

Ram had not even set foot in the Saryu river,
When deep blots of blood started appearing . . .

– Kaifi Azmi, twentieth-century poet

By the end of the 1980s, India was in a severe economic crisis. After the fall of the V. P. Singh government in 1990 came the short-lived Chandra Shekhar government and then P. V. Narasimha Rao's government in 1991. His finance minister Manmohan Singh introduced economic reforms that year.

This increased the role of the private sector and foreign investment in the Indian economy. It deregulated industries by getting rid of quotas and monopolies, and removed several curbs on imports and exports. It reduced the state's role in controlling production.

The early 1990s was also the time when a crisis started brewing in the handloom sector. The market was flooded with cheap power loom-made cloth and sarees that replicated handloom Banarasi designs. Recovering the labour cost and dealing with Chinese yarn prices was difficult.

The income of Akmal's joint family was hard hit by these reforms. After markets opened to the world, there was unrestricted export of yarn. The yarn for Banarasi sarees was no longer available at an affordable price. The family were making and selling only five sarees in a month as opposed to ten or twelve as before. The demand for Akmal's high-end sarees, which used expensive silk yarn, dipped further because of skyrocketing prices.

Handlooms comprise a vast, traditional, unorganized sector. That is the reason why it cannot flourish without state support.

The Banarasi weavers also had to compete with cheap power-loom replicas. Many weavers started moving to Surat district in Gujarat to join the textile mills there. According to estimates, one power loom displaces fourteen handlooms. Synthetic fibres, first adopted by the Surat weavers, were cheaper and it was easy to copy Banaras saree designs on a massive scale on power looms Only the upper classes could buy pure silk and handloom sarees.

The market was shrinking. The sectarian vitriol peddled by the BJP was adding fuel to the fire and deepening the divide.

Poor weavers from both communities in Lohta started competing against each nother.

Weaving was a traditional occupation for many Muslim weavers such as Akmal's family. They were seasoned professionals, knew the craft like the back of their hands and took pride in it too. That was the only professional skill they had – it was their identity. Newer entrants like Purushottam, who had shifted from dairying and similar professions to weaving, continued to do odd jobs while accepting cheaper daily wages as weavers.

Unlike Purushottam, Akmal's family owned many looms, which made a significant economic difference. In an atmosphere of rising religious tensions, this became a cause of resentment against the non-Hindus of Lohta.

By 1992, nineteen-year-old Syeda's two sons Shazeb and Salman were three and two years old respectively. Akmal was still weaving the occasional saree every three months or so but the family felt acute financial pinches now and then – each time the children needed to be taken to the doctor, for instance.

One day, Syeda was rolling yarn onto bobbins and shuttles. That week, her sister-in-law was unwell so she was cooking for two families. There were still empty shuttles to fill, but – tired, sleep-deprived – she nodded off under the soothing winter sun in the courtyard. She was jolted from her slumber by wails and screams; someone was yelling, 'Syeda, wake up! *Gumbad gir gaya!*'

The mosque dome has fallen.

On 6 December 1992, the Babri Mosque in Ayodhya was demolished by thousands of Hindu supremacists under the Sangh Parivar's tutelage.

A mob armed with axes, hammers and grappling hooks levelled the entire structure of the mosque within a few hours. Top BJP leaders such as Murli Manohar Joshi and Uma Bharti were present at the site.

Syeda saw the demolished dome in the newspaper the next day. 'Everyone was in deep shock. No one thought that destruction of a religious place in broad daylight, by thousands of people, in the presence of the administration and the police, would be celebrated in this manner,' she recalls.

There was mourning in the air. Hindu–Muslim riots broke out across the country. There were no immediate riots in Banaras but it was a warlike situation. The military took full control of areas around the Kashi Vishwanath temple, since there was a significant Muslim population in the vicinity.

The only time after Partition that a community had been attacked on such a wide scale was in 1984. This was after Prime Minister Indira Gandhi was killed by her Sikh bodyguards to avenge Operation Blue Star, the army operation inside Amritsar's Golden Temple that she had ordered to target the Khalistani militants, who were demanding a separate Sikh state. Sikhs worldwide saw it as an assault on their identity and religion. Organized anti-Sikh violence that involved many members of the Congress party erupted in Delhi and forty other cities in which an estimated 15,000 Sikhs were believed to have been killed.

Syeda remembers how a famous pharmacy called Sardaar Stores in Lanka, a locality in Banaras, had changed its name to a Hindu-sounding name – Satyendra and Kashinath Stores – after the Sikh owners were brutally attacked and their house burned down.

༺༻

Two days after the Babri demolition, on the night of 8 December 1992, Akmal and Syeda heard that the mausoleum of the Sufi saint Ahmad Shah, where Akmal would hang out when they moved to Lohta, had been damaged at night.

Sufism promotes a more liberal interpretation of Islam (conservative Muslims generally don't like Sufi *pirs* and practices). Political Hinduism also started vilifying all forms of rituals and worships at various Sufi shrines and dargahs, frequented by people from across religions.

As a child, whenever Syeda wanted to eat jalebi, see her father or get a day off from weaving-related work, she would come to Ahmad Shah's mausoleum and ask him for whatever she desired. She sincerely believed this guaranteed the fulfilment of a wish. Without offering namaz or chanting mantras. Without buying chadar, flowers or incense sticks. Hindu, Muslim, Sikh, Christian, it didn't matter. This was the only place in the world where she was granted what she wanted without giving anything in exchange. Unlike with her ammi, abba, dada or Akmal, where service or a certain behaviour was demanded to meet the smallest desires: *Behave like a good girl, Finish the thread cutting for the saree, Don't ask me about today's earnings.*

You just had to walk up, sit next to Baba Ahmad Shah's tomb, say what you had to, and leave. And somehow, sooner or later, your wish would come true. Even a hundred years after he had died he could address the urgency of a little girl's desire to eat jalebi on a par with that of a poor man's prayer to be cured of disease.

Within two days of the demolition of the Babri mosque in Ayodhya, this shrine, this small resting place of a Sufi saint whose life story was woven from myths and folklore, became a 'Muslim' shrine.

Someone tried to smash the enclosure of the saint's dargah that night. And the next day, all hell broke loose.

This act of vandalism was a deliberate attempt to incite religious polarization. It added salt to the wound inflicted on Lohta's Muslims by the Babri demolition.

The wall of the shrine had been broken. The police station was informed early in the morning and repair work began the same day. That morning, there were rumours that a vengeful Muslim mob armed with pistols, knives and sickles was moving towards Choti Bazaar and pelting stones at the houses of the Hindus. The mob had apparently split into two, proceeding towards the villages of Dhanipur and Mehmoodpur near Lohta.

Riots broke out. The violence continued through the day. There were reports that five people in the Harijan Basti had been killed and houses had been looted and destroyed.

At night, there was a war of slogans, with the beating of drums amplifying the competition.

Muslims yelled, *'Allahu Akbar.'* Allah is the greatest.

Hindus yelled, *'Har har Mahadev.'* Hail Lord Shiva.

Next day, the newspapers reported that over twenty-five people had been killed in the Lohta riots. Curfew was imposed once again. Various officials, including the district magistrate, the police commissioner and several contingents of the Provincial Armed Constabulary (PAC), the armed police of the state of UP, reached the spot. They had been given standing instructions to carry out a large-scale operation to clear the area of all rioters.

Akmal's house was made of mud and straw, just like other weavers' homes. There was only one concrete room, built with the money given by a master weaver-cum-trader. The practice was for master weavers or traders to give money to poorer weavers to build a concrete room so that the sarees, looms and raw materials could be protected from the sun and rain.

The police and the PAC were constantly firing outside. 'Everyone in the house, Akmal's brothers, their wives, all the children – we all locked ourselves inside that room and stayed quiet,' Syeda recalls.

Akmal was as usual lost in thought and loitering near the mausoleum during the curfew to check out the repair work. 'When I had no one, I had him,' he would say about Ahmad Shah. The destruction of the mausoleum affected him deeply.

As he wandered around, numbed, several men came running towards him. Tariq, another weaver, yelled at him, 'Akmal, run!'

Akmal instinctively started running with the group, failing to notice they were being chased by a PAC platoon. There were around twenty-five PAC soldiers, who were firing incessantly. It was impossible to stop without facing a bullet.

They all ran towards the railway tracks and Akmal hid with the others in an abandoned railway coach.

Syeda and her family were still hiding in the concrete room when the PAC came to conduct a search operation in the house.

'We heard a loud thud at the door. We didn't open it,' recalls Syeda.

The children were crying but the grown-ups covered the kids' mouths tightly with their palms, to prevent sounds.

But after a few minutes, when the police started to break open the door, Rameez, Akmal's eldest brother, decided to open it.

There were five or six PAC soldiers outside. They had already indulged in wanton destruction. Flowerpots were lying broken on the floor, the thatched roofs of their mud huts had been pulled apart, and the mud wall in their compound had been smashed.

The PAC soldiers pushed Rameez and Alam on to the floor as they asked for Akmal's whereabouts. But no one knew where he was. The men entered the concrete room and started hitting the loom with their rifle butts. 'They threw out all the spools of thread and spilled kerosene from the lamp on the saree stock in the room,' Syeda recalls. She, her sisters-in-law and the children were pushed out, and they squatted on the floor outside, crying in horror. She saw Purushottam standing outside their house, smirking. He was the one who had given the PAC Akmal's address.

They sat in the compound, everyone wailing, Rameez's hand squashed on the floor under the rifle butt of a PAC soldier, Alam sprawled beside him on the floor, his leg under the shoe of another soldier, while the other PAC men dug out all the money, jewellery and valuables from the house.

When they finally left, one of them took Akmal's radio. Another threw a lit match, after lighting a cigarette, into the concrete room that had had kerosene sprinkled over the saree stock. The entire room went up in flames in front of their eyes. Rameez and Alam were thankfully not inside the room.

By evening news came that, officially, at least seventeen people were dead and over fifty had been arrested by the PAC. There was no clarity about which category Akmal was in.

That night, they all took refuge in Bazardiha, in Syeda's brother Kashif's house.

The next day, on 11 December 1992, the PAC carried out a flag march as a peace-building measure. But tensions smouldered. Meanwhile, the Gyanvapi mosque had been declared the next target by the Hindu supremacists after the Babri demolition:

Ayodhya abhi jhaanki hai,
Kashi-Mathura baaki hai.

Ayodhya is just a peek,
Kashi and Mathura are left.

The weekly Friday namaz at the Gyanvapi mosque was held under tight security. Nineteen Muslims offered prayers, led by a mufti. Syeda remembers everyone she knew wore old clothes on that Eid.

❧

The next ten days were nightmarish.

Dr Nomani, a well-known trader and part of the peace committee in Lohta, was beaten to death in police custody. There were so many funerals but no one could turn up at the graveyard because of the curfew. There was no milk for the children, no supplies of groceries.

Many people fled Lohta because of the combing operation by the PAC. Both Muslims and Hindus sent their families to relatives for safety.

Syeda's sisters-in-law, already resentful of Syeda because of her grandmother's preferential treatment of her, used this moment to unleash their bitterness. They had the power to because they were sheltering ten members of her marital family. There were taunts every day about the amount of food they were eating and the expense being incurred to take care of them. That too at a time when supplies were low. There were occasional fights between the two families and peace had to be brokered.

Many local leaders claimed that the killing of people from the Harijan Basti had been planned and executed by Thakurs, upper-caste Hindus, instead of Muslims, to incite riots against the backdrop of the Babri Mosque demolition.

They had also incited Harijans, a name given to the Scheduled Caste community by Mahatma Gandhi, to attack the Ahmad Shah shrine. The police were aware of this but did not investigate. They did not search for rioters despite repeated requests, and instead harassed the common people.

In those ten days, the police destroyed so many looms in the weavers' houses that the threads of Banarasi sarees clogged the drains. Lohta was engulfed in a stench. The looms that once wove stardust turned to ash.

When Syeda entered her destroyed and ransacked home in the wee hours one day to gather some belongings, she tottered. It felt as though her petite frame, Salman in her arms and a gunny bag on her back, would all be swallowed by a volcano opening up beneath her feet. The sarees were still there on the looms, half torn and half burnt.

The black soot on one yellow saree looked like a motif, evenly scattered, a sign of high-quality craftsmanship. When the lantern light fell on the broken zari threads around the loom, it shone like the melting lava from *dozakh*, hell, that she had heard about so often as a child.

A woman who leaves her hair open will go to dozakh.

A man who consumes alcohol will burn in the fire of dozakh.

It was as though the broken zari was telling Syeda to pick up the remaining pieces of that hell and leave. Maybe never to return.

***

Everyone blamed Akmal's thoughtlessness for the destruction of the looms and livelihood, the displacement of the family.

'Why couldn't he be responsible just for once? See what hell his loitering has brought upon us. That's why Ammi and Abbu sent him off with us instead of keeping him at home!' said Alam's wife to Syeda. There was no clarity on how many died during this period, how many were alive, and how many were detained by the police. There was no trace of Akmal for that entire period.

On 21 December 1992, the police carried out *kurki* against all those who were declared 'absconding' in the riots and had not surrendered despite an arrest warrant against them. *Kurki*, or attachment of property, is a big deal for the not-so-rich. Used against loan defaulters or criminals, the seizing or auction of property publicly not just leads to financial losses but almost immediately destroys the respectability and the reputation of a family.

Rameez had anticipated this. Two days before the attachment notice arrived, he sold off their patch of land, which was in his name, to Kamlesh Yadav, a new entrant into the weaving business of Lohta. The police took away all the rest of their belongings – not a glass was spared.

It was a huge setback for Rameez and Alam, who had moved from Chandauli to Banaras for a better life.

Akmal had been hiding in the trader Govind's godown (warehouse) in Godowlia all this while. Govind had sheltered some other weavers too. But word was spreading and he didn't want to invite the wrath of his fellow Hindus. He told Akmal about the *kurki* and persuaded him to surrender. Akmal did so.

Syeda was relieved to know he was not dead.

In Lohta, over 500 looms had to be junked as they were either burned or destroyed in this period. But there was no work for most weavers anyway. And apart from relief materials like blankets and food distributed by Christian organizations, there was little help.

'The government did give a compensation of Rs 10,000 to the riot-affected but we didn't qualify because we had a concrete room, a marker that we are not that poor,' recalls Syeda.

Two months had passed. Akmal was still lodged in jail. Rameez and Alam decided to move back to Chandauli.

Syeda and her kids were left behind at her brother's house.

Kabhi-kabhi jeetne ke liye, kuch haarna bhi padta hai. Aur haar ke jeetne wale ko Baazigar kehte hain.

Sometimes to win, you need to lose too. And the one who wins in spite of losing is called Baazigar.

– *Baazigar* (1993)

Now that the looms had become dust, several women like Syeda stepped out to work. Home was no longer their world. It was confusing. Some Muslim women were allowed to give up the burqa to hide their religious identity while earning a living outside the house. Some families that did not practise purdah earlier now started insisting that their women wear a hijab or burqa: maulvis had told them bad luck had befallen the community because the women were not covering their faces or asserting their religious identity. Either way, it was not the women who took the lead in deciding what to do in this matter. And anyway, they were too preoccupied with the daily survival of their families to have these profound debates.

Five months after his release, Akmal was still not able to muster enough strength to work regularly. He complained of leg aches and palpitations. He had been beaten up by the police for days, starved for over a week to supposedly compel him to reveal the names of the people or organizations behind the riots, and subjected to many other things that he never spoke about.

Syeda pushed him to see a Bengali *baba*, a commonly used term for quacks, who charged less for treatment. The quack doctor kept giving him painkillers that never addressed the root of the decline of his physical and mental health.

Many men like Akmal, who had been in jail for months and tortured in police custody, found their capacity to earn a livelihood eroded.

With husbands in jail or too weak after police beatings or with no confidence to build their lives again, the women took on the responsibility of engaging lawyers, procuring bail, earning for the family – things they had never been trained or prepared for, or even trusted with earlier.

One day, Akmal was lying on the terrace in Syeda's brother's house. 'This is great! We cook, clean, take care of the kids, prepare the warp and weft, and our husbands break their backs to put food in everyone's mouth. And this saheb just lies in the sun and sleeps all day. *Wah bhai wah!*' said Taha, Syeda's sister-in-law, as she swept the terrace to put the red chillies to dry in the sun.

Akmal was awake but kept his eyes tightly shut to avoid any confrontation. It had been almost ten months since the Lohta riots. After five months in jail, he was finally released in May 1993. He had been charged with many crimes, including arson, theft and inciting communal hatred.

They had never had a bank account and Syeda's gold jewellery had been stolen by the PAC. Apart from the Rs 500 she had on her person on the day of the PAC raid, she had nothing. She had begged and pleaded with Akmal's brothers to pay for his bail.

But none of the men on either side of the family wanted to go to the police station to help with Akmal's release. They didn't want to come on to the police radar or be identified as Akmal's accomplices, they said. Rameez had given her Rs 10,000, on the condition that Akmal would not ask for any share of their ancestral house in Chandauli or any money after this.

Syeda started working as an apprentice to a tailor in Godowlia. She would do the hems, buttons, hooks and saree falls. The money helped dilute the taunts of her sisters-in-law.

Syeda's neighbour from Lohta, Tarannum, whose husband was still in jail, had four children to feed. She started working as a domestic worker in Madanpura. She also took on the extra work of carrying finished sarees from Lohta to the traders of Madanpura.

Sumbul, another neighbour from Lohta, found a job in a power mill. She doubled up as a cleaner and a millworker. Several people had set up makeshift power looms in the area by using old parts of the mills in Surat. She informed Syeda that there was a job vacancy there and Akmal could give it a shot.

That day, after silently enduring Taha's barbs, when Akmal stood up on the terrace, he saw the poster for a new film, *Baazigar*. The hero wore a black cap, coat and round sunglasses, with two different actresses pictured on each lens. He had a pistol in his hand. Akmal wanted to watch the film but he had no money.

Syeda was pregnant again, and working for the tailor, and also pitching in with weaving prep work for her brothers. It was tough to keep the two boys and Akmal afloat. She had no money to give him. That day he agreed to take up the Jalalipura power loom job.

When he got his first salary a month later, he took Syeda's entire family to see *Baazigar*.

Things started looking up. In the next few months, they found a small room to rent in Lohta and moved out of Syeda's brothers' house. But she came to Kashif's house, in Bazardiha, in the morning every day for a few hours to do some weaving preparatory work. It was common for married women to do this in exchange for favours in kind. With generations-old contacts and a large extended family in the same occupation, her brothers were still getting steady weaving work compared to many migrants in Lohta.

At the power loom, Akmal found standing for long hours unbearable. Since more women were becoming supervisors, he moved to the more 'manly' unofficial marketing unit, and started taking the finished products to the market to sell, since he had some old contacts in Godowlia and Madanpura.

Religious tensions had cooled down in Banaras. However, every once in a while a Hindu right-wing group called the Kashi Vishvanath Mandir Mukti Samiti (Committee for the Liberation of the Kashi

Vishwanath Temple) and the VHP made attempts to access the Gyanvapi mosque area on Hindu festivals to perform rituals.

In August 1994, Reshma, Syeda and Akmal's third child, was born. While Shazeb's and Salman's births had been celebrated with some fanfare, Reshma's birth was a quiet affair, in a tense environment. Syeda was relieved it was a girl – someone who would take care of her and help her, like daughters do. She finally felt settled again. The boys were growing up too: Shazeb was five and Salman four. She was hoping to get them admitted to school. But within a few months, in March 1995, the power loom owner died and everyone was laid off, including Akmal.

With no monthly income to pay rent, Syeda and her family came back to her brothers' house. But her brothers had also started feeling a cash crunch since competition from Surat was stiff. To expand, to sustain, more money was required but it was impossible to get a bank loan for handloom work. With no entrepreneurial experience, most Banaras handlooms struggled.

Akmal went back to loitering in Godowlia, with no visible signs that he was actively seeking fresh employment. He was not alone in his idleness. According to the official surveys published by the Office of the Development Commissioner (Handlooms), the number of weaver families dropped from 124 lakh in the 1970s to 64 lakh in 1995.

Many skilled weavers left their original craft and became daily wagers, rickshaw drivers and construction workers. But Akmal was a *manmauji*.

One day Taha taunted, 'If you are such a nawab, why don't you move to Lucknow?'

Syeda wanted to get away from the judgemental eyes of her family and start life afresh. She often thought of what Kashif had said about the need for distance between family members to maintain mutual respect.

The *maika* can give a woman care and warmth, but it can also make her feel like an unwelcome guest.

Akmal was on board as long as he didn't have to participate in the planning and execution. The mental load of thinking and communicating what and how things had to be done was hers.

She slowly started collecting all the dues at the tailor, at her brothers' house, and at the power mill where Akmal worked as he never went back to collect his pending wages. Four months later, they decided to move to Lucknow.

Akmal asked the boys, 'Who are we?'

Shazeb and Salman replied, *'Baazigars.'*

He replied, 'Yes. To win, you need to lose.'

2

Raisin

Na kabhi janaza uthta,
Na kahin mazar hota

Had there not been a funeral,
There would have been no shrine

— Mirza Ghalib, nineteenth-century poet

On 3 June 1995, Mayawati became the first Dalit woman chief minister in India.

'Two tickets to Lucknow,' Akmal told the person at the ticket counter.

'Two? But you have three children too?' the man retorted.

'Saheb, please allow them WT. They are too small.'

WT. Without Ticket.

'WT! No. Buy half tickets for each. Three and a half tickets. Total Rs 95.'

'Saheb, that will be a lot for us.'

'Arre, this is the railways, not the *sabzi mandi* [vegetable market] that you are bargaining. Move. There are so many in the line after you.'

'Saheb, please help. You are the *mai-baap*. Whatever you say, we will do. We are anyway going there to find work. If we had money, why would we leave Banaras?'

Mai-baap. Ruler.

'Hmm. Do one thing. You want work, no? Go to Delhi. Even Lucknow–Kanpur people now go there for work. Tickets for the Kashi Vishwanath Express are available.'

Akmal turned around to look at Syeda. She had Reshma in her lap. And she was scolding Shazeb for running around. Salman sat on a pile of belongings they had wrapped up in a big bed sheet.

'Okay. How much will that be?'

'Rs 56. Since there is space on the train, I am giving you only two tickets. If someone asks, tell them the children are all younger than five years. Okay?'

Akmal nodded.

The ticket seller handed him two cardboard tickets. Akmal turned around and walked up to Syeda.

'Delhi! What will we do there? Who is there? And Delhi folks are very cunning!' Syeda was irritated.

'But who is there in Lucknow?' Akmal asked.

The train was to leave in an hour. There was no time for a discussion.

'Let's go. We can always come back,' Akmal said as he put the bed sheet sack on his head, supported it with one hand, and started walking, holding Salman's hand with the other. Syeda followed, muttering to herself.

They climbed on to the overbridge to reach the platform. The Kashi Vishwanath Express was cleaner than most other trains. The ticket seller had told Akmal that VIPs used this train to travel to Delhi and back.

They walked up to the last 'general' coach, with unreserved seating, which was relatively emptier than the others. There were people of all kinds on the train, labourers and the 'tip-top' ones too. There was a row of benches with overhead luggage racks and open windows for ventilation.

Akmal parked Shazeb and Salman on the luggage racks over the seats. Below, seeing a child in Syeda's arms, the five people sitting on a seat meant for three moved and adjusted themselves to create just enough space for her to park a portion of her butt. She sat down with Reshma, less than a year old, in her lap. Akmal sat near her feet on the train floor.

Khata-khat, khata-khat the train went, as it left Banaras station.

Oh, the boys were thrilled: the train was moving. This was the first train journey for both of them. The sound changed to *khatak-khatak, khatak-khatak*. Salman and Shazeb moved forward and backward, in sync with the rhythm. They did this for an hour. Then, they started dangling their legs over the heads and faces of the people sitting below. They giggled each time someone moved their head to dodge their feet. It was so much fun till Shazeb's slipper fell into the lap of a man below.

He got up and slapped Shazeb across his cheek. '*Saale! Babar ki aulaad!*' Babar's child.

He turned and kicked Akmal, who was sitting on the floor. '*Mulle*, that's what you teach your pups!'

Mulle, a term that was more often now used for Muslims in a pejorative manner.

'Saheb, forgive him. It happened by mistake. He is just a child.' Akmal folded his hands.

'Child? Babar's child is worse than a demon.'

Two people in the compartment intervened. Someone vacated the window seat and the man went and sat there. A simple, innocuous-looking man.

Syeda got up and took off Shazeb's and Salman's chappals and stuffed them in the sack. She made them fold their legs and then placed the sack in front of them as a shield that left only their heads visible.

Babar ki auladon ko, goli maaro saalo ko. Babar's children, shoot them all.

Since the Madanpura riots, she had heard that a lot. Babar was the founder of Mughal empire in the Indian subcontinent.

But Babar's actual descendants were quite *mamooli log*. Ordinary people.

Three or four years back, she had met Begum Aqila, a tailor, somewhere in Banaras. Syeda had gone to buy yarn, shuttles and bobbins from a wholesale shop. She was in a rush and asked Munne Mian, the shopkeeper, to hurry up. That's when Munne Mian said, 'Wait. Babar's *bahubegum* is here. Let me get done with her order first.'

Aquila, small and plump, flashed a big smile and said, 'Munne Mian, why are you fooling around?'

Munne Mian responded, 'When did I lie. What is, is.'

Aquila picked up her supplies and walked away with a smirk.

Then Munne Mian told Syeda that Aquila was the wife of Mirza Alamgir, a descendant of Babar. Some descendants of the Mughal emperor Babar had moved to Banaras 200 years ago, according to him. Alamgir's father Fariduddin had even received a pension as a royal family member till the late 1950s. He made a three-storey house with the money he got. Now, Mirza Saheb lived off the rent from this house. He never went to school. And so to make ends meet, he had been making *vark*, silver leaf, by hammering silver wires, for the last forty years. He earned Rs 2 for a dozen.

'There was a time when his ancestors ate in silver plates and now he makes silver leaves to decorate mithai. *Badshah se mazdoor ban gaye, hum jaise,*' said Munne Mian.

Hum jaise, like us – it stayed with her. Like us, *mazdoor*, workers.

Now this man in the train says Babar's children are demons.

Are they demons or workers? Or both? Or just *mamooli log*?

☙

She was lost in these thoughts when the train stopped with a huge jolt. Six hours had passed since the train left Banaras. It was evening. The train was at Jais station, a small town near Amethi.

A number of vendors put their hands through the window to sell samosa, aloo poori, laddoo. Some others entered the compartment to sell chai, peanuts and barfi. Then someone entered to sell chana chaat. Boiled black gram with tomato, onion, chilli, lemon and salt.

Rashid had told her that chana makes you as powerful and resilient as a horse. *Ghode ki taaqat*. And the feeling of fullness lasts for hours. Since then she had always trusted chana.

Shazeb and Salman were no longer visible. They were asleep behind the sack. Reshma was sleeping in Akmal's lap as he stared blankly out of the window.

Syeda stopped the chana chaat vendor and bought three helpings for Rs 5. She gave one to Akmal, one to Shazeb and Salman to share, and ate the third herself. Within minutes, the chaat had been polished off and the newspaper it was wrapped in was clear and readable. '*Pati ne kai hisse kar patni ko tandoor mein jalaya.*' Husband chops up wife into several parts and burns them in a clay oven. Syeda had regularly heard of women being set on fire by in-laws with kerosene if they didn't bring enough dowry. The other story she had heard was of Rani Padmavati who set herself on fire to save her honour. The poet Jais from Jais, the town they had just passed, had written about her.

This was a new one. It was known as Delhi's 'tandoor case'. A man had shot his wife dead and disposed of her body in a clay oven in a restaurant because he suspected her of having an extramarital affair.

Syeda had just finished eating and felt nauseous after reading this. Everyone said Delhi folks were very aggressive. And now Akmal had mindlessly bought tickets to Delhi. She was angry but had no choice. She stared at Akmal but he was, as always, oblivious. In a fit of anger, she snatched up Reshma, who was about to fall from his lap. Akmal looked at her for a few seconds and then went back to looking outside the window. No reaction.

After a few hours, some people got off at Lucknow. It was pitch dark. Syeda asked Akmal to get down. He did not budge.

'What is the difference now? Delhi and Lucknow are the same,' he said.

Syeda was determined to get down. She tried to wake up Salman and Shazeb but they were fast asleep. She asked Akmal again. He pulled her hand, asking her to sit. She stood up again to gather the belongings. By then, the train had moved.

She sat down and leaned her head against the train compartment's ply wall, feeling upset and helpless. Then she dozed off.

When she woke up, it was morning. Daily passengers from Ghaziabad and its neighbouring areas had occupied every inch of the coach. The train had entered Delhi. Within an hour they reached the Delhi railway station. Akmal and Syeda waited for everyone to get off, both trying to think of the first thing to do in this new city where they knew no one.

When the compartment was empty, they picked up Shazeb, Salman, Reshma and their sack from the luggage carrier and got off.

The station was huge. They got off the overbridge to reach the exit. The beggars had many one-rupee coins in their bowls, Syeda noticed. In Banaras, one-rupee coins were a rarity for beggars. Only fifty paise, twenty-five paise.

A number of rickshaw drivers hovered around them at the station exit.

'Rickshaw?'

'Do you want a rickshaw?'

'Auto? Shared auto?'

Several people walked up to them.

A pale man with strong hands, hardened face and lean body stared at them.

Pyaare Lal was a cycle rickshaw driver. He had grown up in Allahabad, three hours from Banaras. In the last few years, he had been driving a cycle rickshaw for a living. He never married because no one ever arranged one for him. He had severed all ties with his family. Now, once in a while he would frequent the brothels on G.B. Road, and even took customers for the sex workers in the red-light area there for a commission.

Many people getting off at the Delhi station needed rides to Old Delhi or Paharganj. Pyaare Lal was more interested in the Paharganj passengers as most of them would end up staying in a hotel, earning him either a ten-rupee commission or a full meal at the in-house restaurants in the hotel. This had taught him how to deal with tourists. Gauge them, switch to their language, make suggestions – all for the cost of a rickshaw ride.

Syeda's conversation with Akmal in Purabiya, an eastern Uttar Pradesh (UP) Hindi dialect, similar to the Bhojpuri language, gave him a hint. Utensils could be heard clinking in the sack. And the cotton quilt and mattress that they were carrying in the month of August made it clear they had left their hometown probably for good to settle in Delhi.

'Kaa-ho? Chalba?' said Pyaare Lal.

What's up? Want to go?

Akmal and Syeda together turned to him. The warmth of a familiar language.

'Yes. But where?' replied Akmal.

'Left home and come? I can see the rolling pin in the sack,' said Pyaare Lal.

'Yes. Now, we will live here only,' replied Akmal as he looked at Syeda.

'Come,' Pyaare Lal said, signalling towards his rickshaw. He started walking.

Akmal and Syeda picked up the sack and the quilt, and followed him without much thought.

Grab the first straw in the pond that keeps you afloat.

Pyaare loaded the quilt and mattress on to the back of the rickshaw and placed Shazeb and Salman on it. 'Hold on to the edge. Don't let go,' he told them.

Syeda sat on the seat with Reshma and Akmal. Pyaare placed their sack of belongings near their feet on the rickshaw floor.

As he started pedalling the cycle rickshaw, he asked, 'Where have you come from?'

'Lohta,' said Akmal.

Syeda added, 'Lohta. In Banaras.'

'Hmmm. You just picked up your bags and came with your family? Do you know this is Dilli? *Dilli bahot behudi.*'

Delhi is very ill-mannered.

'We had heard *Dilli dilwalon ki*,' Syeda said. Delhi belongs to the large-hearted.

'They may have a heart. But do they use it?' replied Pyaare with a smile as he turned back to look at both of them.

As the rickshaw moved through the main lane of Paharganj, the white foreigners, tourists with matted hair and saffron kurtas and long neckpieces, reminded Syeda of Banaras. There was not much difference between this place and the by-lanes near Dashashwamedh ghat in Banaras where similar *firangi*s could be seen making the rounds. In search of peace and Bam Bhole.

Bam Bhole is another name for the Hindu god Shiva. But sometimes, it may also refer to various forms of cannabis that Shiva is believed to enjoy.

'Is there a ghat here as well?' asked Syeda.

Akmal stared at her as a signal to remain silent.

'There is a Yamuna riverbank here. It is full of factory trash. You can't take a dip in it like you can in Gangaji in Banaras,' Pyaare Lal said.

Even the shops here sold the same miniature Taj Mahals, wooden elephant statues, *rudraksh* necklaces, yellow *ramnaami* kurtas, with 'Ram' printed over them, and thin cotton towels.

This must be a welcome sign from Baba. Baba Kashi Vishwanath from Banaras is still with us, Syeda thought to herself. She asked Pyaare, 'Can you find a job for us?'

Pyaare turned back to smile at her. He kept pedalling and entered a narrow lane and stopped at the dead end, next to Chanchal Lodge. It was a three-storey building. He asked the family to wait as he went inside and spoke to the manager.

The manager came out and took them to a room on the second floor. 'Pay me Rs 50 per day. I am letting you stay here without the lodge owner's knowledge. Otherwise, the tariff is Rs 200 per day.' And he left.

Pyaare Lal said, 'Stay here for two days. Look around the city. Meanwhile, I'll see what you can do.'

The room had a double bed and a TV that didn't work. After everyone had washed up, they went out to buy food. The hotel manager looked at them and said, '*Now* you look like you are from a good family.'

After a meal of rajma chawal in a roadside restaurant, their first full meal in twenty-four hours, they slept through the whole evening and night.

༄

The next day, when Syeda went to the hotel terrace to put their clothes out to dry, she met a *firangi* girl, Nikki. She was in jeans and a T-shirt and had matted hair. Syeda smiled at her. Nikki walked up to her and started admiring the embroidery on her dupatta.

Nikki asked, 'Where from?' gesturing with her hand.

Syeda didn't know English but understood the gesture. She replied, 'Banaras.'

'Oooh Banaras!' said Nikki, taking a long drag from an imaginary spliff and laughing.

Syeda smiled and returned to her room.

When she told Akmal what happened on the terrace, he said, 'Do you know she is a *yahudi*? The whole of Paharganj is full of *yahudis*.'

Yahudi. Jewish.

In 1992, India and Israel established formal diplomatic ties. Since then, it is estimated that every year, close to 50,000 Israelis visit India. Most of them are in their early twenties, and come for long stays in India to unwind after completing their mandatory national military service.

Syeda had been told as a child that Jewish people can't be trusted and warned not to befriend them. But Nikki was the first Jewish person she had met. At least that she was aware of. In Banaras, you can never make out. Everyone is just a *firangi*.

It was their third day in Delhi. The hotel bill was Rs 150 already. Plus they had spent Rs 100 in the last two days on food, soap, milk, etc.

Syeda and Akmal had come with Rs 3,000. In their mind, that was a lot. Syeda realized that it would last them just over a month if they didn't actively start looking for work. Pyaare Lal was nowhere to be seen. And Akmal would leave the room in the morning and come back in the evening – but with no work or money.

The next morning, as Akmal left for the day, Syeda went to the terrace to see where he went. He just sat at the bus stop on the main road. When she went back to the terrace around noon, four hours later, to pick up their clothes, he was still sitting there.

Akmal was back to his old ways. Loitering, sitting by the road all day. And this was not even at a shrine, where he could at least earn some blessings. This was a bus stop, where buses were leaving every few minutes but he wouldn't move his arse to hop on to one.

Syeda came downstairs to the room, muttering to herself. Salman was at the door. Nikki, who was in the room opposite, called Salman, offering him a toffee. Syeda went with him. There was a big pile of clothes in the room.

Syeda pointed at it and gestured: 'What is this?'

Nikki replied, 'No laundry,' making a cross in the air.

Syeda pointed towards herself and then the pile of clothes to say: 'I can do it.'

Nikki smiled embarrassedly and said, 'No. No.'

Syeda insisted. She picked up the pile and started walking towards her room. Salman followed her.

Nikki repeated, 'No. No.'

Syeda didn't pay her any heed. Within half an hour, she had washed all the clothes and put them on the clothes line on the terrace to dry.

In the evening, Nikki knocked on Syeda's door. When she opened it, Nikki handed her Rs 30 and a box of sweets and said, 'Thank you.'

Syeda had recovered half a day's rent at the hotel, just as she had hoped.

Bas baatein band, kaam shuru. Deeds, not words.

She had switched on her survival mode unconsciously: this was how she had spent most of the twenty-two years of her life. First, acting as the emotional manager of the family, protecting Mehreen and dealing with an absent father. Then, in the years of her marriage to Akmal so far, she was the one who would step in to clean up everyone's mess, fix everything, stay solid like a rock, one that would just continue to exist, come what may. What other option did she have?

Over the next three days, Syeda did four more loads for Nikki and three for her friends. In four days, she made roughly Rs 250. She did not tell Akmal.

༄

A week later. It was noon and Syeda was hanging out clothes on the terrace when she spotted Pyaare Lal arriving with another set of lodgers. She waved to him and went running down.

'Bhai Saheb, where have you been? Did you find any work for us?'

'Oh! You people are still here? I thought you would have left.'

'But you asked us to wait for you!'

'You were waiting for me?'

'But we have been living here on your assurance,' Syeda replied.

'Bhauji, what did I say that day: This is Dilli. And Dilli is *behudi*!' he replied.

That day Pyaare Lal told Syeda how he had landed up in Delhi. His father worked as a manual scavenger. Every evening, he would come home drunk and beat up his mother. Then one day, his mother died. Pyaare was twelve or thirteen. He ran away from home to the Sangam bank in Allahabad and lived on the alms given by tourists, sometimes doing odd jobs. Carrying luggage, cleaning cars, picking up trash from the stalls on the ghat, and throwing it at the municipal trash depot.

Five or six years later, a tourist told him about Delhi and how it received a lot of labour from UP and Bihar, that wages were higher there. He took the next train to Delhi and reached Paharganj. For the first few days, he earned no money. He would manage half a meal a day from a Hindu temple, and the rest from gurdwaras, Sikh temples, that run free community kitchens.

Rickshaw driving is one of the commonly available jobs in Delhi for new, poor seasonal migrants. Since a large number of the city's population, including the urban poor, depend on this kind of informal transportation, the job is available throughout the year.

Pyaare Lal started hiring a rickshaw on a daily basis from a number of rickshaw contractors in Chandni Chowk. Over the years, he cultivated their trust and that was why he was not required to provide any deposit to rent one.

In all these years, he never thought of buying his own rickshaw. It required not just significant investment but also maintenance work and paying a fee to the Municipal Corporation of Delhi.

Pyaare had to pay roughly Rs 10–20 every day, around 20 per cent of his daily earnings, to the contractor-owner. He worked for ten to twelve hours every day, more during the tourist and festival season, and managed to make Rs 3,000 per month.

Pyaare joked, 'The rickshaw colour should match my mood! When I get fed up of a rickshaw of one colour, I rent another!'

He told Syeda that day, 'Don't take anything at face value in Delhi. I will come in the evening. Tell Bhaijaan to be ready.' And smiling, he left.

Around seven in the evening, Pyaare Lal did come. Akmal was waiting for him near the lodge entrance. The manager said, 'What, Pyaare Lal! My boss is going to come back and they are refusing to leave.'

'Arre Saheb, they are UP-walas. They are still not used to the ways of Dilli.'

Pyaare Lal asked Akmal to hop on to his rickshaw, and twenty minutes later they were in a by-lane of Chandni Chowk.

Chandni Chowk, Moonlit Square, was part of Shahjahanabad, the walled city constructed in 1648 when the Mughal emperor Shah Jahan moved his capital from Agra to Delhi.

There were several hundred handcarts lined up in the lane. At the far end of the lane was a truck. Cart pullers and their assistants were loading cargo from the truck on to their carts and then pulling them past Akmal and Pyaare to the other end.

Chandni Chowk is one of the largest wholesale markets of India. It has narrow lanes. A truck can only come till this loading point. From there, handcarts take the cargo to various godowns. Then, they are taken to the stores. Each cart assistant gets Rs 40–50 a day. The one who owns a cart can earn up to Rs 300.

'You'll find work here,' declared Pyaare Lal.

Akmal looked at the towering load on one cart. Boxes, sacks, one over the other. One person manually pulled the cart, two assistants pushed it from the sides.

'How much weight is on that one?' he asked.

'About 200–250 kilos. When the distance and the weight are more, you get paid more too,' Pyaare said. 'If you manage to buy a cart, the warehouse could even put you on their rolls. Fixed salary every month. And extra if you do some work at night,' he added.

Akmal stared into space.

Pyaare continued without acknowledging Akmal's disappointment, 'For now, start by making as much money as you can.'

Pyaare introduced him to one Ram Khilawan, a cart owner, and it was agreed that Akmal would return early the next morning to assist in taking cargo from the loading station to the wholesale spice market, Khari Baoli.

Akmal came back to the hotel and told Syeda he had found work. He would have to leave for work early in the morning the next day. He also told her to start packing to leave the lodge soon.

He tried to get some sleep but he was nervous. For the past ten years, he had worked on the loom. First on the handloom, sitting all day, spinning yarn. And then at the power loom, standing all day. This was the first time he would be lugging cargo. From a skilled weaver, he would become a porter. That too for just Rs 40 a day.

The next morning at five he reached Fatehpuri Mosque. Ram Khilawan was sleeping on his cart. Akmal woke him up.

'You are here. Come, sit. I will just be back from the bathroom.'

Ram Khilawan went to the public toilet on the other side of the road and returned in ten minutes, his face washed.

Most cart pullers like Ram Khilawan slept on their carts on the side of the road. They did not have a house. They had families back home in the village and would go back once or twice a year, when they had saved enough money.

'Come, let's have chai and then pick up the dry fruits from the truck. Always remember, chai and *beedi* are very important for this work,' he said.

As they were having chai at a roadside stall along with several other cart pullers and porters, it started drizzling. The unpredictable August monsoon.

They reached the loading point. It took almost an hour to load 200 kilos of walnuts, in big boxes, on to the cart. Akmal slipped while trying to push the cart but the cart did not move. It was so heavy. Then Ram Khilawan told him to push it forward from the side. That was when it moved.

Everyone was in a rush. The peak work hours are five in the morning to one in the afternoon. The idea is to do as many rounds as possible in this period to maximize earnings.

It was pouring heavily and so the 2 kilometre stretch to the godown seemed never-ending. At the turn of the road, there was waterlogging and calf-high water. They glided through it. Ram Khilawan told Akmal to tuck the plastic sheet tightly over the walnut boxes. It took them about an hour to reach the godown.

It was a room in an old house in a narrow lane. There were no lights. Ram Khilawan asked Akmal to help load the boxes on to his shoulder to place them in the room. He knew the place well enough to be able to navigate in the dark. Almost an hour later, they were done and walking back to the loading point. They made four such rounds. It was 2 p.m.

Akmal had severe stomach cramps by now. He held his stomach with both hands and slumped down next to the cart.

'What happened? Tired?' Ram Khilawan asked Akmal.

Some of the cart pullers laughed at him. Never much of a talker, Akmal just stared at the open drain by the footpath he was sitting on.

Then one of them said, 'Go, eat something. This work is not done on an empty stomach.'

Akmal's feet were achy and trembling. He stumbled up to a street vendor and ate one serving of aloo poori for Rs 2.50. That was not enough. He had another one and then went off to sleep on Ram Khilawan's cart parked next to a temple tree.

Relief.

By now Khari Baoli was buzzing. Thousands of shops, some very tiny, were selling all kinds of spices. There were, in open sacks, huge mounds of turmeric, nutmeg and rock salt. Cumin, dry mangoes and cinnamon sticks. All neatly lined up, next to each other.

Businesspersons, mostly men, come from all parts of the country to this market, choose what they want after tasting and smelling the spices, and then order in bulk. The bulk order is transported from the godown to the truck by the cart pullers.

In an hour, Ram Khilawan woke up Akmal. For a few seconds, Akmal was disoriented and looked for the tea stall next to his loom.

A *thulla*, police constable, was sauntering towards them to collect a bribe for parking on the road. Before he could come closer, Akmal and Ram Khilawan started walking off with the cart to the loading point again.

'Running after seeing me? No problem, I will see you when you park on the road next time,' the *thulla* yelled.

'What a rascal! Don't look back,' Ram Khilawan told Akmal.

By the time they completed three more rounds of loading and transporting it was 7 p.m. There was no more work till the next morning. 'Unless you want to sleep here and do some loading when trucks arrive at midnight,' Ram Khilawan said.

It was a maze of thousands of people scrunched together. It seemed like everyone was struggling for space: cars, rickshaws, porters, shoppers and pedestrians. And the rain and the humidity!

Akmal said he would come back early the next morning. It was too much for him.

He went back to the lodge. They ate the dal roti Akmal had got packed from Khari Baoli, which was cheaper than the tourist dhaba in Paharganj. He slept off and left at 5 a.m. again the next morning.

The manager had found out that Syeda was doing laundry for the foreigners and making money. He threatened to turn them out but gave her some more time after she agreed to do his laundry for free during their remaining time there. She told Akmal they could no longer afford to stay there.

With the help of Ram Khilawan, Akmal managed to find a small room in Gadodia Market. The rent was Rs 250 per month. They left Chanchal Lodge three days later.

༺༻

On 15 August 1995, internet access was made public to the citizens of India by Videsh Sanchar Nigam Limited.

It was afternoon when the family reached Khari Baoli.

India is the largest producer of spices in the world. It also imports enormous quantities more from around the globe. Khari Baoli, one of the largest spice markets in Asia, covers a 1 kilometre stretch between the Fatehpuri mosque and Chandni Chowk.

They walked through an unassuming tunnelled arch. This was Gadodia Market, a huge multi-storey heritage building complex with floral carvings on the walls. It was crammed with spice shops. Coughing, sneezing, with itchy throats and watering eyes, they climbed up a betel-stained stairway, dodging porters carrying huge sacks.

Their room, damp with seepage, was on the third floor. Through a rickety window frame, they could see the water tanks and terraces of the many interconnected buildings around the sprawling rectangular courtyard of Gadodia Market.

The canopies on the terraces looked like the ones Syeda had seen in Sarnath, a Buddhist pilgrimage site close to Varanasi. Syeda and her family stood there wonderingly. What a huge haveli. Syeda had only seen such structures in films like *Pakeezah* and *Mughal-e-Azam*. There was a small bathroom adjoining the room and Syeda could dry their clothes in the passage outside. The rent for this room was higher because it had a separate bathroom, Akmal told her. It was the former office of a spice trader downstairs.

Akmal left for work and Syeda spent the rest of the day setting up house. Needing to stock up, she stepped out, locking Salman, Shazeb and Reshma in the room with a few salted rotis.

On the ground floor, there were several hundred narrow shops, most of them containing only a desk and a few chairs in front and some samples of rock salt, spices and dry fruits. The rear of each shop was usually a godown stacked with bags of spices. Syeda wanted to buy some groceries but was told to go outside to the retail market. 'This is wholesale,' they said.

She had basic utensils, a mattress and a quilt, a few clothes that she had brought from Banaras. She bought a kerosene stove, a bucket, chana dal, rice and flour with the laundry money. When Akmal returned after the second shift around 9 p.m., the first home-cooked meal in two weeks was ready.

The next morning, before sunrise, they woke up with the *call for morning namaz*. Syeda hadn't noticed that Gadodia Market shared its wall with the Fatehpuri mosque. Akmal left after a cup of tea. In an hour, the market started buzzing. Porters flocked at the warehouses, the small rooms all around Gadodia Market, to load and unload numbered sacks of spices and dry fruits. The cart pullers pulled the carts with an almost feverish frenzy. The shops had neatly laid out sacks of spices, nuts, herbs, tea. By 11 a.m., the market had come fully alive.

Syeda could see a number of women on the terrace. She walked up the stairs and entered another world: a 360 degree view of Old Delhi, with the Red Fort, Jama Mosque and Fatehpuri mosque clearly visible in between countless houses, shops and markets. On the terrace, women and men were cleaning, segregating grains and spices and putting them to dry: turmeric and ginger roots, vanilla pods, poppy seeds, coriander seeds, red chillies.

An old woman in a cotton saree sat cross-legged on the floor, throwing coriander seeds up in the air from a bamboo *soop* – a tray with one side open, traditionally used for cleaning grains and whole spices – and then catching them back in the tray. The seeds gathered at the back, and the dust in front, which she would blow away. She cleaned several batches that way.

Syeda turned around and saw many women doing the same with black pepper, cumin, carom seeds, cardamom and whatnot. She leaned against the parapet wall and watched.

'Who do you want to meet?' the old woman asked.

'No one. Just watching,' replied Syeda.

'New here?' she asked.

'Came just yesterday,' Syeda answered.

Syeda learnt that Kamla, the old woman, worked for a shop for Rs 600 a month. Every day, she would clean three to five bags of spices of 50 kilos each. She would come in the morning at 9 and leave around 6–7 p.m. She had been employed at the shop for the last three years. The shop owner was a ninth-generation trader in Gadodia Market.

Kamla's late husband had been a landless farmer in Bihar. He worked on a farm owner's field in exchange for a portion of the annual crop produce. In 1980, when the Kosi river engulfed the village in the annual floods, he succumbed to the resultant yellow fever epidemic. The patch of land they farmed had also been washed away. Her brother-in-law convinced her and her teenage sons to move to Delhi.

Both her sons worked as porters in Chandni Chowk. Six years back, one of them died of tuberculosis. The other was an addict. He hardly had any savings. Kamla was hoping to save enough money to go back to her village the next year and arrange his marriage. She lived in Daryaganj with her brother-in-law, a widower. Many claimed that they lived as husband and wife but Syeda didn't probe into that.

Over the next few weeks, Syeda developed a deep affinity for Kamla, who introduced her to the ways of Delhi and Khari Baoli. Having lived in the capital city for fifteen years, Kamla's Bhojpuri had acquired a certain roughness. Banaras and Bihar both use a Purabiya dialect of Hindi. Longing for the warmth and sweetness of her language, Syeda occasionally heard it from Kamla.

Akmal would always be too tired and bad-tempered to talk when he came back home in the evenings. There were not many women in the residential complex. Most of the residents were men, from Kashmir, Nepal, Rajasthan, Madhya Pradesh, UP and Bihar. People from one community tended to stick together, cook together. Their families were back home in the villages and they would send them postal money orders every once in a while. That was the template most Khari Baoli porters and cart pullers followed. There were thousands of porters like Ram Khilawan who did not even rent a place to save money and slept on the pavement or on the carts at Aruna Asaf Ali Marg.

Syeda was used to open spaces in Banaras – plants, her own courtyard, clean air – so different from the small dingy room they now occupied and the constant buzz in Gadodia Market. Here, there was not one moment of silence except on Sundays, when the market was shut and the pace of life slowed and people napped. All day, Syeda would wash, clean the room, cook and wait in long queues to fill water from the tap downstairs since the bathroom did not have running water. The water came only in the morning. That was also when there was a long queue for the porters to get ready. The men would bathe there and so she had to wait till they were done. Every alternate day she would end up with no water and so could not have a bath. She hated it but there was nothing she could do about it.

By October 1995, Akmal had started drinking. Someone had told him that it was the cheapest and best way to cure all aches and pains. Occasionally, he would beat up the kids and Syeda too. He had started bringing home less and less money, sometimes only Rs 20 a day.

Delhi was turning out to be more restrictive than Banaras. Syeda still could not work outside because there was no one to look after her kids. She couldn't lock them up in the room the whole day. In Banaras, she could leave them at her brothers' place or even at a neighbours.' Everyone was her own and it was not a big deal. Here, she knew no one, could ask no one for this favour free of cost.

☙

Winter was setting in. The warm sunlight on the terrace was a treat for her and the kids. Nice and balmy, it was a welcome change from the claustrophobia of the room downstairs. Some children, homeless, who lived on the streets, came with their *charkhis*, kite spools, to fly kites. They would ask her for some cooked rice, not to eat, but to use as *laee*, a homemade glue. They would crush discarded glass bottles and then use the *laee* to stick the glass powder on to the string of the kites. That worked as an abrasive to cut other flyers' kite strings.

In spite of these moments of respite, she was not happy.

She told Kamla they had been living on potatoes and rice for a week and asked Kamla to talk to her employer to get her some work. Syeda was anyway helping Kamla every day while chatting. Sometimes Kamla would give the children a Re 1 coin, and a Rs 5 note to Syeda.

'My seth is a *janeudhari*. He had collected money from other traders to send bricks to the Ram temple. But I know another one who will hire you,' Kamla told her.

Janeudhari, the one who wears the holy thread, an upper-caste Brahmin. As part of the Ram Janmabhoomi campaign, the Sangh Parivar had started a drive to collect bricks for the construction of the Ram temple in Ayodhya.

The next day, Syeda went with Kamla to the ground floor where she was introduced to the owner of Shop Number 21. She was given the job of removing the stems from raisins, the agreed rate being 50 paise per 2 kilos.

Every evening, a porter would come and put two bags of raisins, each 50 kilos, on the terrace to be worked on the next day. There was no space in the room, plus the seepage had now reached the floor. Syeda would go up to the terrace with the kids every morning and start removing the stems. For the first few days, she could not complete more than a sack.

'This Banarasi *fursat* won't do here if you want to feed your children vegetables and meat,' said Kamla one day.

Banarasi leisure. When you have a lot of time. When you are in no rush for anything in life. When you can stand for hours on the roadside watching government officials digging a drain. Where the time to do nothing is considered more fulfilling than making extra bucks. Syeda sometimes thought about it but it was Akmal who was actually missing it, sulking about it, given the hard labour he was required to put in every single day. This caused his alcohol intake to increase.

After making only Rs 12.50 every day for two weeks, a total of Rs 175, Syeda had to pick up speed.

She learnt that the raisins were mostly imported from Afghanistan and 100 gram of any variety cost more than her weekly wage. She found out that raisins had different colours. She had earlier seen and eaten only the golden ones, sultanas, in kheer, sevaiyan and meetha chawal on Eid. The seth told her one day that they were coated in a solution to make them dry faster and so they remained golden or pale yellow and never darkened. They were seedless and tangy. In contrast, the munakka raisin was made from a ripe grape and then dried in the sun. They were longer, darker and sweeter. There were other varieties too: malaga, muscat and currant.

The cleaning of raisin stems was done in stages. First, the bigger stems and twigs were removed. Then they were shaken in the bamboo tray to break up the clumps and separate the raisins. The final and the most difficult stage was to remove the cap stems that linked the grape to the vine stem. Syeda figured out that spinning them in a vessel a number of times with a rolling pin would quickly loosen the cap stem.

By working on the terrace at night, with a makeshift kerosene lamp, even though it was cold, she graduated to three sacks, Rs 37.50 a day. She had hoped to make at least Rs 1,100 each month at this speed. But daily wage work was available only twelve or thirteen days in a month, which added up to less than Rs 500 a month.

At least Akmal had still been going to work for the last five months. His earnings took care of the rent and the cheap rice and wheat she bought from Naya Bazaar mandi, the stuff that didn't meet quality control and was sold at a far cheaper price.

With her earnings, she bought milk and vegetables, and meat waste from the butcher shop once a month.

Wages might be higher in Delhi but so was the cost of living. In Banaras you could get 250 gram of bhindi for Rs 5. Here, you got the same amount for Rs 7. Mixing potatoes in everything to bulk up the quantity of the food was a necessity.

Syeda had been called a *batod*, a chatterbox, in Banaras. From *nautanki* to film heroes and heroines, to the latest neck patterns in kurtas to loom parts, she could talk about anything. In Delhi, she had switched to communicating in monosyllables and signs. Except with Kamla, her sons and two or three other porters from UP and Bihar.

Not that there wasn't much to say. But it was hard to understand Delhi's language. The 900 kilometre distance between Banaras and Delhi meant switching from Purabiya Hindi to Khari Boli Hindi, Punjabi, Urdu and a mix of all three. Everyone would talk in Delhi as if they were scolding you.

They also had a *taqiya kalam*, a pet phrase. *Bhencho*.

Bhencho, why do you people pack your bags and come to Delhi to find work?

When will you get done with the work, bhencho?

Let's have chai, bhencho!

And one day, Shazeb, while flying kites on the terrace, said, 'Rahul, you *bhencho*!'

Her six-year-old son had acquired the local lingo.

Kamla explained to her one day, '*Bhencho* is like *Bhonsdiwale*, a punctuation, an exclamation point in a sentence, that you Banarasis use.'

Both the Hindi words were literally abuses targeted at women.

Over the next four months, Syeda switched from cleaning raisins to other spices. By March 1996, she had done the 'big four' of Indian masalas: brown cumin seeds, red chillies, yellowish green coriander seeds and yellow turmeric roots. They were available in all shops in Gadodia. The minimum purchase for each of them was 40 kilos.

She could now identify at least three types of *jeera*, cumin seeds: brown for everyday use, black for Bengali food, and shahi for Mughlai food. She also found out that *hing*, asafoetida, was a pinkish white resin and not a seed, and that wheat flour was mixed in it before it was sold.

℘

On 19 October 1995 Dilwale Dulhania Le Jayenge, *starring Shah Rukh Khan, released. The movie has been playing in a theatre for over 1,000 weeks since its release.*

It was February and preparations for the 1996 general elections had begun. Chandni Chowk is the smallest of Delhi's seven Lok Sabha constituencies. That year there was tough competition between the Congress's J.P. Aggarwal and the BJP's J.K. Jain.

J.K. Jain was the owner of Jain Studios and a pioneer in the use of electronic media for electoral canvassing. That year, *Time* magazine had described him as 'the country's leading maker and distributor of political videos, a potent new force in Indian politics'. Jain Studios had started making videos for election campaigns in 1987. Special graphics, montages, skits, everything was used in these videos for political leaders.

Many, including big guns like Shatrughan Sinha, Vijayraje Scindia, Rajiv Gandhi and Bal Thackeray, got videos for their campaigns made by Jain which became all the rage. Jain Studios also made videos for the Ram Janmabhoomi campaign and circulated them widely between 1989 and 1993, when the Sangh Parivar tried to lay the foundation stone of the Ram temple in Ayodhya, popularly known as *shilanyas*. Jain Studios was quick to shoot, edit and disseminate their videos in large parts of India through the Sangh Parivar's networks. Hundreds of copies of the videos were made, circulated and shown in these years through television and VCR. This helped in the recruitment of many part-time Sangh volunteers known as *karsevak*s who were the ones who demolished the Babri mosque. Jain's videos were also shown all over Banaras after the Babri demolition.

In the 1996 election, when Jain contested on a BJP ticket in Chandni Chowk, he positioned television sets in street corners and squares and got the local cable network to show his videos.

These visuals reminded Syeda of a past that she wanted to erase.

In the 1996 general elections, the key points in the BJP's agenda were following principles of Hindutva that aimed at shaping India into a Hindu state, banning cow slaughter, facilitating the construction of the Ram temple at the disputed site in Ayodhya, introducing a uniform civil code to replace the laws applicable to various religions and communities, removing Article 370 of the Indian Constitution that gave special status to Muslim-majority Kashmir, and maintaining a national register of citizens (NRC). They had also brought up the 'tandoor case' because the murderer was Sushil Sharma, a local Congress member.

On 22 April, just three days before the country was to go to the polls, an explosion in a three-storey building in Paharganj killed seventeen people, including eight foreigners. Two separatist groups that took responsibility were seeking to halt the elections in Kashmir.

Thirty people were injured, including Pyaare Lal, who was trapped under the debris of the building. Akmal heard about it from Ram Khilawan, and by the time they found out he was at Ram Manohar Lohia Hospital, he had succumbed to his injuries. His body had been stored in the mortuary as 'unidentified'. Claiming it would have meant paperwork. They did not have any identity cards, which meant they would have had to bribe the cops. And then who would bear the expense for the funeral? 'He is anyway dead. How does it matter?' said Ram Khilawan. Akmal told Syeda that had three or four people chipped in, he would have ensured the cremation, but left it at that.

'*Dilli bahot behudi.*' Pyaare Lal was right. In just a few months, it made you lose your decency and you could declare that organizing a funeral for the dead was irrelevant.

Jain lost the election by a margin of 20,000 votes in Chandni Chowk. But the BJP, led by Atal Bihari Vajpayee, staked its claim to form a government at the Centre, for the first time; it lasted only thirteen days before it was replaced by a third-front coalition government.

The only good thing Syeda heard in these elections was that Phoolan Devi, the dreaded woman bandit from Chambal ravines, had been elected to the Lok Sabha. In the 1980s, many teenage girls like Syeda had been in awe of Phoolan for taking up guns against the feudal landlords. Folklore had it that Phoolan sponsored weddings of poor girls, even sent some to school. These tales were translated into local *nautanki*s.

༄

Both the blast in Paharganj and Jain's campaign vitiated the old city.

In the next few months, investigation into the blast picked up speed. Delhi had seen a few more blasts after that and so every nook and corner of the old city was searched aggressively. It was like the *talaashi* in Madanpura and Lohta after the riots there. Several rickshaw drivers and porters were regularly picked up for questioning.

One day, the *thulla* Jagdish whom Ram Khilawan regularly dodged to avoid paying *hafta*, protection money, to park his cart and sleep on the road, caught hold of Akmal who refused to pay him too.

Over the next few months, Jagdish threatened to get Akmal picked up for questioning. By then, Akmal was a complete drunk and hardly managed to work ten to fifteen days a month.

Syeda needed more work to make ends meet, and actively started looking for jobs outside Gadodia Market.

Her first visit to the 'burqa park' was a revelation. Waiting for a contractor in this park, just at the end of the Khari Baoli road, she noted the comings and goings of women. Women would enter from one end, take off their burqa, and proceed to the market from the other end of the park. Similarly, from the other end, women would enter, put on their burqa, and exit towards the bus stop. These were women who worked in the market. The park also served as a place for women to interact with fellow workers, meet prospective contractors, and redefine freedom in their own terms. It was now clear to Syeda that many women like her were, in their own ways, eking out a living despite restrictions.

The contractor got her work in a namkeen (savouries) factory which occupied one room of a residential quarter in a back lane of Khari Baoli. It shared its premises with a clothes dyeing unit.

Akmal would watch the kids on days when he didn't go to work. But on other days, they would just roam around Gadodia Market. Reshma, however, was too young so she was sometimes left with Kamla and at other times accompanied Syeda to work.

In September 1996, a major outbreak of dengue haemorrhagic fever affected more than 10,000 people in Delhi and neighbouring areas, lasting till December. Lok Nayak Hospital in the vicinity was full of dengue patients. Fever, abdominal pain, vomiting, bleeding were the primary symptoms. Several porters, including Kamla's surviving son, Vishnu, also caught it. Kamla stopped going to work.

The following October and November were a nightmare for Syeda. A drunk Akmal abused the cop Jagdish one day, and was thrown into the lock-up. He was released the next day but had been beaten up brutally.

Syeda was upset at Akmal's recklessness. He had not been on the other side and didn't have a clue about the effort it took to procure bail, running from police station to lawyers to courts. And in Delhi, she did not even know anyone. She was angry he had got into trouble again here, just like he had in Banaras – the very reason they had been uprooted from their hometown.

She took the help of the Chanchal Lodge manager. Thankfully, no case was filed and Akmal was let off after a warning. In return, she did a month's laundry for the hotel free of charge.

It took a month for Akmal to recuperate. But since he was home, she could at least leave the children with him when she went to work in the namkeen factory.

According to a 1989 World Health Organization report, in terms of suspended particulate matter, Delhi was the fourth most polluted city in the world. Environmentalists across Delhi geared up to demand action in the matter.

In March 1995, the Supreme Court heard a plea by lawyer and environmentalist M.C. Mehta and took note of the two most polluting factors in Delhi: vehicles and industries.

The next couple of winters in Delhi, the air was black with smog.

In December 1996, the court ordered the closure of over 1,300 highly polluting industries. Over 90,000 units were notified for relocation from Delhi in a bid to improve the capital city's air quality. Many were to be relocated to the neighbouring states of UP, Rajasthan and Haryana. This move affected a large section of Delhi's migrant population.

The Delhi Master Plan clearly says all polluting industries must ultimately be asked to shift out of the city. But many felt the government and court should have also cracked down on vehicular pollution which contributed more than 50 per cent air pollution at that time in Delhi.

At any rate, all industrial units located close to residential areas were to be shifted. The namkeen factory, like 500 other similar units, had two options: to shift or to shut down.

The namkeen factory owner decided to move the factory to a small village on the outskirts of Delhi, Sabhapur. Some portions of this village, dominated by the Gujjar community, came under the state of UP. The rest was in Delhi. The namkeen factory owner asked Syeda to move to Sabhapur, promising a salary of Rs 2,500 a month and a place to stay.

She decided to move there with the children. From Central Delhi 6 to Outer Delhi 94. Akmal decided to continue working as a cart puller in Old Delhi, promising to visit them every week.

3

Gajak

Phir main zehreele karkhaanon mein,
Zinda rehne ka kaam karne laga,
Saaf inkaar kar nahin paaya,
Woh mera ehteram karne laga . . .
Laila ghar par silai karne lagi,
Qais Dilli mein kaam karne laga . . .

Then I, in poisonous workshops,
Started working at staying alive,
Couldn't outrightly say no,
They started venerating me . . .
Laila started sewing at home,
Qais started working in Delhi . . .

– Fehmi Badayuni, twentieth-century poet

Syeda and family packed up all their belongings and left Khari Baoli in an autorickshaw. The radio was on full blast. The radio announcer mentioned the Australian cricket team's decision not to play in Delhi because of the smog and pollution. An Indian cricket commentator shot back that this was just an excuse for Australia's bad performance in the 1996 World Cup. All said and done, Delhi's pollution had become an international issue.

Reshma, Shazeb and Salman had fallen asleep over the bedding near Syeda's feet. Akmal was sitting in the front seat with the auto driver. He would occasionally get out to push the auto when it got stuck in the potholes of the non-existent roads in 'Yamuna Paar'. It had been hours now in the auto.

The Yamuna is the only major river in Delhi. For centuries, all major Delhi rulers had set up their capitals on the west side of the Yamuna, which has a higher elevation compared to the east side. This helped protect the settlements from flooding.

The region called 'Yamuna Paar' or 'Jamna Paar', Trans Yamuna, refers to the eastern flood-prone bank of the river which started getting settled after Indian independence. In many ways, it demarcates who can be considered the inner and the outer citizen of Delhi.

When the government sought to implement a *slum* removal scheme in inner Delhi in the 1950s and then again during the Emergency in the 1970s, the poor were removed and sent off Yamuna Paar. When Bangladesh was created in the 1970s, the refugees from East Pakistan settled there. When people were evicted to make Delhi a 'world-class city' in the late 1970s in the run-up to the Asian Games of 1982 they were again thrown into outer Delhi. Space in the inner city had to be freed up to construct five-star hotels for guests and athletes, flyovers, the Jawaharlal Nehru Stadium and the Talkatora swimming pool complex. Since Delhi did not produce its own labour, the workers who came from outside Delhi to construct these things, once done, also settled in this periphery.

For the longest time, Jamna Paar was Delhi's least developed area, with very few basic civic amenities. Over the years, leftover construction material, sand, bricks and whatnot have been used by residents themselves to make this soft, marshy *pushta* slightly liveable, tolerable.

Pushta. Riverbank.

All of east Delhi is Jamna Paar.

In 1996, after the court order to oust industrial units from inner Delhi, many small units moved there and even expanded.

When people were evicted from inner Delhi, they lost not just their homes but also their livelihood. There were few transportation options from that bank of the Yamuna into central Delhi and the long commute time left people with no option but to look for work closer by, in the informal economy that gradually emerged in Jamna Paar.

Every day, people from UP, Bihar, West Bengal and Rajasthan, from the most marginalized sections of India, get down at the Shahdara railway station, Kashmere Gate bus terminal or Anand Vihar railway station – the three train and bus terminals closest to north east Delhi – and join the workforce in Jamna Paar.

That day, it took Syeda and her family almost three hours to find Sabhapur. In this time, you could reach Allahabad from Banaras, Syeda thought.

But Delhi is a country in itself.

Sabhapur village is one of Delhi's estimated 360 villages. Located on the outskirts of Delhi, it borders UP's Loni town in Ghaziabad district and is roughly 17 kilometres from Chandni Chowk. About 30 per cent of Sabhapur village is part of Ghaziabad district in the state of UP, whose agricultural and industrial policies differ from Delhi's.

The auto took a muddy track that led to the village. It had small mud houses, shanties, with houses that still had thatched roofs but very big compounds around them. There were very few concrete buildings. You could see farms at the end of the village. But it was not the kind of village Akmal had seen in Chandauli. It was bigger, an urban village, rural in the sense that it lacked the infrastructure of a big city but was culturally influenced by the ways of urban life.

The namkeen factory site consisted of a tin shed with no walls, just a stack of bricks. Nabi Ahmed, the owner of the namkeen factory, a short man in jeans, jacket and sports shoes, was waiting for them.

Akmal unloaded all their stuff in the compound, opening the bedding for the children to lie down. The auto guy wanted to leave before it got dark.

Nobody wanted to come Yamuna Paar. It was considered a jungle. Jamna Paaris were known as tricksters or crooks. But then the poor are always thought of as criminals, encroachers, thieves. For the longest time, people from other Delhi localities did not marry their girls or boys into households in this area. It was called *beehad*.

Beehad. Wilderness.

It was winter and the days were shorter. On top of that, there was a power cut in the village and there were rumours that the Sabhapur

Gujjars were catching hold of anyone on the main *pushta* road, robbing them and beating them to a pulp for even fifty bucks.

The driver asked Akmal to hurry up if he wanted to go back with him to Chandni Chowk. There were no regular public buses from Sabhapur to Chandni Chowk. Within half an hour Akmal was gone. He said he had to work the next day; a big consignment was expected.

Syeda was scared, frustrated, anxious, doubtful, vexed – all at once. Did Akmal even care? In the past year, he had grown more and more distant. What was he thinking when he abandoned them in an unknown village under a tin shed with no food and water? That too in Delhi. For a second, she wondered if he was abandoning them forever.

Akmal must have thought that, as always, she would figure out something. As she did, come what may. But was it such a good thing after all? To take care of everything and not to be cared for at all? Her sisters-in-law were better off. They took no responsibility. They just ate, did housework and weaving work, and slept. But such luxury was not available to her. What did she think life would be like outside Banaras? It may have been a bad decision to move.

It was bitterly cold in the tin shed without walls. A year in Delhi had taught Syeda how much tougher Delhi's December was than Banaras's. That night, she lit a fire using the twigs lying around. It lasted only an hour or so. She sat huddled with the children in a quilt, Reshma weeping continuously, and did not realize when everyone dozed off.

The next morning, just as the sun was rising, a stout woman, dressed in a salwar kameez and shawl, walked in. 'Come, all of you. Have this tea and namak ke paranthe,' she said authoritatively as she sat down without introducing herself.

She poured tea from a brass vessel and looked up to smile at Syeda. 'Does the infant have fever?'

Syeda shook her head. 'She is just hungry.' She sat down quietly next to the woman – her name was Raziya, she learnt – watching her serve the food. Relieved that for a few moments someone had lifted the burden off her shoulders.

Thank god for women, humanity is alive! she thought to herself as she saw Shazeb and Salman with mouthfuls of parantha rolls, chewing at breakneck speed. Men make rules, have discussions of what should be done and how it should be done. But who keeps it all going? Who sustains humanity? Or steps up without being told to? Or takes the initiative to think of the mundane and the ordinary to hold it all together?

Raziya Begum was from Shahjahanpur, a district in UP, 400 kilometres from Delhi. She came to Sabhapur in 1990 when her husband, a construction worker, moved with a contractor to Delhi.

Housing in Trans Yamuna is relatively affordable compared to the rest of Delhi because it has fewer civic amenities. According to some estimates, 46 per cent of migrants from UP live in the Trans Yamuna area, 19 per cent in other middle-class areas in Delhi.

This is also the reason why this edge of Delhi became a hub of large working-class settlements.

After moving to Delhi, Raziya started working as a mason's apprentice. Many women in Sabhapur did construction work before they joined the small factories that were springing up in the vicinity. Nabi Ahmed had hired Raziya and her husband, Mohd Israel, to make a brick-and-mortar structure at the factory site in a week's time, to get things started.

The children and Syeda gathered around Raziya and ate. Within a few minutes it was all over. The food eased their anxiety a bit. It was their first meal since leaving Khari Baoli almost twenty-four hours ago. Kamla did pack some raisins and almonds for the kids. But they were long over.

Raziya looked at the polished-off plates. Syeda was embarrassed. Raziya smiled and said, 'One does feel more hungry in the winters.' She was trying to put Syeda at ease.

Within a week, the brick-and-mortar structure was ready: a huge enclosure with gaps on the upper parts of the walls for ventilation. A tin roof was placed and screwed on iron angles over the brick wall. A handpump was installed within the premises. Nabi Ahmed had promised Syeda a place to stay in the factory. The enclosure was divided into two halves by three iron trunks. One side had a large clay oven which they used for the namkeen factory. The other side was where Syeda had laid their bed and placed their belongings. This side was home.

This was the first time in nine years of marriage that Syeda was staying away from Akmal. They were in the same city but their family had been split up.

'Families separate in Delhi. You can either earn a living or live with your family,' said Raziya.

She told Syeda that such an arrangement was not uncommon among workers in Delhi. Men work and stay elsewhere and visit their families once in two weeks when they save money. Sometimes children are sent to live with grandparents, uncles and aunts or other relatives, and study in the village schools because working parents in Delhi cannot watch over their kids during the day. There are also no creche-like facilities at the workplace.

'At least you have your children here with you! And anyway, if he sits drunk all day in front of your eyes, you will only burn your blood. As it is, you are so tiny!' said Raziya.

She soon became Syeda's confidante. She would always give things a funny, positive twist.

The soul uplifter, Syeda thought. Raziya was a Sufi. 'Raziya Sufi', Syeda started calling her.

Raziya called her 'Banarasi', a name several others would pick up in the coming years.

The very first month, one day when Syeda was walking back from the fields after relieving herself in the morning, she saw a woman her age leaning against a mud wall. She was dressed in a collared shirt and ghaghra. Her dupatta was neatly balanced on the edge of her forehead and hairline.

She yelled at Syeda in a thick Haryanvi accent, *'Aye! Kahan se aayi tu?'* Hey! Where have you come from?

Is this how people talk to strangers? It felt like a stone hitting her chest.

Impolite. Discourteous. The impudence increases as you go from central Delhi to the periphery, she thought to herself.

'Banaras. Where Banarasi sarees are made.' The added trivia was her attempt at breaking the ice with the woman.

'Which saree?'

'Banarasi saree. The one with woven gold and silver,' Syeda tried to explain by drawing a banarasi motif in the air.

The woman had no idea. How could any Indian woman not know what a Banarasi saree was? After all, Banarasi sarees were world famous. This was something one heard in Banaras all the time.

She cursed Akmal under her breath for bringing her to crass Delhi instead of cultured Lucknow. But then if the women did not wear sarees, how would they know?

'But all Hindu women wear sarees, isn't it?' she asked Raziya later.

Gujjar and Jat women, Hindu or not, don't wear sarees, Raziya told her.

'But why the collared bush shirt? Why not a nicely fitted kurta with some colour and design?' Syeda asked Raziya.

'You tailor, weaver! How did you land up in a Gujjar village in Delhi?!' Raziya had a good laugh.

The collared shirt was a fashion style that Jat and Gujjar men had picked up while serving in the British Indian military. And it slowly became customary clothing for the women too.

Neeras. Flavourless, Syeda would call them.

Raziya and Syeda became, what they called in Banaras, *odhni badal* sisters. Friends so close that they could even wear each other's clothes.

Nabi Ahmed decided that along with namkeen snacks, they would also make gajak. Across north India, the demand for gajak rises in winter. Gajak is a sweet snack made of sesame and jaggery – both thought to warm up human bodies.

Kallu Ram, the chef famous for frying super crisp samosas in Chandni Chowk, was hired to prepare the namkeen fried green peas, fried chickpeas, besan sev and namakpara. Syeda was to assist him.

Shakeel and Aftab, newly minted gajak experts from Shahdara, were also hired. Both of them, in their mid-twenties, had run away from Rampur ten years ago. They claimed both sets of their parents were dead and that they had no other siblings or family. They were always buying gifts for each other and blushing like lovers. Syeda always thought that there was more to their story.

Nabi procured sesame from a wholesaler in Jhansi, a district in south UP.

In a few days, Syeda had 'by-hearted' the gajak recipe.

The five of them would start work at nine in the morning.

Shakeel and Aftab would first roast the sesame seeds in a huge iron utensil over a big urn-shaped clay oven made with bricks, cow dung and mud. When the white seeds turned pinkish, they would remove the kadhai from the heat. Then, on the same flame of the open clay oven, they would melt jaggery that came from western UP and Haryana – known as the sugarcane belt – in the vicinity of Sabhapur. The jaggery's consistency would become like kneaded dough. Once that was done, they would stretch the jaggery dough into rope-like structures. These would be hung on a nail on the wall and then stretched, whipped till they started shining evenly. This was done to make them more consistent and smooth in taste. These ropes would be rolled over the roasted sesame and divided and cut into several pieces. All this would take at least three or four hours.

Then Shakeel and Aftab would sit down to pound these pieces with a wooden hammer to flatten them. Once the pieces were flat and even, they would be cut into uniform squares using a steel frame.

It was fascinating to observe the procedure the first few weeks.

The gajak had to be immediately packed to prevent it getting soft. A half kilo box sold at wholesale for Rs 25.

Syeda did the packing. She was assisted by Shazeb on days when work carried on past 8 p.m., so that she could cook dinner. On those days, Syeda would feel agonized about not managing to send the children to school yet.

※

Since moving from Banaras, Syeda had wanted to send the children to school. But the situation had never been conducive.

By the time the family found their footing in Chandni Chowk, it was time to move to Sabhapur.

Nevertheless, she had tried to teach the children whatever she could: numbers and the Hindi alphabet.

After three months in Sabhapur, once their lives had again settled down somewhat, she decided to get the kids admitted to the only private school within accessible distance. But their applications were rejected repeatedly for one reason or another.

Shazeb was seven, Salman six and Reshma almost three. One day in May, when Ratanjot, the principal of the school, once again refused admission to the children because Syeda could not produce an address proof – a bank passbook, ration card or voter card – she broke down outside the school gate. She slumped against the school boundary wall and howled.

Suddenly she felt a shadow over her: a tall, hefty middle-aged man in a white kurta pyjama and a frown on his face was walking towards her. Syeda froze in fear.

He stopped a few feet away from her and said in a loud baritone, 'What happened? Why are you crying like someone has stolen all your buffaloes?'

'What?!' Syeda thought to herself. And then quickly reminded herself of what Raziya had told her. *They are not being rude. That's how they talk.*

Syeda was still wiping her face with her dupatta when Ratanjot came out of the school gate.

'Arre, Tau! Come, come,' Ratanjot said effusively.

'Why is she crying?' the man asked authoritatively.

'She doesn't even have a ration card and yet comes every day to get her children admitted,' Ratanjot replied disdainfully.

'As if you run a government school that you need government documents for children to learn A-B-C-D! The children will tease you, "The master has no brain!"'

Ratanjot quailed. 'But we need to keep records, Tau! Plus, she is a Muslim. She could even be Bangladeshi.'

Over the years, many refugees from Bangladesh have made India their home because of growing economic distress back home. The Sangh Parivar made it a political issue, with the propaganda that the influx of Muslims from Bangladesh would increase their numbers and put the Hindu population in danger: *Hindu khatre mein hain.*

'Don't try to be a politician! I gave the land to the school to have more schoolgoing children than Chauhanpatti. Not to think of Hindu–Muslim,' replied the man as he looked at Syeda.

Ratanjot was staring at the drain lining the school wall.

'Tomorrow I want to see her children in the school.' With that, the large man stalked into the school.

Ratanjot told Syeda, 'Come at seven in the morning tomorrow.' He followed the man inside.

Syeda later recounted the incident to Raziya. Raziya identified the man as Sukhbir Singh Gujjar. One of the biggest landlords in Gujjarpatti.

The Gujjars, a pastoral community living in parts of north and west India, mostly engage in livestock farming and dairy work, and own large patches of land in and around the Delhi National Capital Region (NCR). They constitute roughly 7 per cent of Delhi's electorate and have a sizeable population in Yamuna Paar. Over the years, the Gujjars have sold large patches of their land, which has brought both huge sums of money and also raging consumerism into the community.

Sabhapur has two sub-villages: Gujjarpatti and Chauhanpatti. Gujjarpatti has a population of 4,000 while Chauhanpatti has roughly 800 people. Chauhanpatti is dominated by Thakurs, a landowning, upper-caste, warrior community, while Gujjarpatti is dominated by Gujjars, who are struggling to get reservation in government jobs and colleges under the OBC category.

Sukhbir was one of the biggest employers of farm labour in Sabhapur. He grew potatoes, okra, tomatoes, sugarcane and wheat, and occasionally, brinjals and beans on his farms. His terms of employment were straightforward: payment in kind. For every ten hours of work, he would give 2 kilos of wheat and sometimes even let the workers pluck fresh vegetables to take home. Cash payment was always out of the question.

The next day, all three kids were admitted in the school. Shazeb in Class 4, Salman in Class 3, and Reshma in Nursery.

Since the past one year, Shazeb was becoming shy and introverted, always keeping to himself, like Akmal. He was also tall and muscular like him. On one occasion, when Syeda slapped him for eating gajak straight out of the packaging tray, he went missing for an entire day. Aftab, one of the gajak makers, found him sitting in a tomato farm.

On the other hand, when Syeda slapped Salman for making paper planes and aiming them at the kadhai where the jaggery was melting, he stood firm in front of her and said, 'It doesn't hurt, slap me once more.'

This horrified Syeda.

Reshma was contented with coloured pencils and a 'rough copy', a notebook to scribble in. She kept herself busy with it. She would eat whatever she was given, even go and pee and poo on her own. She didn't need much looking after.

Salman soon became friends with Vikram, Sukhbir's youngest son, by teaching him how to make paper planes and aim them at the teachers when they wrote on the blackboard.

Vikram had a habit of muttering to himself all the time. He was fair with curly hair, the tallest in their class. Salman was dark and seemed to have taken after his petite mother.

Often after school Salman would hang out at Vikram's house which had a huge compound with two tractors, two jeeps and a couple of bikes. It was a joint family with over twenty people living in the same house, including Vikram's two uncles, aunts, their children and his grandparents. There was always something cooking on at least one of the five clay ovens in the huge courtyard behind the tall building that had eight to ten rooms on two floors. The first time Salman visited them, Vikram took him straight to the courtyard. Vikram's mother, dressed in a collared shirt, ghaghra and dupatta, was chopping vegetables.

'Why did you bring him inside the house? What if Dadi finds out?' she asked Vikram with a smile.

'Dadi will do this.' Vikram clawed his hands in his hair, making a funny face.

'Keep quiet,' she said with a smirk. 'Come and eat.'

Vikram and Salman were both served fresh rotis from the clay oven, fried bhindi and a tall glass of buttermilk each. Vikram got a brass plate and Salman a white ceramic plate.

'I want to eat in a ceramic plate too,' said Vikram.

'No. Those are only for guests,' his mother said.

Salman had never been treated as a special guest. So this made him happy. Many years later, he learnt that ceramic plates are used for Muslim guests because of religious discrimination.

He took out a piece of gajak wrapped in a newspaper from his pocket and offered it to Vikram's mother. She smiled and asked him to keep it on the floor next to her. Salman wondered why she did not take it from his hand.

From that day onwards, Salman was a regular at Vikram's place at lunchtime.

Very often, Vikram's mother would give Vikram's old clothes to Salman. And Salman would wear them happily. That is what close friends do. Wear each other's clothes. Like Syeda would say, *odhni badal* friends.

Meanwhile, rents had started soaring in the village. The number of factories were growing and so the demand for houses increased.

This was the time when Iftekaar, a tall, lean man from the neighbouring Loni area, acquired a huge patch of land in Sabhapur. Dressed in a white kurta pyjama, always chewing tobacco, with a small rexine pouch under his arm, he walked with the swagger of a prince in the muddy tracks of Sabhapur. Except that no one treated him like one.

Raziya had told Syeda that Iftekaar used to work as a mason in Loni. He charmed his childless maternal uncle. So when the uncle died, he was left lots of money. Iftekaar bought this land with that money.

In spite of his newly acquired money, the climb up the social ladder was difficult. Iftekaar would still sit on a roadside stone or a wooden log and interact with regular workers. 'Rich people shouldn't do that if they want to be treated as rich,' Raziya once said.

Iftekaar divided the land into small plots, roughly 200–250 square feet each, just enough to make two small rooms, and put them on sale for Rs 1.5 lakh each. He offered them to the settling workers on an instalment of Rs 2,000 per month for twenty years.

The local Gujjars including Sukhbir Singh were particularly peeved by this. They wanted the workers to stay in Sabhapur. They could get them to work in their fields for hours in return for a few kilos of wheat or tomatoes instead of a fixed daily wage. But they definitely didn't want them as permanent settlers right in their own backyard, on what they saw as their land. 'This is the land of brave Gujjars, not of labourers and scrap dealers,' Sukhbir would say.

Every day Iftekaar would go and sit in a hut occupied by four or five workers, convincing them to buy land on instalments. And his success rate was high.

Many settlers like Syeda had been uprooted from their ancestral land. Some were born into landless families. Many of them had faced displacement within Delhi multiple times. Owning land in Delhi also meant you had arrived in life in some way.

'Who doesn't want a permanent roof over their head?' Iftekaar would always end with this question which would seal the decision for most people.

One day, he came to the namkeen factory. He squatted on the mud floor, popped a few freshly fried green peas into his mouth, and asked Syeda, 'So, you plan to stay here, or go back to Banaras?' Syeda hadn't even thought about it herself.

But owning land was her desire too. Particularly after Akmal had cashed in his share of his family assets and ancestral land in Chandauli.

Raziya had already bought a patch from Iftekaar. Often the water from the neighbouring farms would collect in her yard. Iftekaar had carved out the plots in a low-lying area. The new landowners placed wooden slabs over the water to sit, to walk around, to cook. And wooden *takhats* to sleep on.

When Syeda once asked Raziya why she did not complain to Iftekaar, she said, 'We know this is all we can afford. If it means floating on water, so be it. At least this is ours.' Syeda was perturbed with Raziya's resigned attitude.

She discussed the property question with Akmal, who was visiting that night. She told him they should also try to buy, adding, 'Iftekaar is one of us even though he is rich.'

By now Akmal would come home with Rs 200–300 once in two weeks. In contrast, Syeda was earning Rs 2,500 per month at the namkeen factory. Other cart pullers who also worked in Chandni Chowk and had family in Sabhapur told Syeda that Akmal spent a lot of time sleeping or hanging out at the tea stall and would work for only three or four days before coming home. 'Just enough to take care of his bare minimum expenses and bring something home.'

Akmal was convinced they would not be able to afford a plot of land from Iftekaar given the amounts he and Syeda earned. After paying the children's school fees and other expenses, there was hardly anything left to pay the instalment. He dissuaded her, saying, 'We'll buy something better later.'

By now Syeda had realized Akmal was not at all interested in taking on the load of the primary breadwinner. No matter how many times you appealed to his masculinity, or questioned it, or compared him to other men, it did not make a difference. In Banaras, at least he would hit the jackpot once in a while with his masterpieces. Even the taunts of his sisters-in-law were helpful in pushing him. But one and a half years into their life in Delhi, there was no one to goad him that way. He had created the life he seemed to want for himself: eat, sleep, hang around and earn just enough to survive.

Just like her mother Mehreen had learnt all those years ago, Syeda understood that more prodding and poking from her could even lead to Akmal withdrawing completely and stopping even his bimonthly visits to see them.

Over the next few months, Iftekaar sold off plots of land to over a hundred workers on the UP–Delhi border that existed within Sabhapur. Tarpaulin, bricks, bed sheets: whatever each one could afford at that point was used to set up tents and shacks.

From Vikram's terrace, it looked like a shanty town.

'Like *Krantiveer*,' Vikram told Salman. *Krantiveer* was a 1994 masala Hindi film about a slum in Mumbai. The villain regularly tries to build a resort on the slum land and is eventually killed by the protagonist. Both Salman and Vikram had seen the film together one day after school on cable TV.

'*Love rap, aa aa aa aa aa,*' they sang the popular song from the film. They had even been punished in school for singing it while the Hindi teacher was giving them a dictation test.

Around this time the Brahmins and the Gujjars of Sabhapur were increasingly at loggerheads.

The Brahmins, highest in the Hindu caste order, the varna system, account for only 12–14 per cent of the total votes in Delhi. But with their early access to education, they have government jobs and influential positions in the bureaucracy and judiciary. Most may not have been politicians but they play the role of political gurus in Delhi politics.

The Gujjars, lower in the varna system, are not only witnessing an astronomical rise in their wealth due to land prices, but many of them now even have family members in government jobs – mostly in the police and armed forces. This is also changing their degree of expected deference towards the Brahmins.

Subhash Pandit, who was the priest of the village temple, was part of a group of Brahmins which advised politicians on seats, vote shares and even campaign strategy in Sabhapur and neighbouring areas of east Delhi.

Subhash Pandit and Sukhbir Gujjar had been at odds for a long time. Subhash had asked the village panchayat for more land for the temple. Sukhbir and many other Gujjars believed Subhash, the trustee of the temple, was acquiring money and land for himself in the name of the temple, and were cut up about it.

Sukhbir had openly declared in the village panchayat that the Gujjars did all the labour while the Brahmins never gave up asking for alms! They should at least bring their begging bowl. This was a disparaging reference to the tradition of Brahmins living on alms – land, wealth – donated by landowning castes.

Subhash had taken Sukhbir's comments personally. And that was why the last four years had seen both sides displaying their superiority. The Gujjars with sheer wealth and the Brahmins with influence, getting politicians and bureaucrats to pull strings for them.

When Sukhbir Gujjar bought his second car, Subhash was heard saying, 'You can buy cars but the blue light on the car is with us.'

Brahmins account for a large segment of Indian bureaucrats, who customarily travel in government cars with flashing blue lights.

But now, it seemed they were united in their hatred of the poor outsiders: these new settlers who were mostly from landless, marginalized communities.

One day when Iftekaar was walking towards the shanty town, Sukhbir approached him. 'Heard you are selling land?'

Iftekaar nodded.

'Sell it to us! Why are you settling beggars next to us? We'll give you more money!' Sukhbir exclaimed.

Iftekaar walked away with a smile. There was more money to be made by selling small patches in instalments with interest.

And the respect! The respect that he got from the workers. Some had even started calling him 'Zamindaar Iftekaar'. Landlord Iftekaar. It felt good.

He wouldn't barter the reverence he was enjoying.

There were similar encounters with Subhash. One day, when Iftekaar reached the shanty town, there was police checking the paperwork of the small-plot owners. He later heard that Subhash had asked his cousin – who was a member of the Legislative Assembly (MLA) – to send in the cops to get rid of these *jhuggiwalas*. Thankfully, the paperwork was complete in most cases.

They were not *jhuggiwalas*, squatters. They were landowners.

༄

Vikram had told Salman that the Brahmin Samaj Sanstha and the Kalsyan Khap Panchayat of the Gujjars had planned a meeting on the day of Holika Dahan, the day before the festival of Holi, at his place to solve the 'Iftekaar problem'.

On Holi, revellers thronged the narrow lanes of Sabhapur. Akmal had come down for a few days because Chandni Chowk was closed for the festival. He had been missing since the morning and was later found inebriated in a tomato farm. Shazeb and Salman were dripping with blue-coloured water when they returned home at 4 p.m. They had a bath but the blue colour on their faces couldn't be washed away so easily. They ate the poori aloo Syeda had made and the gujiyas Vikram had given. Everyone was tired and went off to sleep early.

Around 11 p.m., Syeda heard the thud of a metal pot falling on the ground. Everyone else was fast asleep. She got up and tiptoed through the factory. Only the shadows of the clay oven and big pots were visible.

She was scared. Could someone be hiding behind the pile of sesame bags, or perhaps there were monkeys?

But then she spotted Iftekaar. He was sitting slumped, his head between his elbows, near the plastic water drum in the corner.

Syeda saw that he was wounded: there was an thick, ugly metal bullet embedded in one leg, poisoning the blood. He lifted his head. His eyes were glazed with the fear of death. They looked like those of a wounded dog, petrified of another attack. Even his long, curly beard was trembling with fear. He was clutching his leg with both hands.

Blood flowed from his open wound. Syeda opened an old steel trunk and took out a dupatta to bandage the wound.

Dogs started barking outside. Iftekaar held on to the edge of the plastic drum to get up but collapsed in pain. Syeda helped him sit in the corner, gave him some water to drink. She asked him how this had happened.

He whimpered, 'Sukhbir Gujjar and Subhash Pandit.'

In the evening when everyone had cleaned themselves after Holi, Iftekaar, drenched in colour, was sitting on the road near his patch of land. He was still intoxicated with bhang, a traditional preparation made with Cannabis leaves, which he had drunk in several houses to mark Holi.

Sukhbir and Subhash, along with a few others, walked up to him and wished him for Holi. They asked him to come home with them to have some gujiya.

'*Holi ke din dushman bhi gale mil jaate hain,*' said Subhash in his hoarse voice.

On Holi, even enemies hug each other.

Iftekaar got up and joined them. As they walked towards Sukhbir's house, Sukhbir offered to show him the new lot of sugarcane they had just harvested from the field. Iftekaar agreed.

It was almost dusk. The planted sugarcane in the field was taller than Iftekaar. Sukhbir asked him to enter first.

It was a bit odd, Iftekaar thought. But he was too charmed by this extension of the hand of friendship by the two most powerful men of the village to say anything. He thought they were finally treating him as one of them.

As he entered the field, he heard some commotion. There were whispers and some hurried footsteps. He ran instinctively. Sukhbir aimed a gun at him. The bullet hit Iftekaar's leg as he ran from one sugarcane field to another. He managed to hide under a bundle of recently harvested sugarcane. They hunted for him for an hour, and after they finally left, he dragged himself out to Syeda's place which was the only dark, silent house in the vicinity. Most other houses had Holi guests.

Syeda discovered him after an hour.

It was now 3 a.m. Shazeb had woken up. He walked up to Syeda and Iftekaar.

They could still hear batons and loud conversations down the street. People were looking for him. Syeda shushed Shazeb.

Iftekaar was still bleeding profusely.

Shazeb said, 'Let's call the police.'

Both Iftekaar and Syeda were resistant. But there seemed to be no other way to get out.

Shazeb said he would quietly go to the plastic tap factory which had a phone connection. Babu Ram, the supervisor, who had also bought a patch from Iftekaar, might be able to help.

They dialled 100, the police helpline. The cops wanted to know if the shooting had occurred in the Delhi part of Sabhapur or the UP part. It was difficult to tell. Earlier the UP part had the sugarcane farms and the Delhi part had vegetables, mostly tomatoes. But last year, in 1996, the minimum support price of sugarcane was raised, and all farm landlords ditched the other crops in favour of sugarcane.

The phone conversation went on for almost half an hour. Reluctantly, Delhi Police arrived at 6 a.m.

Iftekaar had somehow stumbled out of Syeda's house at her request. She didn't want to give the wrong signal to Sukhbir about her loyalties.

The police jeep arrived with a red light flashing on top of it and stopped at the tea shack where Iftekaar had fainted on the wooden bench.

Sukhbir, Subhash, Ratanjot, Bulle Mian, the local contractor, and Babu Ram all stood next to Iftekaar.

Iftekaar's leg was still bleeding and his white pyjama was crimson.

The subinspector (SI), a tall, well-built young man, asked all of them if they knew how this had happened and, more importantly, where it had happened. It was critical to know this, not just to determine under which police station's jurisdiction the case would be filed but also if Iftekaar could be taken to a government hospital in Ghaziabad, UP, or in Karawal Nagar, Delhi.

When the SI asked Syeda, she flatly said, 'I don't know this man.' Shazeb looked shocked, gave her a look, but kept his mouth shut. Syeda looked away.

At 7 a.m., the Ghaziabad police arrived. A young woman SI got down from the jeep.

The two SIs got talking. After a few minutes, Sukhbir said, 'Inspector Saheb, do your love story setting later!'

Everyone laughed. The young man was too embarrassed to respond. He got back into his jeep to make a wireless call to communicate that the UP police personnel, the young woman SI, would be taking Iftekaar to the nearest government hospital in UP.

As they were preparing to lift Iftekaar into the jeep, he stopped breathing.

At the hospital, he was declared dead on arrival.

Iftekaar had a genetic disease called haemophilia which does not allow the clotting of blood. A large number of haemophiliacs fall in the low-income bracket. Haemophilia occurs in one of every 5,000 male births. If not treated properly, a nick or cut could see a patient bleed to death. Iftekaar had had a bullet fired into a leg and had lain bleeding for a long time.

Iftekaar's childless wife observed *iddat*, a period of mourning for four months and ten days, which Muslim women practise when they are widowed or get divorced. As soon as it was over, she sold off Iftekaar's remaining land to Sukhbir Gujjar. Within a year of Iftekaar's death she had married her second cousin.

Salman observed that Iftekaar did not, after all, turn out to be a *krantiveer*, a revolutionary, who defeated the feudal gangsters.

Apan gand hawai,
dusr ke kare dawai

Trying to cure someone else
When your own butthole is infected.

Razia had this to say about Iftekaar. He could have easily made a huge house for himself and started a farming business. But he wanted to be a landlord. He yearned for respect, power and admiration. He wanted to climb up the class ladder.

Iftekaar is now a forgotten entity. Though Syeda often thinks of him as her missed opportunity for having her own house in Delhi.

༄

On 13 May 1998, India declared itself as a full-fledged nuclear state after conducting five underground nuclear tests in Pokhran.

In Sabhapur, whenever Syeda looked up at the sky, she missed Banaras. Here, the sky was always dark, covered by a filthy grey haze. To save the national capital from pollution, the black soot-emanating chimneys of the small factories and brick kilns had been moved to the outskirts, the margins. For the people on the margins. So that the people within Delhi could breathe clean air.

In Banaras, the sky was blue with snow-white clouds in which one could see the odd cat, the face of a bear, a flower.

Raziya and her husband had built a boundary wall and managed to lay down a concrete slab for a room. Her sons, Junaid and Javed, were enrolled in Class 5 and Class 6 but they were much older than the rest of their classmates. They would occasionally assist their father Mohd Israel in construction work.

There came a time when almost every month they would be laying one concrete slab in the shanty town Iftekaar had built. The annual goal for so many families was a concrete slab that symbolized permanence. Something that indicated roots, stability. This also brought them respect and admiration from fellow dwellers and folks back home.

Alongside the growth in the number of these residential units, there was also the influx of unrestricted and unauthorized industries. They had access to cheap labour and zero infrastructure cost. Most of the factories were on the UP side of Sabhapur which was more lax about rules. No one checked for permits, licences or clearance from the pollution control board to operate factories in residential areas.

Gandhinagar in east Delhi is 12 kilometres from Sabhapur. It is believed to be among the largest wholesale markets for readymade garments in India. In the 1970s, when the street vendors who sold readymade clothes near the Red Fort were evicted, they moved here, built houses, started making garments at home. It later grew into a manufacturing hub.

Conservative estimates suggest that 31 per cent of Delhi's labour force is employed in the garment manufacturing sector. Even though it is the biggest employer in Delhi, it pays the lowest wages.

There are two types of garment manufacturing industries in NCR. In the first category are the export houses that produce garments for national and international brands. Even though production is done in the factory, people are employed on a short-term contract basis.

Another type of garment manufacturing is done through millions of home-based workers on a piece-rate basis through a chain of contractors, subcontractors, suppliers, etc. They make garments for the masses, unbranded and affordable. More than half of the garment manufacturing in Delhi is done this way.

When Syeda moved to Delhi, in the 1990s, Indian markets had already opened up to the world. Jeans were always aspirational for Indians. Men were thought to look cool in them; male models in most Indi-pop music videos in that decade would invariably be in a white shirt and blue denim jeans.

It was also the item of clothing that women from conventional Indian families most dreamed of wearing. They would take surreptitious baby steps towards Western clothing by quietly slipping into a pair under a kurta, or posing in jeans on their honeymoon at least.

But global denim brands were unaffordable. This is when Ruf N Tuf, an Indian brand endorsed by Bollywood star Akshay Kumar, broke the barrier.

It launched ready-to-stitch denims with the tag line 'The distance between you and these well-fitting jeans is just the distance between your tailor and you.' It not just brought the price down but also suited Indians who were still not used to readymade clothes. The brand hit the jackpot.

Within two years, a number of local garment manufacturing units had not just started counterfeiting their product but also started offering low-quality copycats at competitive prices. This became such a common practice that for the first time in India, in 1997, Arvind Mills, the company that owned Ruf N Tuf, even set up an anti-piracy cell. It was meant to check the large-scale copying of their jeans.

In a short time, jeans accounted for 50 per cent of garment manufacturing in Delhi. It is estimated that the Gandhinagar wholesale market sells roughly a hundred thousand pairs of jeans on a daily basis.

Wholesalers hand out the order to contractors who get it manufactured through the home-based worker economy. At least ten to twelve people – master tailors, their apprentices, thread workers, buttonhole makers, button fixers, stitching and dyeing unit operators, and washers – are involved in making one pair of jeans.

Sabhapur became a hub of jeans manufacturing units. These were what put food in the plates of many migrant workers and their families.

℮

Kadam Singh Gurjar, a dairy owner, with twenty buffaloes and five cows – a pretty low number by Sabhapur Gujjar standards – who was earning a living by delivering milk on his bike to the nearby areas, decided to venture into the jeans business. He entered into a partnership with Sarfaraz Alam, a twenty-five-year-old contractor from Gandhinagar. Kadam invested the money and Sarfaraz ran the enterprise.

Sarfaraz Alam had worked in a jeans factory and knew the tricks of the trade. And Kadam Gurjar wanted to do something different to generate a new source of income.

In the chain of supply, Sarfaraz was the contractor who obtained the fabric from Gandhinagar. The fabric originally came from Gujarat, Rajasthan, Maharashtra or UP.

Sarfaraz set up two teams: a stitching team and a washing team, aligning all the cogs in the wheel perfectly. He outsourced the cutting of the jeans to master tailors. They would use a machine and cut the denim cloth into different designs and sizes, making sure that the measurement of the pockets, and other accessories were proportional and exact.

Each master tailor had at least two helpers in the factory. Together, they managed to cut 500 pieces a day and were paid 60 paise to Re 1 per piece. Sarfaraz paid them Rs 50–60 per day and kept the rest.

Once the pieces were cut, Sarfaraz would pick them up for fabrication. This included stitching the pieces together, threading, transportation.

Sarfaraz and Kadam Singh bought some sewing machines and hired a few tailors who would stitch the pieces together at home. Sometimes two threads were used for stitching. In better quality jeans, three threads were used.

Sarfaraz would dip into the large pool of Muslim migrants who were hereditary tailors and had moved from north India to Delhi in search of work.

He would repeat the common proverb: *'Darji ka put jab tak jita tab tak sita.'*

The tailor's brat will do nothing but sew all his life long.

Additionally, Sarfaraz engaged buttonhole makers who had special machines to do just that; they charged 15 paise per hole and ended up making almost 700 buttonholes per day. Once the buttonholes were done, buttons and rivets were fixed separately for 10 paise per hole by other workers. Finally, the threading work – removing loose threads from the finished pairs – was outsourced to the women in Sabhapur. They were paid 30 paise per piece. Most of the time the women were helped by their children. Syeda would do it in her free time and managed to complete up to 50–100 pieces on good days. That would mean an extra 10–30 bucks a day and Rs 300–900 per month.

Earlier, the denim cloth was washed at higher pressure before stitching but as designs evolved and the faded look became all the rage, a number of washing units started washing the pieces after they were ready.

Raziya's son Junaid was now fifteen years old and a school dropout. He joined Sarfaraz's washing team. He was trained to put pairs of jeans on a dummy and then scrape them with sand paper to give them a weathered look. Sometimes he would also use white spray to enhance that look.

Once this was done, the pieces were put in huge water containers to remove the excess colour and chemicals. Sometimes, to enhance the texture, they would even use softening agents. After several rounds of washing the pieces to get rid of the toxins, they would dry them in the sun. Washers like Junaid were paid Rs 1–3 per pair of jeans.

The dried pairs of jeans were eventually ironed and packaged to send to Gandhinagar. Sarfaraz managed to make roughly 5,000 pieces per month and made a profit of about Rs 5 per piece even though payment was delayed by six months on average.

Each pair was sold to the wholesalers of the Gandhinagar market for Rs 50–80 depending on their quality. The wholesalers would sell it on for Rs 140–500. In the retail market, as a rule, they sold for at least double that price. These kinds of profit margins were only possible because of the cheap labour and per-piece agreements used in manufacturing them.

Soon enough, Sarfaraz realized there was quicker money to be made in washing units, with much less headache, than stitching set-ups.

According to new pollution control laws, dyers in Delhi had to obtain a no-objection certificate and put up a wastewater treatment plant. No one checked for that in the dyeing units in Sabhapur.

In 1998, several washing units for denims were set up in Sabhapur.

Textile is one of the largest water-consuming industries, next only to power and steel. On an average, it takes 75 litres to make one pair of jeans.

There wasn't any significant government water supply in Sabhapur but there were plenty of privately installed borewells for irrigating farms.

Within three months, Sarfaraz had put together a team of fifteen people in the washing unit that started operating on autopilot.

With no drainage and sewage system, the liquids from dyeing, washing and the acid baths from the jeans washing units started collecting in the low-lying areas of Sabhapur. These wastes were never treated. During monsoons, this water did not just collect on the roads but also seeped into the ground, polluting the water of the handpumps and tube wells.

During heavy rains, Vikram, Salman, and other children played in these waterlogged streets where frogs leaped and hopped against the legs of passers-by.

One day, when both of them were completely drenched, they came to Salman's home.

Salman dried himself and changed his clothes. He gave Vikram a change of clothes so that he could do the same.

Vikram said, 'I can't wear your clothes.'

'But I wear yours all the time,' Salman replied.

'But those are my discarded clothes that I don't wear any longer,' said Vikram.

'But what is the problem with you wearing my clothes? Will you fall sick?'

'Because my father owns farms and your father works as a cart puller,' Vikram replied.

After Vikram left that day, Salman cried the whole night. Syeda tried to explain to him not to take it to heart. That this was life and he should accept who he was. Something changed for Salman that day. He started comparing himself to others.

Each year, the floodwaters from the Yamuna battered the shores of Sabhapur and the village flooded just like all the low-lying areas of Yamuna Paar.

The water entered the houses in the shanty town. It mixed with the acid water from the factories. Within a couple of years, a swamp had formed in the public grounds outside Sukhbir's farms.

One day, a cow got trapped in the swamp and after hours of struggle to pull it out, with everyone pitching in, it died. The Gujjars made a huge deal of this and blamed the migrants for this threat to their dairy businesses and cattle. It was due to their washing units and factories and shanty town that this swamp had been created, they said.

The Brahmins made it an attack on Hinduism by citing the holiness of the cows that were losing their lives because of the jeans washing units run by Muslims.

Kadam Singh, Sarfaraz's partner, was under a lot of pressure to get rid of Sarfaraz and other Muslims from his business but he didn't buckle under the pressure.

Over the next three years, hostility was displayed over the most basic of things. With the level of ground water falling, the availability of fresh water for the growing population of Sabhapur had become a problem. During summers, government water tankers started to arrive twice a day.

One day, as Raziya was waiting to fill water at a tanker, Sukhbir Gujjar said, 'This water is not for you. This is for Dilliwalas. You UP-walas get your water from the UP government.' The land Raziya had bought from Iftekaar was on the Delhi–UP border in Sabhapur.

'Water is water. It does not differentiate between people in the same village. I am not going anywhere,' Raziya said as she stood in the water queue with a stoic expression, making no eye contact with Sukhbir.

He was peeved with Raziya for not only buying land from Iftekaar but also constructing houses for others on the land he had sold.

Her other son, Javed, had now also set up a separate jeans washing unit with the money he had saved from construction and got his brother Junaid, who used to work for Sarfaraz and Kadam Singh, to join him. The new unit was right next to Sukhbir's farmland, which was slowly disintegrating into a swamp because of the waste acid water.

Javed also had a showdown with Sukhbir's elder son Satbir who threatened them with dire consequences if the water from the jeans washing factory continued to flow into the swamp.

Subhash Pandit got the area raided by health inspectors who said that the wastewater was increasing cancer cases, dengue and malaria in the vicinity. But the washing units remained functional.

Javed and Junaid had brought the family some stability. They had added a floor to their house and were even thinking of constructing a toilet within the house, something most settlers still didn't have.

One day Javed was instructing some new recruits to his washing unit on how to stir the denims with great force so that all toxins were removed.

That was when he heard that a calf had got stuck in the swamp. By the time he arrived at the scene, the calf was dead. It belonged to Sukhbir's dairy.

A month later, Javed's body was found in the same swamp. There were investigations over the next few months but no one could be pinned down. Kadam Singh bought Javed's washing unit; it remained functional for many years.

Fear for her other son, Junaid, settled inside Raziya like a ghost. She gave up construction work and completely entered the per-piece work life, slicing almond rejects for biscuits, cakes and ice cream for Rs 20 per kilo, finishing up to 3 kilos per day.

Syeda tried to lift Raziya Sufi's spirits sometimes.

Raziya's husband remained locked in his own silence and started working in Karawal Nagar, an emerging hub of small-scale industries, just 6 kilometres away. Junaid started working in Gandhinagar full time.

In May 2000, India's population crossed 1 billion.

The poor are never provided infrastructure but always blamed for living in unhygienic conditions and spreading disease. Instead of discussing measures to fix the situation, the court and the media both blame the Jamna Paaris for polluting the Yamuna river.

Within four years of Syeda moving to Sabhapur, once again, in November 2000, the Supreme Court cracked down on polluting industrial units in residential areas. They set a one-month deadline for their closure in 'non-conforming' areas, including urban villages like Sabhapur.

This caused the unorganized sector workers all over Delhi to go on a rampage. There was a riot-like situation, buses were torched, and fights between the crowds and the police cost three lives. It took a while for the situation to calm down.

After this, Akmal moved to Sabhapur for good. This was the first time in the last four years he had shown any concern for his family. He said he would look for work close by.

The namkeen factory was still running in full swing. The production had increased many times and so two more women were hired to help Syeda.

The new women had to mix green colour and food soda and put them on the dry peas. Kallu would fry them. The besan sev was now mostly made of rice flour, and not besan, to cut costs.

Syeda often raised objections. Once the owner, Nabi Ahmed, turned around and said, 'Don't try to be a man.' She did not bring up the matter ever again.

One day, a man came to the factory early in the morning. Syeda was by herself. He said he wanted to take samples and place an order. Syeda handed over one packet each of the gajak, hara matar and sev.

It turned out he was a food security officer from Delhi and found the food adulterated.

Shakeel and Aftab, the gajak makers, had started mixing starch and hydrogen peroxide to clean the unprocessed sesame seeds. They were also adding selam powder – an anaesthetic drug – to increase the weight of the gajak and cut costs. A huge fine was imposed and the factory was sealed.

Nabi Ahmed, who had already bought a house in Karawal Nagar and was also running a small namkeen factory there, ran away and was nowhere to be seen. Aftab and Shakeel were absconding too.

This was when Syeda found out she was pregnant again. She was now twenty-seven. She didn't want to have more kids.

Raziya suggested, '*Safai kara lo.*' Get it aborted.

Syeda didn't want to discuss it with Akmal. He would be stuck on the anti-abortion tenet of Islam even though drinking alcohol, which is also prohibited, was fine by him.

Till as late as the 1960s, abortion was illegal in India. The first discussion on changing the abortion law in India started in 1964 and it was finally legalized when the Medical Termination of Pregnancy [MTP] Act was passed by Parliament in 1971.

Syeda first tried some home methods. She had a concoction of jaggery and betel nut to terminate the pregnancy on her own. She bled a little but it did not lead to a termination. She also had shooting pains in her abdomen.

All government hospitals provide subsidized abortion facilities. Syeda borrowed money from Raziya and visited the government hospital in Ghaziabad.

The doctor refused to conduct the abortion without her husband present, even though the law does not require this. They even refused to accept 'unwanted pregnancy' as a good enough reason to terminate. Frustrated, she came back.

Raziya had found out from her husband that there was a private clinic in Karawal Nagar where abortions were done discreetly.

The next day, Raziya accompanied Syeda to Karawal Nagar. They got the procedure done within three hours; by evening she was home.

Salman and Shazeb had made a small hole in the brick enclosure to enter the sealed factory, which was still their home.

In a week, Kallu Ram, the chef had arranged for a job for Akmal as a rickshaw cart driver at a bag factory and for Syeda to make cycle parts in Karawal Nagar.

With no job and a sealed home, they had no option but to move to Karawal Nagar. Syeda was sad to leave Raziya's company. Vikram came to say bye to Salman. Both of them had grown apart and had made other friends now but stayed in touch.

4

Doorknob

'Ek aur aa gayi aakash naapne.'
One more has arrived to measure the sky.
One more woman has come to measure the immeasurable. When Syeda moved to Karawal Nagar, Roopmati said this about her. A few years later, Syeda repeated this for Seema who then said the same for Khushboo. No one remembers the source of this adage. But it continues to be said for every new migrant woman who joins the workforce in Karawal Nagar.

Astronomers measure the sky in degrees, minutes and seconds to confirm if a star has moved closer to the moon. The women workers of Karawal Nagar count the pieces, the dozens, the kilos, of things they prepare, to measure how close they are to survival.

When Kallu Ram told Syeda he had fixed up a cycle parts job for her, she imagined herself standing in a factory assembly line. The *dhak-dhak-dhak* of big factory machines. A long, endless hall as in the Dilip Kumar film *Mazdoor*. With workers standing next to each other who laugh and work together. And sing songs in the break time as they share food from their tiffin carriers.

Instead, she found herself sitting in her mouldy, dark, one-room house doing the cycle parts manufacturing work.

I will hit you so hard, your teeth will fall off!
I will beat you to pulp, your intestines will hang from your body!
Salman and Shazeb brawled all day.
You shut up, mongoose's offspring!
Seven-year-old Reshma regularly yelled expletives at the tenants. She had to push buckets full of water as big as her from the shared

handpump. She would spill water all throughout the corridor while dragging them to their room every day.

Khichdi simmered on the clay oven the third consecutive day, much to the kids' disapproval. This was the one thing about which all three were in silent solidarity.

In this domestic commotion, Syeda struggled to make cycle brake wires. Nathu Ram, a thekedar, subcontractor, had provided her the raw material: steel strands and plastic sleeves. The rate for preparing 12 dozen brake wires, 144 pieces, was Rs 80.

In Sabhapur, she had seen women do per-piece work in their free time. But Karawal Nagar offered it as a full-time occupation to all women.

Things that are necessary for a common person's survival – food, snacks, spices, cosmetics, stationery, garments, automobile parts, books, prints, spare parts, decoration pieces, toys, kitchen appliances, hardware, carpentry tools, plumbing material, building material, devotional items, festival goodies, medical supplies, electric goods, electronic goods – everything is made and packaged here by women on a per-piece basis.

After Indian independence, while Mumbai and Kolkata saw large-scale industrial development, Delhi's Master Plan ruled out similar industries here. But within the next twenty-five years, Delhi as a power capital also emerged as the single biggest centre for small-scale industries and one of the largest wholesale centres of north India.

In the 1980s and 1990s, a number of multinational companies either shifted their production sites or outsourced goods production to poorer countries with surplus labour and cheaper wages. After India opened up its economy to the world in 1991, it became more market and export focused. A number of global companies created multilayered local subcontracting networks for manufacturing work. Instead of setting up factory floors that complied with existing labour laws, it was easier and more profitable to outsource the work to home-based workers.

Home-based workers are those who are directly or indirectly employed by an employer and work at home, or premises other than the workplace of the employer, for remuneration. They are paid piece-based wages, mostly per 12 dozen or 144 pieces, not time-based ones, like those received by workers in a factory who work in shifts. That helps to circumvent the minimum wage set by the government. Syeda was one of them now.

Karawal Nagar is an industrial town and home to several small-scale industries. Like Sabhapur, it was earlier a village, called Dhodhi, on the Delhi–UP border. It had a large Rajput population engaged in farming, a Gujjar population engaged in cattle rearing, and a significant Dalit population. In 1973, a few months after the Delimitation Act of 1972 came into effect which increased the number of Parliament and assembly constituencies all over India, a big chunk of Dhodhi village land was acquired by the government to carve two new assembly constituencies out of it: Karawal Nagar and Mustafabad.

༄

Syeda's first five months in Karawal Nagar, from February to June 2001, were a whirlwind for the family. Unlike the namkeen factory in Sabhapur which also had a living space, this job did not come with accommodation: they now had to rent their own living space.

Akmal had found a place near Kali Ghata Road, in West Karawal Nagar. It took two whole days of going from lane to lane, looking for a vacant place that had doors and, most importantly, a separate toilet. Reshma had flatly refused to poo or pee in the open. She was growing up. Their new dwelling was a ground-floor room, the size of one of the bathrooms in Sukhbir Gujjar's house. It was all they could afford for Rs 500 per month.

The decade Syeda moved to Karawal Nagar, its population doubled. According to the 2011 census, between 2001 and 2011, the population increased from 1.5 lakh to 2.3 lakh. This was also the decade when the number of internal migrants in India doubled.

There was an influx of people looking for accommodation close to income-earning opportunities here. Karawal Nagar mostly had tiny, one-storey independent houses on small plots. Most of them were made in a piecemeal fashion. When a plot-owning family received a payment for the jobs they did, they could decide to buy bricks and prepare a structure. Another payment, they could plaster. Doors? Could be installed when the next round of payment came through.

Often, many families lived in rooms next to each other along with the house owner. They shared the same toilet, if there was one. In the house in which Syeda's family was renting a room, there was just one Indian style toilet at the end of the house. A makeshift cloth enclosure had been put up around it by the tenants. The children would count other people's farts and speculate about who had diarrhoea as they waited in the queue to use the toilet in the mornings.

The house had only one handpump that everyone had to share since the municipal water supply was minimal or of extremely low pressure.

The room Akmal and Syeda rented was so small that if three of them lay next to each other without any gaps in between, there would be no room for the other two to also lie down. February in Delhi is cold and so sleeping outside the room was out of the question. Inspired by other tenants, Akmal fetched some discarded wooden planks from a local timber shop. He propped them up on one wall to create a bunk bed structure as a sleeping arrangement for the other two people.

Thrilled at his own *jugaad*, he told the boys,' See. You like train berths, na? Now you can experience it every night'.

Jugaad. Hack. Frugal innovation.

Shazeb was almost twelve and Salman eleven. It was not easy to impress them any longer. They knew by now that *jugaad* was done due to a lack of resources. It is born more out of necessity than creativity.

With no choice, they slept on the upper bunk every night, their long legs dangling off the so-called berth over the heads of Syeda, Akmal and Reshma, who slept under them on the floor.

They had a gas stove but no official papers to obtain a gas connection. The gas cylinders available through the black market were unaffordable. So they made a clay oven in the common area, like everyone else. For cooking fuel, it was cheaper to use twigs and dung cakes, which they bought from the dairies in Karawal Nagar.

Syeda often told the kids that chulhe ki roti, the smoke-flavoured chapattis of the clay oven, eaten with garlic and smoked red chilli chutney, was the best food in the world. The children never agreed.

Akmal, now thirty-one, had silver sideburns. After a series of setbacks to his self-worth and demotions in the last decade from a super-skilled handloom weaver to a power mill sidekick to a cart puller, he got his first promotion.

He had got the job of a cart rickshaw driver at a monthly salary of Rs 3,000. He had to ferry raw material and finished products from a bag factory. Bags of all kinds: school bags, luggage, office bags and whatnot. And unlike Syeda's, his was a real factory with ten to twelve workers.

'Arre, all work comes to a halt when Akmal *Mian* does not turn up,' the thekedar would say. Akmal had not felt so important in a long time.

Perhaps he needed that ego boost. He was now also the primary breadwinner since Syeda was still struggling with per-piece work. He wanted to be the man he had not been so far since their move to Delhi.

Get me chai!

Massage my feet!

You greet a man looking like a chudail when he comes home after a long day of work!

Chudail. Witch.

It is true that with her dark circles and freckled face she looked like the oldest twenty-eight-year-old ever. Her love for finely cut kurtas and fancy necklines was long lost. She had not trimmed her hair in three years. The split ends in the braid made it look like a broom. Where was the time? To sleep or look in the mirror. And when there was, she didn't want to.

The boys were now taking mental notes from Akmal even though they had never thought much of him. But Akmal had a renewed interest in himself. He started colouring his hair and ironed his clothes before work.

This caused the other tenants heartburn. Not because of his dashing good looks but because the monthly electricity bill was shared by all the tenants equally, even the cost of his ironed shirt.

'Ironing your shirt will not make you look like a *hariyala banna!*' Badshahi, their middle-aged neighbour, would yell.

Hariyala banna. Freshly bloomed groom.

In retaliation, Akmal would switch off Badshahi's immersion rod for heating his bathing water, whenever he could.

'*Ye lo, Badshahi ka badshahi hamam,*' Akmal, a man of few words, would add.

A royal bath for Badshahi.

'By Allah's grace, you will fall in a drain today. May lightning strike your rickshaw today!' Badshahi would curse him.

Akmal and Badshahi's exchanges livened up everyone's mornings. They didn't have a TV but this was good entertainment.

The one appliance Syeda's family had was an electric fan, which seemed possessed. It changed speed, stopped, started, all on its own.

❧

When Syeda started her bicycle wire work, she just couldn't make head or tail of it. The only cycles she had used or seen were the ones with linear pulls, not disk brakes, for which these wires would be used.

She was slow, often twisted her fingers, and bruised her fingertips.

When Nathu Ram came to collect the first batch of cycle brake wires from Syeda, she hadn't even prepared half of them. He said, 'Arre, you think you can make brake wires with bare hands? You need tools!'

He asked her to buy a combination plier, which could both compress and cut the wires. The pliers cost Rs 150, almost thirty hours of work wages.

With the pliers, she could wind steel strands and bind them with an anchor at the end and cover it with a plastic sleeve. She gradually picked up speed.

She also requested Kallu Ram to help, through his contacts, to get Salman and Shazeb admitted to the Government Boys Senior Secondary School in the Dayalpur area of Karawal Nagar, a twenty-minute walk from their house. Shazeb was admitted in Class 7 and Salman in Class 6. They had to repeat a class since they had left the Sabhapur school in the middle of the academic year, without appearing for their final exams. Reshma, on the other hand, was bright and was admitted directly to Class 3 after Class 1 at the Municipal Corporation of Delhi Primary School, a fifteen-minute walk from home.

Even though Kashif, Syeda's brother, had enrolled all his boys in a madrasa, an Islamic school, Syeda never thought of sending her children to one. Even though the madrasas provided free education and sometimes lodging.

'What will they do by becoming a *hafiz*?'

Hafiz. One who knows the Quran by heart.

At least in government schools they will learn Hindi, English, maths and computers, she thought. Akmal didn't have much of an opinion on this. He had never been to school and never wanted to either.

By the time the children started school in Karawal Nagar in July 2001, she had got the hang of her per-piece home-based work.

On 28 November 2001, the midday meal scheme came into force which required all government and government-assisted primary schools to provide cooked midday meals.

Over the next few months, Syeda made wooden, metal and plastic photo frames and was paid Rs 70 for 144 pieces.

She then made door hangings, bouquets of plastic flowers, and decorative pieces out of discarded bulbs which were crocheted with wool for Rs 60 for 144 pieces.

She picked up thread and needle work too. She stuffed soft toys with fibre or cloth scraps and stitched them up for Re 1 per piece. She stitched cloth bags for 50 paise per piece on a sewing machine.

She embroidered sarees for Rs 5 per piece and motifs on garments for Rs 30 per 144 pieces.

She finished and packaged school bags for Rs 60 for 144 pieces.

Using wires and beads, she made jewellery for Rs 50 per 144 earrings.

She assembled plastic guns with springs for Rs 25 per 1,000 pieces.

No one knew who decided these abysmal rates for working on these products but there was no option but to do it. If you didn't, there would be many others who would.

Most of these jobs had to be done simultaneously. It took fourteen to sixteen hours a day, that too with Reshma's help. Syeda's monthly income would rarely go beyond Rs 1,000. The minimum wage for unskilled labour in Delhi was roughly Rs 2,600 per month.

The thekedar would collect the finished products from Syeda and hand them over to the supplier: often a contractor or a wholesale dealer who would deliver them to the exporters for multinational companies. That's how these products made by Syeda and other home-based workers reached their invisible employers: the multinational companies.

Since every house had a home-based worker, Syeda had learnt that the most common way to find work was to get out and ask around. No one gave any instructions or training to make these things. No one told you which tool you may need to get the job done. If you didn't know how to do something, all you had to do was go help another woman with her domestic chores so she could squeeze out half an hour from her busy life to teach you how to do it. There was always piece-based work available because of the number of wholesale markets and the wide range of factories in north Delhi.

If you didn't negotiate for a high per-piece rate or ask too many questions, and bought your own tools and delivered the products on time without excuses, and did not ask for an advance or for help during an illness or calamity, and if you could put up with delayed payments, then there was work to do.

Finding this kind of work is not just about contacts and networks. It is also about following the news cycle.

Major events trigger demand and supply. When Kalpana Chawla became the first Indian-origin woman to go to space in 1997, women in Chandni Chowk and Sabhapur dressed up plastic dolls in hand-stitched white spacesuits. During the 1999 Cricket World Cup, everyone wanted faux leather balls, so the women sat in Sukhbir

Gujjar's farms and stitched hundreds every day to be supplied to the Sadar Bazaar wholesale market. In 1999, when Prime Minister Atal Bihari Vajpayee made a goodwill visit to Pakistan on the inaugural trip of a cross-border friendship bus service between the two countries, they stuck India–Pakistan stickers on several miniature buses to be sold in toy shops. In 2001, when 'monkey man', a roughly 4 foot tall creature with a helmet, metal claws, thick black hair, glowing eyes and buttons on his chest, became an urban legend and was reported to have attacked several people in Delhi but was never caught by the police, they made monkey man masks to be sold at traffic signals.

Syeda learnt to keep track of upcoming festivals a few months in advance. She had perfected making rakhis for Raksha Bandhan using coloured threads and foam cut-outs. They prepared mehndi cones and decorated *karwas*, earthen pots, for Karwa Chauth, the day Hindu married women fast for the long lives of their husbands. Before Navratri, there was a rush to stitch *mata ki chunri*, a red colour scarf offered to Hindu goddesses with *gota*. For Ramzan prayer rugs had to be prepared. Two months before Diwali, orders for strings of fairy lights were handed out. She tried to complete them in advance to keep the week before Diwali free. During that week, she made garlands out of fresh ashok leaves and marigolds. Christmas meant preparing tiny decorative pieces and Santa dolls for Christmas trees; for Basant Panchami, Goddess Saraswati's clay idols had to be dressed; Lohri meant packaging rewri, gajak and popcorn; and New Year brought orders for making paper confetti and coloured paper streamers. For elections, they made flags, keyrings and caps for various political parties. For the new academic year, they packaged crayons and school bags and bound books.

She was all-in-one – worker, material manager, production manager, finance manager, personnel manager, marketing manager, chief executive – of her business.

Over time, she put together a toolbox, which she fondly called her *jadoo ka pitara*, treasure trove. Reshma later started referring to it as her 'CV' – the only comprehensive testament to the variety of jobs she had done for years. It was an iron trunk as big as a coffee table – her constant companion. It contained pliers, screwdrivers, wrenches in all sizes, a screw gauge, needles of all shapes, threads of varying thickness, nuts and bolts, sequins and beads, tapes and aluminium wires, among other things.

⁓

'Get up! That World Cup order is coming.' Syeda woke up Shazeb.

'World Cup? That's next year. Let me sleep!' he replied.

'Not cricket. This is football,' she said.

'Football World Cup? Since when do you care about football?' he asked.

'You don't need to be a saheb to know the news. The football World Cup is this year,' Syeda told Shazeb, chuffed with her knowledge. The FIFA 2002 World Cup was scheduled to be held in June that year.

Shazeb, like any arrogant teenage boy, woke up with a dismissive expression on his face and grudgingly took Syeda on the bicycle to the *pushta* road.

After the Parliament attack in December 2001, and the Gujarat riots in February 2002, where according to some estimates 2,000 Muslims were killed, she had stopped asking Akmal to accompany her anywhere in the wee hours, like she would have before. Delhi landlords were getting arrested left, right and centre for not getting their tenants verified by the police. Her landlord, Kamesh Bhadana, had warned them that if anyone was caught in any mischief, they would be thrown out without notice. And she was not going down that road once again. The decade between the 1992 Babri riots and the 2002 Gujarat riots had changed her life. But Akmal was still the same, even though he had been arrested twice in this period. She could not risk him walking absent-mindedly into a volatile situation now.

The Global March Against Child Labour, a worldwide campaign to end child labour, had reported that Pakistan and India were the main centres for the manufacture of footballs for top multinational companies sponsoring the 2002 FIFA World Cup. After a lot of backlash, FIFA, international labour unions and the multinational companies that were sponsoring the World Cup pledged that they would follow labour laws and procedures, and ensure that cheap labour was not used for making their products.

Even though prominent multinational companies had made this pledge, they did little to overhaul their manufacturing chain of contractors, subcontractors and home-based workers. Paying legitimate wages was not part of their profit-making revenue model. Instead, they found it easier to insist that workers and contractors not get caught while manufacturing these products.

As a result, now the raw material for the World Cup items started arriving at odd hours, in secluded spots, to escape the eyes of activists, labour inspectors and others.

It was three in the morning when Syeda and Shazeb reached *pushta* road and disembarked from the cycle.

'When is Bhagwan Das coming for the World Cup work?' asked a woman on the way.

'How do I know?' Syeda replied as she walked past her.

Shazeb was used to Syeda's lies. He had perfected his disdainful look for her at such moments.

'What?' she protested at Shazeb's silent chatisement. 'She will take the entire order. All her five children will help her. Will you sit with me and stitch footballs?' Syeda was irritated at his growing self-righteousness.

While Banarasi weaving had common family labour, home-based work was not always like that. Syeda could force Reshma to help her but Salman and Shazeb were learning how to be men from Akmal. And Akmal just wouldn't pitch in with Syeda's piece-based work. Most men in Karawal Nagar preferred time-based jobs that gave at least a bare minimum daily wage. Her boys only agreed to do 'manly' jobs like picking up and delivering goods.

Syeda was on good terms with Bhagwan Das, a subcontractor who regularly brought her different kinds of orders. In return, she would volunteer to occasionally cook for him and his guests. Since his family was vegetarian, he would ask Syeda to cook him meat dishes.

Make chicken pasanda today, I will be bringing some people over.
It is getting cold. When will you make mutton paaya?

Syeda, you haven't made kebabs in a while. What's the matter? You want work or not?

When he brought his guests over, the children had to stay out of their tiny one-room house. On those days, Syeda made an effort to dress up: she wore better clothes, put kajal in her eyes, and oiled her plait. Often, there was not enough meat to feed Bhagwan Das, his guests and the children, too. So the children were served only the remaining curry without meat pieces, or worse, their most dreaded meal, khichdi.

Though it was not a direct demand in exchange for orders from Bhagwan Das, Syeda did find it frustrating sometimes. But overall, she didn't think of it as a big burden in exchange for regular inflowing orders from him.

Shazeb was uncomfortable about his mother hosting, entertaining, befriending and serving food to these men. Particularly because Bhagwan Das only came during the day, when Akmal was not at home.

That morning, Shazeb and Syeda waited for an hour with other women on a mud road for the truck to arrive. Bhagwan Das had picked up the raw material from the train station. When he came, he distributed large bags containing hexagonal leather patches and stitching instruction diagrams to Syeda and the others to take home.

March afternoons in Delhi are bearable. The wind blows strongly enough to dry the sweat of the workers in the dark, dingy, hot alleys of Karawal Nagar.

School exams were over. Reshma was almost eight and had passed her annual exams with good marks. Syeda asked her to skip classes to assist her. Reshma was upset but had no option.

Akmal was taking a nap. His stint as the main breadwinner of the family had come to an end in eleven months. He had been fired by the bag factory for missing days of work because he was down with cholera.

Doctors would say, 'Maintain hygiene! Wash your hands!' for prevention. But without proper sewage and drainage lines, and given the garbage heaps full of flies, overflowing privately constructed septic tanks, and waterlogged streets with mosquitoes, it was common for people to catch cholera, typhoid, malaria or diarrhoea every few months.

It wasn't that Akmal was lying to the factory people! But they didn't consider the situation.

With Reshma's help, Syeda was preparing eight to ten balls in fifteen hours daily. At the rate of Rs 5 per ball, they were making up to Rs 50 per day.

The finished balls were to be collected by Bhagwan Das. He had to send them back to New Delhi railway station from where suppliers apparently delivered them to established sports goods companies that in turn exported them to companies like Nike and Adidas in other parts of Asia and Europe.

Syeda decided to take a nap too, next to Akmal. Reshma was busy stitching the hexagonal patches as the newly acquired second-hand transistor played songs from the latest supernatural film, *Raaz*, where a female ghost screams in people's ears.

Ye shehar hai aman ka,
yahaan ki fiza hai nirali...
Yahaan pe sab shanti shanti hai...
Yahaan pe sab shanti shanti hai...

This is a city of peace,
The air here is unique...
There is all silence silence here...
There is all silence silence here...

Suddenly, they heard screams from their lane. The iron door of the house they lived in was pushed open with a loud thud. A woman and two men piled into their room. Syeda sat up.

'There is one child here too. Take her,' said one of the men, pointing at Reshma.

No one introduced themselves. They took photos of Reshma sitting next to the hexagonal patches, grabbed some raw material, and dragged Reshma out of the house. She was pushed into a jeep, with some other children from the neighbourhood.

A man tapped on the jeep's bonnet and asked the driver to drive away.

Syeda ran behind them. Parshuram, a bindi subcontractor from the adjacent lane, stopped her.

'Where are they taking Reshma?' Syeda asked Parshuram in a panic.

'Children under fourteen are not allowed to work. But don't worry. They'll be back by evening,' he replied.

Karawal Nagar has numerous small workshops, manufacturing units, in each house. They are casually called 'factories'. Activists like to call them sweatshops. From dingy basements to 8 foot by 8 foot rooms in houses, to makeshift spaces on terraces, people manufacture something in every second house. Set up in residential areas, in violation of several laws and Supreme Court guidelines, these factories are places where home-based workers and others come and do the required work, or collect or deliver finished products.

Parshuram had set up one such makeshift factory on his small terrace with tarpaulin and tin sheets. A number of boys between the ages of six and twelve, from different parts of rural Bareilly in UP, who called him 'Chachu', made bindis for him there. The radio started playing in the morning when the children started work at 7 a.m. and stopped only at 8 p.m. in the evening.

He took orders from wholesale traders for bindis. Like all bindi subcontractors, he bought the raw materials for bindis himself. The boys first applied gum on sheer velvet and covered it with thin paper. Then they cut out bindi dots or stylized shapes with metal hand tools.

Like all subcontractors, Parshuram wasn't well off. Everyone in the family was part of this venture. Mala, his wife, would serve chai and two slices of bread to his worker boys in the morning. Some of the children had learnt to plaster their bread with Iodex, an anti-inflammatory balm that has high chloroform content. This gives the children a high and they work with almost robotic efficiency. No one knew who introduced them to this or to the practice of inhaling whitener fluid. At night when they finished their shift, they would get a small portion of meat and two chapattis or dal chawal for dinner.

Salman had started spending time with Ganesh, a distant nephew of Parshuram. He needed a hideout to skip school: he hated it and had even flunked a year. Ganesh wanted a break from the substandard food that Parshuram's wife made in bulk. Ganesh would let Salman hang out at the factory to listen to the radio and acquire a taste for Iodex toast, in exchange for the tiffin Syeda packed for him every day.

On the day of the raid, Salman was at Parshuram's factory. When they realized the area was being raided, on cue, in Parshuram's factory, some children hid in gunny bags, some were asked to go out and play with a bat and ball, and some were told to stay back and pick up books and pencil boxes from the shelves. A roller writing board was put out and Ganesh started 'teaching' them. It was a well-oiled, nicely rehearsed routine taught to them by Parshuram who knew how to escape the raids of the anti-child labour activists and the police.

On hearing Syeda's and Reshma's screams, Salman had asked Parshuram for help. Which was why he had gone up to Syeda on the street and told her Reshma would be back by the evening.

Syeda was irritated that Akmal hadn't even gotten up. He was making casual inquiries as he lay on the mattress, a pillow under his head. As if nothing had happened. Shazeb was at school. She asked Salman to put away all the raw materials for the footballs and left for the subdivisional magistrate's (SDM) office with Parshuram.

After a number of raids and news reports about the use of child labour, top clothing and sports goods brands had stopped putting tags, logos or other branding on unfinished products during manufacturing to escape accountability. So the punishment was doled out to the immediate employer – in this case, home-based workers or subcontractors-cum-factory-operators – who were supposed to prepare the products for a pittance, rather than the multinational corporations who made the profits.

Parshuram had tutored her to say that Reshma did not do any per-piece work. She was merely playing that day.

At the SDM's office, over seventy children had been made to sit in a queue. Some were as young as five. Some had poor eyesight, injuries, broken fingers, crooked backs and torn clothes. The floor was cold, their toes were curled. Activists were noting down their names and taking details of the work they did.

The children had been picked up from homes while making sports goods, accessories and imitation jewellery, and some from factories that made footwear, plastic spoons, biscuits, zari. From welding units, dry fruit factories, jeans and stitching units.

'Who brought you to the factory?' asked an activist, taking copious notes.

'I don't know,' replied the seven-year-old child with twisted fingers from the imitation jewellery factory.

'How much are you paid?' the activist asked.

'I don't know,' replied the child.

And so it went on:

'Where are your parents?'

'In the village.'

'Which village?'

'I don't know.'

'What's your father's name?'

'Babloo.'

'Where is he?'

'In the village.'

'Okay, sing a song from your village,' the activist asked in an effort to guess the dialect of the child to identify her hometown.

'*Kisi disco mein jaaye, kisi hotel mein khaaye,*' the child sang – a regular Bollywood number.

'Didn't you tell your parents that your fingertips are crushed?' the activist persisted.

'What is the point? They will worry unnecessarily,' replied the child.

Similar mature-beyond-age children thwarted all attempts by activists to map out the child labour chain or child trafficking in unregulated factories.

'Sir, she is my daughter.' Syeda pointed out Reshma to the activist.

'What is the proof?' he asked.

More than 50 per cent of child workers in India are coerced into these professions by relatives or acquaintances.

'See, we both have moles at the same spot on our stomachs.' Syeda started to lift her kurta on one side to show him.

'Are you mad or what! Stop this,' exclaimed the activist.

'Sir, it's true.'

'You make the child work instead of sending her to school,' the activist accused her.

'Sir, she goes to school. I was the one making those balls. She was just playing around,' Syeda lied.

'You are lying. I am sending her to a government shelter home,' the activist replied.

'I am not lying. Ask her anything. She just passed Class 3,' retorted Syeda, certain that Reshma would perform well.

'Okay. Beta, do you know the table of 7?'

'Seven oneza seven, seven twoza 14, seven threeza 21 ...' Reshma moved her upper body forward and back as she sat on the floor, perfectly demonstrating the rote learning typical of Indian schools.

'Okay, Okay,' conceded the activist. 'Get her school report card,' he added.

After a few hours, the SDM, a man in jeans and T-shirt, clicked a picture with the children queued up in front of him with a banana and samosa in each one's hands.

He walked up to Syeda and the other parents who had brought documents to prove their relationship with the children. 'Next time we find the children working, we will arrest you all.'

'No, sir. It won't happen. Promise.'

The children whose guardians could not be confirmed were taken in a jeep to be presented at a Child Welfare Committee office so that they could be sent to a government shelter for child rehabilitation.

Syeda slapped Reshma as soon as they sat in a rickshaw to go back home. 'Couldn't you have gone and hidden somewhere?'

'How could I have known what was happening?' Reshma started crying. 'Now try and make me work for you!' she said, her eyes dilated with rage.

'What did you say?' Syeda slapped her again.

'You want to make me like you, *anpadh, ganwaar*,' she replied. Illiterate and uncouth.

'I am teaching you some skills. That will help you more than schooling when you grow older,' Syeda replied.

'They should have taken me with them. At least they would let me study,' Reshma retorted.

'Study? They would have sold you to a brothel in G.B. Road.'

'I would have worked in a brothel. Just like I work at home. What is the difference?' Reshma replied.

Syeda was livid. She slapped her once more.

Teary-eyed, Reshma looked away. Her dislike for her mother was growing.

'Dhakkan Salman, train mein aag kyun lagaayi?'

Dumbass Salman, why did you set the train on fire?

In February 2002, the state of Gujarat saw large-scale violence. A coach of a train carrying over fifty RSS *karsevak*s, volunteers, from Ayodhya was set on fire at Godhra station in Gujarat. Rumour spread that the attack was engineered by Muslims. As a result, over 2,000 Muslims were killed in the state by Hindu supremacists. Narendra Modi was then the chief minister of Gujarat and accused of polarizing the atmosphere on religious lines.

His government displayed the charred bodies of the *karsevak*s to the public just a day after the train coach was set on fire. This fanned sectarian sentiments and riots continued in Gujarat for almost three months. CDs with these visuals were distributed across RSS *shakhas* in the country to provoke anti-Muslim attacks.

In June the same year, many months after the riots, a summer vacation camp, called Kishore Varg, held for young boys by the RSS repeatedly screened the video of the charred bodies of the *karsevak*s to emphasize political Hinduism and the fight against the 'invaders': Muslims and Christians.

The Government Boys Senior Secondary School was situated in the Dayalpur area of Karawal Nagar, a Hindu-majority area with a strong RSS presence.

Eleven-year-old Salman was already known as *dhakkan*, a dumbass. He was not just weak in studies – he had flunked a year – but also had trouble staying tidy and being on time. He was thin, with a gaunt face, scrawny legs and hands. 'He looked like a scarecrow in the fields in his school uniform,' said Syeda.

He was always unfavourably compared to Shazeb who was more dutiful, sincere and valued by the family and had moved up to Class 8. Salman, just a year younger, was still in Class 6. Syeda would ask Shazeb for advice and for help in collecting payments from contractors and delivering finished products.

All this frustrated Salman no end. He did not want to attend the same school as Shazeb. The new academic session in school started in July and it was already taking a toll on him. He would look for excuses to miss school every second day.

Syeda was on the warpath with Salman over this. In fact, this was one of the rare times that Akmal had also scolded Salman, giving his own example of not being able to do much with his life. 'If you don't go to school, you will never go beyond being Salman rickshawala,' he said.

Soon to hit teenage, Salman detested his father. The trick worked to get him back to school.

One day, he was accosted outside the school by a group of boys, led by a student called Adarsh, and asked that question:

'*Dhakkan* Salman, why did you set the train on fire?!'

'Which train?'

'The one they are showing on the CD.'

Salman, often bullied, would project himself as tougher and meaner than he was.

'Yes, I did. So?'

He didn't know what they were talking about but was too proud to show that he didn't.

'See!' said Adarsh, as he grabbed his collar.

Salman was short in stature. Adarsh, though the same age, was taller than him by almost 2 feet.

That day Salman came home barefoot, shirtless, with some bruises on his arm and face, but unfazed. It was not uncommon for boys his age to get into fistfights. Syeda did not pay it much attention.

The next day, Syeda was summoned by the school peon to school.

By then she had started working in a tea strainer factory. Home-based work alone was not generating enough of an income. At the factory, she had to punch the steel net of the strainer using a machine and fit it in a steel frame. She was paid Rs 1,500 per month for working from 9 a.m. to 7 p.m. in a dark dungeon with a single bulb as the light source. Workers like her had to slave away surreptitiously for unauthorized manufacturing units to escape the labour inspections that were shutting down such units in residential areas.

The other worker at the factory had taken off so this was an opportunity for her to earn an additional Rs 50 per day working overtime. There was no time for her to go and meet the headmaster.

One day as Syeda was getting ready to go to the factory, Shazeb told her that Salman had been expelled from school.

She rushed to the school.

'He talks back to his teachers, he picks up fights with other boys. But I ignored all of this,' said Sudershan Lal, the school principal.

Lal was a strict but a dedicated teacher who made sure he knew every student in his school by name. He would stay back after school, even visit students' homes sometimes to keep a tab on them.

While parents appreciated this special attention, teenage boys, making their journey into adulthood, resented the presence of another patriarch in their lives. No matter how much he physically thrashed the boys, no parent, not even the feudal Gujjars, objected.

'I always believe in giving children a chance. Puncturing others' cycle wheels, hiding people's school bags, small fistfights are common. But he actually flashed a saw at some students. And then at me too,' Lal told Syeda.

Syeda begged him and made every possible promise to control her son. Eventually, Lal agreed to take Salman back.

That day, after her meeting with the principal, when Syeda reached the strainer factory, another woman had replaced her. 'The order needed to be completed on time. I couldn't wait for you,' the factory owner told her.

That's how quick the turnaround rate was in this line of work. A five-hour delay could get you replaced. It was so commonplace that Syeda expected it.

From that day onwards, she started locking her 'toolkit'; she knew Salman had flicked the saw that he flashed at school from it. The one she used to make wooden photo frames.

When Salman came home, she thrashed him dutifully, as she believed all good mothers should, and told him how Shazeb never got her into these situations. Then it was back to business as usual.

Over the next few months, Salman got into several fistfights with Adarsh and other Gujjar boys. Shazeb would stop him, drag him back, instead of lending a fist in support. This irked Salman further. Even though they still shared a 'train berth' at home, at some point he completely stopped talking to Shazeb.

By the time Delhi's first metro line started in December 2002, from Shahdara to Tis Hazari, he had stopped going to school.

And so, the name *Dhakkan* Salman stayed.

❦

Tamaam rishton ko main ghar pe chhod aaya tha,
Phir uske baad mujhe koi ajnabi nahin mila ...

I left several relationships back at home,
After that no one seemed like a stranger to me.

– Bashir Badr, twentieth-century poet

In these years of non-stop working, there had always been some emergency. Was it acceptable to sit and have a cup of chai without doing anything else? To sleep for an entire day even when you were not sick. To not work for a day? Sunday? What is Sunday?

Syeda had almost no contact with her family back home. Just an annual phone call from her brother out of duty on Eid that she received on the landline of the grocery shop next door. A customary call devoid of any affection from the past.

But even those rare phone calls with her family drew her into a strange competition: who was more miserable, who had more problems.

'Salman failed again.'

'Both my children get such bad marks,' replied her sister-in-law.

'The house rent is so high in Delhi.'

'In Banaras, it is even higher', comes the reply from the other side as if hinting she should never think of coming back.

They had no space for her, physically or emotionally, any longer.

She felt burdened while talking to them. She didn't share any good news, or anything positive, fearing they would be offended or cast a jealous evil eye.

Like, how dare she say that she had bought a second-hand TV and a bed box or that Reshma was doing well at school? How dare she be okay when her relatives said they were miserable?

Just because she was part of that family, and they had once supported her when she was most vulnerable, made Syeda feel responsible for them. But they also hurt her by not including her, informing her, pretending that her presence or absence did not matter in a family wedding, or even when someone died, as at the time of her dadi's death.

In those moments, Syeda felt comforted that she had her own family, her own people: Akmal and her children. She had some people to go back to: to talk over her days with, get some warmth, at least sometimes when Salman would hug her to sleep or Reshma would get worried if Syeda took too long to get back home after work. Or when they discussed the films shown on Doordarshan on Sundays. Or when Akmal occasionally asked her to pay attention to herself.

~

At some point after she lost her job at the tea strainer factory, Syeda started working at Ram Kumar's door hinge factory. She was moving towards working in factories, or workshops, or sweatshops: different people called these workspaces different names depending on their needs, morality and worldview.

It was difficult to get home-based work for more than twenty days a month. These factories provided time-based wages instead of piece-based wages. The monthly salary could be anywhere between Rs 1,500 and Rs 2,500 for a twelve- to fifteen-hour shift. Some of them even gave a weekly day off. It was still less than the minimum wage.

Ram Kumar's factory was in a shoebox-sized house with two floors. His family lived on the ground floor, the factory was on the first floor. Syeda and three other women took the staircase through a narrow passage where his old mother was a permanent fixture on a cot. With a *rudraksh mala* in her hand, and a wrinkled cotton saree, she got into a tizzy each time she saw Syeda.

'Don't touch anything in the house. I don't have enough Gangajal to purify everything!'

Gangajal. Ganga's pure water.

Syeda would laugh. 'I can source you the best Gangajal from Banaras!'

The old woman would make a face in disgust.

Most factories, unlicensed, unregulated, were inside the living quarters of the subcontractors.

There was a running joke in Jamna Paar.

Once a south Delhi boy delivered the famous rich, posh, south Delhi line: *'Jaanta hai mera baap kaun hai?'* Do you know who my father is?

The Jamna Paar boy asked, 'Who?'

The south Delhi boy replied, 'My father owns many factories.'

To which the Jamna Paar boy replied, 'Abbe, everyone's father owns a factory here!'

Unlike in south Delhi where the affluent and the working class are segregated, in Jamna Paar, factory owners and workers live next to each other: in *slums*, resettlement colonies, unauthorized colonies, urban villages, and planned residential and industrial areas. There was homogeneity with a pinch of egalitarianism.

There were many Iftekaars here: people who had risen from the same ranks as other people, with no idea how to actually behave like a saheb. There wasn't a world of a difference between the lives of a factory owner and a home-based worker.

Since the water and electricity connections were residential, and not industrial in nature, the voltage was always low, and so was the water pressure.

If these houses-cum-factories had toilets, the workers used them. If they didn't, everyone had to go pee in the corner of the drain. Rooms and floors were added randomly over each other without municipal clearance, and the stairways were extremely narrow – nowhere close to fulfilling fire safety norms. Often there was no space for a window for natural light or ventilation.

Sab ghar ki baat thi. Everything was the internal matter of a household.

They worked like members of a household that was chaotic, feudal, complex, dysfunctional but somehow operational.

This was a common sight in the factories: dark, stuffy, seepage-lined spaces, chipped-off plaster on walls, a single electric light source illuminating the workspace, raw materials and finished products stacked up high. Some rooms had a fan, others didn't. There were as many clacking machines as could be accommodated, with cots or mattresses in corners, often with masturbating men – these could be the factory owner, his relatives or workers – who lived on the premises, cooked and slept there.

To escape that last visual, the whisper network of the women workers of Karawal Nagar had only one guideline: work in those factories that have families. Even though this meant giving a hand to the subcontractor's family for domestic chores.

That was why Syeda took Ram Kumar's mother's barbs in her stride. She had to make up to 2,000 door hinges a day by putting the metal piece in a machine and turning its lever with full force to punch holes. Those who didn't pay attention lost their fingers. There was no compensation for it. The shift was from 9 a.m. to 5 p.m., the monthly salary was Rs 2,500, Sundays were off.

A lot of times Syeda could not identify the things she made but door hinges she could. She had learnt how to make them all right but what was the use, what did it look like when fitted into the final product – no one explained and not many wanted to know because these products usually could not be sold on their own without the chain of subcontractors, contractors and suppliers. There was no time and need to delve deeper to understand the function of these parts. For instance, the rubber lining for car wipers or helmet buckles made no sense as standalone objects.

*

Every morning when Syeda walked to Ram Kumar's factory, she saw an old children's walker on the fourth floor of a cramped house-factory in a garbage-strewn lane in Shiv Vihar. She recognized the walker though she could never afford one herself for Shazeb, Salman or Reshma.

This walker was grubby, faded by sunlight, and worn out by rain and wind. The owner of the factory, Babloo, a pious, thirty-something man, who garlanded a picture of Baba Vishwanath, Lord Shiva, every morning after a bath, ran a unit that assembled plastic wheels for these walkers.

He did not have a family. One day, as Syeda was walking by, Babloo asked her if she was interested in working in his factory. He offered Rs 3,500 for a fifteen-hour shift. Syeda decided to flout the guideline for women workers and agreed to work in this single man's house for better pay. Even a raise of a few hundred rupees made a big difference to the family budget. Switching jobs, getting fired, coming back and working for the same amount, at the same place, was all part of this line of work. The priority was continuous work, because missing even a single day could lead to a survival crisis. No one seemed to mind or make a big deal about changing jobs. It was after all not a corporate office with contracts and notice periods.

One day, as Syeda was busy assembling the plastic wheels, two policemen barged in and took Babloo into custody. Babloo tossed the keys to Syeda nonchalantly and said, 'Take care of things till I return.'

There had been a fire in a nail paint factory in the Moonga Nagar area of Karawal Nagar. The inflammable liquid used to make nail paint had caught fire because of faulty electrical wiring. The gunny bags that lined the walls, full of nail paint bottles, were also ablaze. There was no window or ventilator, and the whole place went up in flames.

No one was hurt but it took six fire tenders to douse the flames. The neighbouring area was filled with toxic fumes for almost a day.

Syeda didn't know that Babloo owned that factory too. Babloo kept to himself. He was fond of dressing up, and dyed his hair like Akmal, and just like him enjoyed his bottle of hooch in the evenings, but lived frugally, with hardly any belongings. He had many high-profile visitors and calls to make through the day and did not meddle much with Syeda or the other workers.

The next one week, Syeda ran the walker factory, dutifully garlanding the Baba Vishwanath picture in the morning, and continued work as usual. Babloo was released on the eighth day. He gave Syeda a monthly raise of Rs 500.

Akmal's latest job was in a cardboard factory as a cart rickshaw driver. He may have been careless at home and with his family but he never lost a single piece of material or product while taking them to and from the factories and godowns. That was a good reputation to have and it helped him get a cart rickshaw driver job whenever he tried to.

Shazeb and Reshma were regular at school. Syeda had forced Salman to keep going to school and he had flunked Class 6 once again, the third time in a row. Now Reshma and he were in the same class. Reshma left no opportunity to rub that in. Mostly because even though she was Syeda and Akmal's most responsible child, since she was a daughter, she received little attention.

Babloo's factory was close enough for Syeda to go home once in a while, check on the children, supervise Reshma's per-piece work, cook lunch and return in time.

They were slightly more comfortable now, money-wise. They had moved to another room on the terrace of a four-storey building. It had a tin roof and field rats but the room was bigger and they were allowed to use the terrace space. The field rats danced between the tin sheet layers at night, making horrible rustling noises. But they got used to it.

In 2003, for the first time in the eight years since they had arrived in Delhi, the entire family went to watch a film in a theatre. The film was chosen by Shazeb and Salman, one of the rare times when both were in sync.

The movie *Jaani Dushman* is the story of an *icchadhari* snake couple: shape-shifting serpents who are cursed by a saint. A thousand years later, when they acquire human form in the modern world, the female serpent is raped and killed. The male serpent avenges her death by punishing an ensemble cast of the top macho Bollywood actors of that time: Suniel Shetty, Akshay Kumar, Sunny Deol. Dressed in a black trench coat, the male serpent flies, walks on water, rides his scooter in the sky, turns into liquid metal and dodges bullets.

Akmal, Salman and Shazeb loved the film. Syeda was thrilled too. Reshma was bored but didn't mind the outing because she got a day off from making things by the dozen at home.

For the next few months, Syeda continued working at the walker factory. Babloo was fond of cooking. One day, he offered to make atte ka halwa for everyone. He was about to pour the wheat flour into the hot *ghee* in the vessel when the police arrived again. Syeda switched off the gas as he was dragged away.

This time, the fire was in a plastic factory near Yamuna Dairy in Karawal Nagar. It produced buckets, plastic mugs, soap dishes, laundry brushes and so on.

On the day of the fire, three workers were sleeping inside the factory. It was locked from outside for fear of theft. Since over ten machines were installed in the factory, there was no room to move around. The workers cried for help over and over again. They were finally rescued with a makeshift ladder propped against the home-factory. But one of them fell from the third floor, cracked his skull and was rushed to the hospital. Since the factory was located in a cramped lane, there was no space for the fire brigades to enter. It took ten hours for the fire tenders to douse the fire.

None of these factories had fire clearances or firefighting equipment. This time, Babloo was in jail for almost a month. Syeda again took over the running of the walker factory. Bhagwan Das – for whom Syeda would cook sometimes and who gave her the football-making assignment – ensured a steady supply of the raw material and collected the finished plastic wheels on time. She got another raise of Rs 500 when Babloo was released. Her salary was now Rs 4,500 per month.

Babloo was arrested a third time that year, this time when a jeans dyeing factory was sealed. Shiv Vihar had a high number of cancer cases because the chemicals used for dyeing had started polluting the area. Approval from the Delhi Pollution Control Board for any of these illegal dyeing units was out of the question. This time they sealed the walker factory too, calling Babloo a repeat offender.

Syeda took up work in a factory that made wooden electricity socket boxes for Rs 4,000 per month on a twelve-hour shift with a weekly off on Tuesday. When she was fired for falling sick, she started working at a plastic pipe factory that was bigger and paid Rs 200 more than her last job.

Babloo was released six months after his arrest.

'How many factories do you own?' Syeda asked Babloo when she went to collect her dues from him.

'You still don't get it.' Babloo smiled.

'What?' Syeda probed.

'I am an owner only on paper. Each time there is a raid, closure, a fire in a factory, I serve jail time to protect the actual owners, subcontractors and suppliers,' he replied.

There were many such proxy prisoners like Babloo in Karawal Nagar. He was compensated for these services. Unlike Akmal, whose prison term cost them their past life and inheritance, at least Babloo was using it to save money to buy land back home in Badaun for his family's future.

ᛋ

On 23 August 2005, the government passed the Mahatma Gandhi National Rural Employment Guarantee Act to guarantee the 'right to work' to every rural household for 100 days annually.

Ensnared by hooch, Akmal had slipped into inactivity once again. He had been persona non grata at his father's funeral in Chandauli in August 2005, his first visit there in over ten years.

One day, while he was lying drunk at home, someone stole the ludo and chess pieces that Reshma had been tasked to pack after school. Syeda was to be paid Rs 20 per 144 sets of the games.

Even though Karawal Nagar was just 6 kilometres from Sabhapur, there was a difference of decades between them. Unlike the rural, conventional, collective Sabhapur, Karawal Nagar was urban, forward and individualistic. Karawal Nagar was all business; there was no time to waste. You were always running against the clock. People were cut and dried, professional, kept to themselves. No one would show leniency, not even Bhagwan Das whom Syeda had fed special meals more times than she could remember.

She missed Raziya, or someone like her.

Bhagwan Das, who had given Syeda the chess and ludo packing work, was livid and refused to pay her previous dues of Rs 1,000, deciding to keep that as compensation for the lost material. Syeda thrashed Reshma for not keeping the raw material safely.

Word spread that Syeda had lost raw material; you could not afford to have that reputation as a home-based worker. Her orders dried up for some time.

Syeda racked her brains for ideas on how to run the house. She needed at least two or three jobs at one time. One in a factory and up to two that could be done at home. She was buying more potatoes, less meat and almost no milk.

All attempts to rehabilitate Akmal were turning out to be fruitless. Syeda was desperate. One day, she instinctively walked into the tent of a Bengali Baba – a roadside quack dressed in black, with matted hair and a beard, who claimed to cure everything from drug addiction and alcoholism to infidelity and infertility. He guaranteed results and gave her some herbs to administer to Akmal and an amulet to tie on his arm. In exchange, she handed over her gold earrings, the only piece of gold she had.

She was now working at a factory that made Sarva Shiksha Abhiyan bags. Sarva Shiksha Abhiyan is a government programme to provide free elementary education to all Indian children under fourteen. She made Rs 3,000 per month for finishing and packing 250 bags per day.

To salvage her reputation as a responsible home-based worker, she had started personally collecting raw material and handing over finished products, instead of entrusting the children with these chores.

It was a Sunday, that day. Syeda liked Sundays, not because it was her a weekly off like the rest of the world, but because on Sunday she could get the children to help her out, the precise reason for which the children hated Sundays.

For her home-based work of colouring and polishing carrom board pieces and making the corner nets of the boards, Syeda had gathered the raw material in a brightly coloured cloth bundle, which she was ferrying home.

Her head was rigid, the bundle steady as a rock, while her brain was occupied with how to find more work. The cloth bundle was neatly balanced without the touch of a hand, without a wobble, without a quiver, even when she walked into and out of a ditch to dodge the traffic.

There was a traffic jam in the lane. It was only as wide as a car, and one had entered from one side and blocked all the traffic from the other side. A car wheel had got stuck in an open drain.

Oh, a woman driver in the car. These women, these rich women, that's how they drive. They don't know where to go, or where not to. Must be some NGOwali, like that one who came and gave lecture on how all children should be sent to school. What did they know about everyday survival and children flunking their classes? mused an irritable Syeda.

Some boys on a motorbike started honking at her and the other women carrying bundles on their heads. From the top, the colourful bundles, steady on their heads, looked like gold fish navigating a sea of trash.

The woman in the car called out to Syeda. She was Dr Meena from Kush Hospital, a small private medical facility, where Syeda had gone for her own abortion and had accompanied other women later. 'Come and meet me tomorrow!'

℮

The next day, when Syeda met Dr Meena, she offered her a job as a cleaner and a sanitary attendant for Rs 4,500 per month. Syeda accepted instantly.

The hospital was a recognized maternity care and abortion clinic, with a few rooms, four to five beds, an X-ray room, an operation theatre and a doctor's clinic. She was tasked to do the cleaning and assist with deliveries.

A lot of caregiving work for pregnant women is usually done by female family members. Since most women in Karawal Nagar were migrants, they didn't have that kind of support. The husbands or the children would bring women to the nursing home and then they were left to their own devices. And they would pretty much resume work within two days of childbirth or abortion. Syeda emulated Raziya in how she treated the other women but realized she did not have the infinite reserve of patience of Raziya Sufi. Still, she tried to do as much as she could to help these women.

Within a few months, she had learnt how to assist in child delivery and abortion, sometimes even supervising it all on her own when the doctor was not available at night. She knew which medicines to give and what kind of post-care to prescribe.

The clinic was frequented by college girls from all over Delhi. Gynaecologists were as sexist and moralistic as anyone else. Many doctors interpreted the abortion law as allowing abortion only if the pregnancy posed a risk to the woman or if the foetus was damaged or if the woman claimed she was coerced into sexual activity or in cases of contraceptive failure. That too only for married women.

As a result, single pregnant women looking to terminate a pregnancy would find help only in clinics like these which did the work discreetly. Dr Meena had trained Syeda not to ask such patients personal questions.

At home, Syeda had taken up bindi pasting work from Parshuram – the bindi factory owner who ran his enterprise on Iodex-toast-fed child labour. Over the past year, many children from Parshuram's brigade had been taken away by child rights activists. He figured that it was easier and more cost effective to outsource this work to home-based workers than host so many children at his place.

After Parshuram's army had cut out dots or fancy stylized shapes for bindis with metal hand tools in the factory, they had to be pasted on the brand's packets that were provided by wholesale traders.

Parshuram also dealt directly with small-time local retailers who printed their own brand names on the packets: Lady Care, Lady Kiran, Asian Beauty, Sneha, Prerna and Shringar.

Syeda would receive the packets with instructions on the arrangement or display of the bindis inside the packets. She was paid Rs 12 for 144 packets, with each packet containing five to fifteen bindis. She managed to complete 720 packets in seven to eight hours every day, making approximately Rs 1,800 in a month additionally.

After her shift at the hospital, she would come home to this work: peeling off the thin paper under the velvet bindi cut-outs with her nails or teeth, and sticking the bindi under the cellophane window of the packet. Reshma had been tasked with cleaning the house and doing laundry. In the absence of a job, Akmal was doing the cooking, which was a huge relief.

Reshma loved bindis with embellishments in various shapes and sizes. Salman would scold her for that, saying Muslim women didn't wear bindis. Syeda kept asking him from where he was learning all these religious diktats.

Salman had started hanging out with the local madrasa kids who empathized with his alienation at school after the train incident. Some madrasas had started following the Wahabi sect of Islam which aims to return to 'authentic Islam' and the way of life that existed in Arabia at the time of Prophet Muhammad. The composite syncretic Islam that has existed in the Indian subcontinent, which permits cultural practices like wearing a bindi and saree, shaving one's beard and Sufi influences like music, is according to this sect 'un-Islamic'. Salman had learnt this from some of his madrasa friends.

Syeda managed to get additional work by doing polio duty for the Delhi government for a few days. She had to administer polio drops to children under five and was paid Rs 50 per day. An additional Rs 300.

Things had started looking up, though she was terribly sleep deprived. She could be summoned at any time of the night. The cleaning work was too much. Additionally, Dr Meena would often call her home to help with her domestic chores and she couldn't say no.

In 1994, India had passed the Pre-Conception and Pre-Natal Diagnostic Techniques [PCPNDT] Act to stop sex-selective abortions and control the declining sex ratio in the country. Yet even after twelve years of implementation, over five million girls went 'missing' because of the preference for a male child in the country.

Affluent, posh south Delhi was under a lot of surveillance. It had the lowest sex ratio in the national capital, at one point as low as 798/1,000.

While the super-rich were travelling to Thailand and other neighbouring countries to get sex-selective abortions done, some found remote, unassuming places like Kush Hospital for a quick procedure.

In Kush Hospital, doctors would use different coloured pens or ask for a jalebi or a laddoo as a code language to indicate the sex of the foetus.

Syeda remembers several women coming in big cars, decked in diamonds, who left within two hours. They would leave hefty tips for cleaners like Syeda.

In March 2006, the first ever conviction under the PCPNDT Act took place when a doctor and his assistants were handed a jail term of two years and a fine of Rs 5,000 for sex-selective abortions in Palwal, Faridabad.

This was almost a year after Syeda began to work at the clinic. One day, a woman came in a blue car with a man posing as her husband. They met Dr Meena, the sex of the foetus was determined as female, and the man requested an abortion immediately. While Syeda was cleaning the operation theatre, a number of cops entered the hospital and arrested Dr Meena and took her away. Within half an hour, the hospital had been sealed for violation of the PCPNDT Act. The hospital didn't reopen for almost a year.

℘

In May 2006, the Arjun Sengupta Committee report on Social Security for Unorganised Workers revealed that 93 per cent of all non-agricultural workers in India work in the unorganized sector.

According to this report, in urban areas, 96 per cent of women workers are part of the informal sector, which account for roughly 50 per cent of the national product. Over half of these women are home-based workers. This was the first time the Indian government had officially acknowledged home-based workers as part of the Indian economy.

The report also stated that after agricultural work, the largest working sector for women in India is home-based work. More than 80 million women – around 7 per cent of the Indian population – do this work, but are not counted as 'workers'. The average monthly income of a home-based worker is one-fifth of the legal minimum wage in Delhi, according to estimates.

Syeda was back to doing per-piece work again and not making more than Rs 2,500 per month. The rent hadn't been paid for over three months.

At least the herbs and the charm from the Bengali Baba had worked. Akmal was hired again as a cart rickshaw puller at the bag factory. But things were still tight. The recognition by the Arjun Sengupta report did not really impact her life.

***

On 25 July 2007, Pratibha Patil became the first woman president of India.

'Arre, I know how to sew. My father was a tailor in a *nautanki*. I can make all kinds of styles. That's what I did in Banaras for two years!' Syeda told Pintoo, a subcontractor, coaxing him for a job at one of the bigger garment factories.

'Chachi, you cut jeans threads, you stitch buttons on shirts, you do trimming, you do embroidery. But a tailor is the one who puts all of this together. In the *factory*! The one who sits in the *factory* for hours to make a complete garment,' Pintoo countered.

'So why don't you hire me in your *factory*. I will make double the number of garments they are making,' she urged.

'You sit comfortably at home. Your men bring the raw materials and deliver the finished products. Between cooking and taking care of the children, you cut some threads and think you can be a tailor,' he replied.

Unlike earlier when the entire garment was stitched by one tailor, now different parts of the garments were prepared separately and put together in the factory by stitching operators.

The kind of work outsourced to home-based workers, in this case women, was pattern-making, processing the fabric, cutting, zipping, button work, embroidery, trimming, threading, washing, spot removing, ironing and packing. They were kept away from the assembly floor. They could only be the tailor's apprentice, not the tailor.

'Money comes to you while you sit and soak the sun at home with ease. And then you buy saree after saree,' Pintoo said.

That's what he thought of women? That's what everyone thought of women, except the women. When was the last time Syeda bought new clothes, she couldn't remember. She would alter Dr Meena's discarded salwar kameezes to her size and wear them.

Pintoo was repeating what several discussion papers by the Ministry of Labour had stated about home-based workers. They defined home-based women's wages as *supplementary* to the family income because they had flexible hours and worked from home.

After repeatedly coaxing Pintoo and many other subcontractors for a job in a bigger factory with a fixed income, Syeda finally landed a job in Tronica City.

Koop mandook. A frog who lives in a well and hasn't seen the world. She could hear her dadi's words.

Home-based work also means social confinement.

Syeda had not left Delhi 94 in the last nine years. There was no time or need to go anywhere. There was no time to loiter. Akmal, Salman, Shazeb, on the other hand, had mapped the length and breadth of Delhi for some reason or the other. But she had only heard of the Rashtrapati Bhavan, India Gate, Qutub Minar, south Delhi, with its wide roads, foreign embassies and fancy shopping malls.

'Remember, 227. Don't sit in any other bus,' said Shazeb as Syeda packed dal roti in a plastic tiffin box.

'I know how to catch a bus,' Syeda snapped.

'Really? Tell me, when did you last go outside Karawal Nagar?'

She kept quiet.

As she waited at the Shaheed Bhagat Singh Colony bus stop in Karawal Nagar for the Delhi Transport Corporation (DTC) bus number 227.

The bus was full. She entered through the front door and stood near the ladies' seats. A college girl held her bag as was the practice in DTC buses. The ones who had a seat were obligated to hold the bags of the ones standing in the aisle. Syeda held on tightly to the seat in front of her. She was too short to reach the straps above her. She was nervous but calm. The bus passed Sabhapur crossing, Khajoori. It all looked the same – stuffed with people and matchbox houses propped next to large open drains, waterlogged roads with people hopping from one dry spot to the next to get to the bus stop.

Half an hour later, when Syeda was about to get off, she asked for her bag. When she took it off the college girl's lap, they realized the dal from her tiffin had leaked, soaking and staining the girl's clothes. She kicked up a fuss. Syeda apologized. She did not know that daily commuters should only pack dry items in the tiffin.

The bus dropped her off at Tronica City, an industrial township created in the 1990s to develop the industrially backward area of Loni in Ghaziabad district. The city was divided into twelve residential sectors and eight industrial sectors. It was full of actual factories, like the ones she had seen in films, in newspapers, the ones in her imagination. Big buildings with chimneys, soot, an entry gate, an exit gate, guards, the cacophony of big machines.

Over stretches of kilometres there were innumerable factories with assembly-line production. Ones that made auto parts: coils, ignitions, side mirrors, rubber caps, gaskets and indicators. There were pipe manufacturing units that made industrial hose pipes, high-pressure hoses, automobile hose pipes, hydraulic hosepipes, flexible hosepipes, industrial pipes. Some made steel wire ropes and slings, welding wires, spring steel wires and cold heading wires.

But most of these heavy industrial units did not employ women.

Factories that employed women in Tronica City were the ones that made ice cream, biscuits, jeans, mushrooms, power brakes, hardware, bed sheets, furniture, wax-coated papers for commercial use. Also the ones that make hospital equipment – surgical tools, furniture, stools, things Syeda was now familiar with after her stint at Kush Hospital.

From the bus stand, Syeda had to walk almost half an hour to the factory.

༄

Pintoo had found her a job at a wedding card manufacturing unit. It was an eight-hour shift for Rs 4,500 per month. With four hours of overtime every day, she could make up to Rs 6,500.

There was a big, well-lit hall with workstations. Syeda had to sit on a stool for up to twelve hours colouring the cards. Years of squatting on the floor and working in a bad posture had given her a crooked back. This was so different from Karawal Nagar factories where any free minute meant taking a quick trip to check on the children. Unlike here, where once you entered the gate, you couldn't leave till the end of the shift.

During lunchtime, they sat in the backyard to eat and sometimes take a fifteen-minute nap too. There was a supervisor who sat in a glass cabin with a computer to keep an eye on the thirty-five women who worked there. Many of her co-workers took buses from Loni, Karawal Nagar and other parts of north east Delhi to work here.

Within two weeks she had learnt how to do screen printing for wedding cards. The usual templates had Hindu God Ganesh on top of a Hindu wedding card, Guru Nanak on the Sikh wedding card, and some calligraphy on a Muslim card. Some cards with Hindu names did not have Ganesh but instead a partially bald man in glasses, and a suit and tie. She initially thought it was someone's father but later found out it was Dr B.R. Ambedkar, who drafted the Indian constitution and was an anti-caste activist who along with thousands renounced Hinduism for its oppressive, discriminatory caste system and embraced Buddhism.

She had to pack the cards in envelopes, the expensive ones with an extra layer of cellophane, the super expensive ones packed in boxes with bags for other goodies. The scale of manufacturing here was bigger than anything she had seen so far. Thousands of cards were made from start to finish within a day. They had big tempo carriers for deliveries. The workers were not allowed to have a direct conversation with the factory owner who came in a big car once in a while, flanked by a personal bodyguard.

There was no *ghar ki baat* concept here. Even chatting was not allowed during work, unlike in the mini-factories of Karawal Nagar.

Syeda would reach home by ten every night. But since the bus was full, she didn't feel scared.

Akmal, Salman, Shazeb and Reshma were thrilled not to have her home. No one was asked to go to work, no one was asked to go to school or stopped from going, in Reshma's case. Just before Syeda reached home, there was a flurry of activity when the food was cooked and the house cleaned. She was living the life of a man.

After a long time, she felt she had a little more mindspace. Her gaunt face started filling up. She would even watch TV serials once she came back home. In her absence, the children had hacked the neighbour's cable TV connection and connected it to their TV.

Once the wedding season was over, the factory started making notebooks. Syeda was used to changing jobs every few weeks and so she adapted well.

Reams of paper were folded, cut to size in a separate machine, and stapled in another one. These were not the regular copies Syeda made in Karawal Nagar but ledger books, attendance books, accounts books as big as a 2 foot ruler.

She had just been seven months in this job when one day the generator room caught fire and burned down the paper stock. A guard got locked in and eventually lost his life. The factory was sealed.

Syeda managed to get work in a toffee-packing factory in Tronica City but that lasted only two months because they started outsourcing the job to home-based workers in Loni. For a month, she worked at a fruit conservation centre where they were tasked with making pickle, jam and squash. The payment here was Rs 20 per 2 kilo bottle. This brought down her income to Rs 4,500, the same as what she was making in Karawal Nagar, with no extra time to pick up more work.

After ten months at Tronica, she was back working in Karawal Nagar full time. Meanwhile, Akmal had been unwell with jaundice, metabolic syndrome and liver issues because of the medicines given by the Bengali Baba. He had stopped working altogether, once again.

Syeda got a job at the pressure cooker factory in the lane adjacent to her house. It was a huge hall on the ground floor of a residential building where everyone roamed around with silver patches on their clothes and faces from the coating that was done on the finished products. She fitted cover brackets on the cooker handles and packaged the finished pieces. The packaging of these pressure cookers had names of big brands like Hawkins, Reliance, Godrej, etc. There was no knowing if they were genuine or replicas.

There were almost twenty people employed here who worked on a twelve-hour shift, 9 a.m. to 9 p.m.; Sundays were off. The men were paid Rs 5,500 and the women Rs 4,000. No one challenged this gender pay gap. It was universally accepted.

She worked here for a year and a half from 2007 to 2008 while taking up two more jobs on the side.

In all these years, even when Syeda was hired and fired a couple of times, she did not hold grudges. She kept *dua-salaam*, always exchanged greetings, to keep alive the possibility of getting rehired.

￼ ❧

In 2008, the North East Delhi Lok Sabha constituency was carved out of east Delhi after delimitation.

The North East Delhi district now has the highest population density among the eleven districts of the national capital. It extends from Seemapuri in the easternmost part of Delhi, bordering UP, to Burari in the north. And has as many people as the country of Latvia, or the state of New Mexico in the US. North East Delhi shares its northern and eastern borders with Ghaziabad. More than 70 per cent of the constituency consists of illegal colonies, including Seelampur,

Gokulpur, Karawal Nagar, Rohtash Nagar, Ghonda, Burari and Seemapuri. Some areas have authorized pockets like Yamuna Vihar, Timarpur and Dilshad Garden.

Both Salman and Shazeb had stopped going to school now – Salman because of flunking repeatedly and Shazeb because most of his classmates had dropped out to take up jobs to help their families. He too saw no point in continuing while his family lived in a perennial financial crisis.

By October 2008, on Sundays, Syeda had started work with Kalim in his scrapyard. She had to dismantle the spiral binding metal spine from calendars using a snap machine.

At home, she was cleaning cardboard packaging of home appliances for recycling. The cardboard factories did not employ women except to clean the premises. Her house was already stuffed with raw material which she worked on at night after dinner for three to four hours. She made about Rs 60 in a day by cleaning 7–8 kilos with Reshma's help.

Syeda preferred dismantling metal in Kalim's scrapyard because there was no space left at home to store any more raw material. That was where she met Nisha Radiowali.

More than forty-five jobs in twelve years, more than sixteen hours of work every day, and living in perennial crisis mode had changed Syeda's core personality. From a chatterbox who loved films, music, colours, she had become an irritable, bitter, quiet woman who kept to herself. Then, when she met Radiowali, things changed. It was as if there was an explosion that resuscitated her old self.

5

Almond

Shaadi ke baad sab kuch badal jaata hai
Jaise us din ye fark, ye nikhaar, sabne pehchana,
Siwai inke, akhir husbands hote hi aise hain.
Fair and Lovely...
Bheetar se melanin seemit rakhein,
Sirf chhe hafton mein laaye naya nikhaar, ek naya andaaz.
Jeevan mein ek naya nikhaar...
Hahaha... husbands hote hi aise hain.
Fair and Lovely.

Everything changes after marriage,
Back then everyone noticed the difference, my glow
Except him, after all, husbands are like this only.
Fair and Lovely...
It restricts the melanin from inside,
In just six weeks, it brings a new glow, a new style.
A new glow in life...
Hahaha... husbands are like this only.
Fair and Lovely.

– Fair and Lovely TV advertisement, late 1990s

'What did she say? Husbands are like this, offering flowers and swinging their wives in their arms? Then who are the ones we have?' asked Roopmati.

'They are not Hus-Band. They are just *Band*!' answered Rani.

Band. Closed.

The women watching the Fair and Lovely TV ad where a husband starts romancing his wife after her face complexion turns lighter from using the skin whitening cream Fair and Lovely at Radiowali's, Syeda among them, had a good laugh.

After meeting at Kalim's scrapyard, Syeda had developed a solid friendship with Nisha Radiowali.

Syeda had briefly worked at a small factory where she packaged tubes of Fair and Love. This was a knock-off of Fair and Lovely, which for generations had advertised how women could get the attention of their husbands, family and co-workers only if their skin tone was lighter. The factory was later sealed for counterfeiting the original product.

At Radiowali's place, she saw many other television advertisements that reminded her of the things she had made. Many of the women preferred to watch television at Radiowali's than at home where children and husbands dictated what to watch at all times of the day. The last few months of 2008 were full of TV anchors sitting on a rocket announcing the launch of Chandrayaan-1, India's first mission to the moon, and visuals of the terrorist attacks on Mumbai by the Lashkar-e-Taiba.

Radiowali's place was their *adda*, their hangout. They jokingly called it Radiowali ka ashram. Someone or the other would drop by, often bringing homemade *saag, parantha, halwa, matthi, achaar*. Radiowali would make chai for them. Her place allowed them a few moments of leisure which they couldn't get at home or in the factories.

Syeda was now thirty-five; Radiowali was thirty-seven, older than her. When Syeda looked at Radiowali's tall, broad body, glowing, moisturized skin, and nicely braided hair or neat bun at the back of her slender neck, her brightly coloured sarees with well-fitting, matching blouses, she felt older than she actually was.

In Radiowali's company, she became more conscious of her rounded shoulders, mismatched dupatta salwar, matted hair, dry skin, crow's feet, frown lines on her forehead, and smile lines even though she rarely smiled.

She had stopped polishing her face with mustard oil, except on Eid, never bothered to apply the creams that she packaged herself, had not bought a lipstick in years. Unlike Radiowali, who had no problems sitting and chatting with people in a warm, affectionate, fully present way, Syeda no longer liked to engage in casual conversation. She was always preoccupied.

Bas kaam se kaam. Mind one's own business.

Like professional Delhi people. The insides were empty and there was nothing to give to anyone, not even a smile.

⁓

By the 1970s, Delhi had the highest concentration of small-scale industries in India. Noida, New Okhla Industrial Development Area, was set up in 1976, in UP, adjoining Delhi, as part of the urbanization drive during the Emergency period in India. It is located on the floodplains of the Yamuna river on non-fertile land. Noida is now part of NCR, the National Capital Region. It is classified as a special economic zone where industries, factories and real estate grew exponentially in the following decades.

Nisha started making radio transmitters when she was fifteen. In the mid-1980s, she had moved with her family from Mathura to Noida to work at a construction site. She was one of many girls her age who watched over their younger siblings at the construction site while their parents worked.

This was the time when the electronics sector in Noida had become huge, with an initial thrust on making radios and for components of black-and-white TVs. In contrast to the male-dominated engineering units, the electronics sector had a special demand for nimble fingers and dexterity to handle sensitive parts. Adolescent girls like Nisha in shanties, slums and construction sites were often identified, trained and employed as interns or apprentices for years on low wages. This was illegal but a common way to cut costs.

When Indian technology companies started setting up shop in Noida, the demand for such trainees grew. Companies were now also making optical instruments, photographic equipment, watches, clocks, calculators, computing machinery, transmitters and many similar things.

Unmarried girls were preferred for this work. They were young enough to not have an opinion of their own and were under the strict control of their fathers and brothers. There was less baggage to deal with.

Nisha's father collected her salary every month. Initially, she resisted working at the factory. Long hours of sitting in dungeon-like rooms, no leave even when you had a fever, and the watchful, lecherous looks of the supervisors were too much to deal with for the adolescent girl. The father had more trust in the supervisors than in Nisha's reports of her experiences. After a couple of beatings from her parents for complaining, she surrendered.

When her father died in 1995, she became, at age twenty-four, the sole earning member of the family. Both her younger brothers, even though married by then, only worked sporadically: a construction site here, an office attendant's job there. Her salary paid the rent of the two-room house they lived in. The brothers occupied the two rooms with their wives. She and her mother, who had lost the privilege of having her own room after she was widowed, slept in the small courtyard at the back.

In the late 1990s, Bhagirath Palace in Chandni Chowk, near Red Fort, emerged as one of Asia's largest electrical and electronics markets. It was a one-stop destination for a variety of electrical equipment and accessories, for both domestic and industrial use. Colourful decorative tube lights and bulbs, electric heaters, switchboards, wires and every other imaginable piece of equipment – the shops had it all and offered generous discounts. The market also emerged as a hub for the import and export trade to Sri Lanka, Pakistan, Maldives and Bangladesh. It had more than 2,000 wholesale shops that started setting up their own small in-house electronic and electrical manufacturing units.

Kamal Kumar, the supervisor who had trained Nisha and many other girls to assemble radio transmitters, had moved to one of these wholesale shops. It made electric heaters, and electronic watches that could display the ambient temperature. Kamal was married with kids. He was twenty years older than Nisha. He was the only one who would spend his own money on her, sometimes to buy a plate of chowmein, sometimes a cold drink or coffee. He was the only one who ever told her to 'get some rest'. Over the years, their mutual affection and intimacy grew. There was no name for their relationship but a lot of comfort in it.

Nisha had heard that women are harassed and neglected in the *paraya ghar*, the house of someone else, that of their husbands, the marital home. But she felt she was facing that abuse and indifference in her own parents' home.

She was not allowed to make friends. If her brothers found her eating chaat on the road or talking to a man at the bus stop, they would question her character. She was expected to bear with the insults to maintain harmony at home. Everyone was allowed to have an opinion on her actions, even her niece and nephews.

Her brothers were more important to her mother than Nisha. She bitched about her sons to Nisha, but when it came to taking a position, it was always the boys that she sided with.

Poor guy didn't take home-cooked lunch to work today! Poor thing has a headache but still went to buy veggies from the market! The mother had plenty of sympathy and praise for the sons. But not a word of approval or affection for Nisha – the one who was regularly earning and feeding them all. No acknowledgement. Nothing.

Nisha was now twenty-seven, but no one ever mentioned her marriage or made any efforts to arrange one for her. If not marriage, is there another way to get a new life, break out of this family, and see the world? she wondered. To her, a married woman seemed to have more rights. An unmarried woman like her was always the apprentice in the house, secondary, never in the foreground. Unlike her, a married woman could wear make-up and colourful clothes, have a room of her own, get gifts as part of religious rituals, get rest, even get pampered when pregnant, and go to her parents' home once in a while to relax.

Her younger brothers and cousins were married and were more respected at family gatherings than her. No one ever got up to offer her a chair or make her a cup of tea.

She was expected to hand over her entire salary to her mother. Many of her co-workers had a similar story: their families got used to their salaries and never attempted to get them married.

One day, she heard her mother talk about her distant aunt who was unmarried and lived all her life working in a government school as a sweeper. 'She must have been cursed in her past life that she did not get married. She is frustrated and has no one to control her or watch over her. Some people are born to die a lonely death.'

Her mother didn't even notice that Nisha was sitting right there.

Nisha had a perennial feeling of being isolated at home, uncared for.

The electronics industry had started employing so many women that even though under Section 66 of the Factories Act women were prohibited from working in factories between 7 p.m. and 6 a.m., in 1998, they lifted the ban for women in electronics.

Within a year of Kamal moving to Bhagirath Palace, Nisha also decided to move there.

When she told her family, her mother instantly blamed Kamal. Nisha was slapped, cursed, abused. They swore to cut all ties with her and locked her in the house for a week. But she knew she wanted to move not so much because of Kamal but to get away from her dysfunctional, selfish family that only wanted to squeeze her for everything she had but offered no warmth, no respite. She did not realize her resolve to leave them had become so strong.

One morning, she packed her bags and escaped, without a note, without saying anything to anyone.

A number of women who worked in Bhagirath Palace lived in a three-room semi-hostel in the same building. There were eighteen of them. Sometimes they slept in shifts, sometimes they just squeezed into whichever bed they found space in. Nisha moved in there. She liked this new world, with lots of young women and chitter-chatter. They would cook their own food, sometimes buy it from outside, and share. There were fights about who used whose bucket, or toothpaste or took more time in the bathroom. But there was laughter too, and care. If you had a fever, everyone would ask about your health. The women would even ask each other if they had eaten or not. Perhaps they knew the importance of being asked.

Nisha was instructed by one of her hostel mates, 'Don't go out and lean against the pillar or Begum Samru's spirit will grab you from behind and possess you.'

Like many hostels, this one was also rumoured to be haunted.

Bhagirath Palace is at least 200 years old. The original owner was Farzana, a Kashmiri nautch girl living in Old Delhi who married Walter Reinhardt, an Austrian mercenary, in 1767. Reinhardt had acquired the nickname 'Le Sombre' because of his dark complexion. It was distorted to Samru and after marriage, Farzana was known as Begum Samru.

By the early 1800s, after her husband's death, Begum Samru had become a prominent political figure. She was the only Catholic ruler in India, reigning over the Sardhana province in north India's Meerut for fifty-five years. In 1806, Akbar Shah II, the father of the last Mughal king, Bahadur Shah Zafar II, gifted her a plot of land across the Red Fort where she built a palace. It had classical Greek columns and magnificent gardens where she hosted grand parties that were attended by the high and mighty.

After her death in 1837, her adopted son sold off the palace. After passing through several owners, it was finally bought by Lala Bhagirath Mal in 1940 and its name changed to Bhagirath Palace. For many years, it was used as a banquet hall. Around 1985, it transitioned into an electrical market. When Nisha moved there in 1998, it was flourishing.

One night during the second week of Nisha's stay, there was a commotion in the hostel. The women were jumping in fear and excitement. 'Is she here?' one of them yelled. 'I don't know but someone is running around on the roof!' replied another. 'Yes, I can hear too!' confirmed a third. Then, according to Nisha, the bulb and the tube light in the room started flickering.

'She is definitely here! Light the incense stick in front of Durga's picture! Or she'll come to our room!' screamed the first as she hurried towards a corner in the room where pictures of several gods and goddesses were placed.

'Oh, I can see someone in a white robe moving in this direction,' said the second as she stood up on her bed.

'I see some shadows,' said the third as she peeped through the window.

The windows suddenly started to shake. Nisha was scared. She stood behind the hosteller who was peeping out from a crack in the door. She thought she saw a figure in a white robe moving towards the terrace. She couldn't see the face, just dark, flowing hair and sparkling jewels that shone brightly in the darkness of the night. The figure moved from one end of the terrace to the other for a while and then disappeared into thin air at the break of dawn.

Nisha was mesmerized. The hostellers claimed that it was Begum Samru's spirit that often visited and registered her presence this way. Discussing Begum Samru's many lovers – a Mughal prince, a British official, an officer in her private army – was a favourite pastime in the hostel. She was called Zeb un-Nissa, the jewel of her sex, a child-free female ruler. The kind of woman they had never heard of in the king–queen–family folk tales they had grown up with.

Begum Samru's tales were music to Nisha's ears. She had entertained, socialized and lived life on her own terms. Two hundred year later, why was the same lifestyle disapproved of for single women, she often thought.

୬

By the 2000s, the nature of electronics manufacturing was changing. Mobile phones had entered the market. The demand for cheap labour surged.

In the six years that Nisha worked there, till 2004, she never met her family. Driven by the guilt of prioritizing herself, she kept sending money to her family every once in a while through postal money order. The money was accepted but no one ever wrote to her or checked in on her. Disentangling yourself from family does come with its own share of loneliness but also the freedom to eat, chat, loiter, laze around and form your own worldview.

In 2004, the Election Commission of India decided to use Electronic Voting Machines (EVMs) in all 543 Lok Sabha constituencies for the first time in the Indian general elections. They were exclusively manufactured by Bharat Electronics Limited, Bangalore, and Electronics Corporation of India Limited, Hyderabad.

Electoral fraud in Indian parliamentary elections had become a major issue. Multiple voting, voter intimidation, vote buying and booth capturing were some of the major challenges faced by the Election Commission. EVMs were introduced primarily to address booth capturing, where criminals deployed by political parties and candidates would capture the polling station and stuff the ballot boxes with a large number of votes for their favoured candidate.

The EVMs were designed in a way that it was impossible to cast more than five votes per minute. This meant criminal politicians had to ensure the capturing of booths for a longer time, making it riskier and more expensive.

Each time a new electronic product came into the market, the electronic markets of Delhi buzzed with cheaper replicas. This was the first time they were dealing with EVMs. Nisha remembers that small electronic workshops were commissioned to hack EVMs, change their configuration, manipulate the counting system, and even make replicas, and were working overtime to do so.

A few EVMs that were stolen from Andhra Pradesh had been brought to Bhagirath Palace through the alleged involvement of some Election Commission officers. Kamal had been commissioned to change the five-vote-per-minute configuration of the EVMs so that more votes could be cast in less time during booth capturing.

He explained to Nisha and others that the EVM used a hardware called microcontroller, designed to perform dedicated applications. The workers in Bhagirath Palace were familiar with these generic microcontrollers used in the EVMs because these were extensively used in home appliances, electricity meters, office machines, toys, etc.

The strategy was to procure the same make of microcontroller as used in the EVM, which was as cheap as Rs 100. Seasoned electronic workers would have to fuse tampered software on to them to increase the number of votes per minute. After that they would replace the microcontroller in the EVM using a desoldering machine.

They had already practised this on a couple of replicas and could apparently rig the whole thing in minutes. This was reported widely by newspapers, researchers and political leaders.

It was not safe to do this in central Delhi. Kamal arranged for a place in Karawal Nagar, which by then had gained notoriety for its small, unchecked manufacturing units. Nisha was put in charge of the assembly of the tampered EVMs.

But when the day arrived to transfer the EVMs from the safe house to the factory, the police raided the house, arresting Kamal and detaining some of the women workers. The cops used the age-old tactic of threatening the women with prostitution charges. That scared them enough to reveal the details of Kamal's plan.

Nisha, waiting for the machines in Karawal Nagar, decided to stay back there to escape police scrutiny. The last thing she wanted was prostitution charges that would have proven her family's prophecy for her future. Meanwhile, she started working at Kalim's scrapyard, which also had an electronic-waste recycling unit. That was where people started calling her Radiowali.

❦

Radiowali had an advantage. The IT sector generated enormous amounts of e-waste. With her experience, she could identify specific electronic parts. Once segregated, they could be tested, refurbished and sold off to repair shops.

Kalim Ahmed, the owner of this scrapyard, hired Radiowali as a supervisor. She had to train women to identify specific circuit boards from phones, radios, VCRs and computers collected by waste-pickers or small-time scrap dealers who would roam door to door, lane to lane, mostly on foot, collecting discarded scrap or buying it for a small price.

Once the electronic parts with the potential to be repaired were separated, the women had to dislodge the metal from the leftovers. The cable strippers had the most difficult job. They had to use knives and blades to extract the copper from the wires, causing skin infections and blisters, even tetanus.

It is especially difficult to strip the cables in winter because the plastic covers become hard. Children accompanying the women were taught the easiest way to extract copper: by burning electric cables, even though the fumes generated were toxic and caused respiratory diseases. At times this required bathing the electronic items in acid. A dedicated team melted the metal in a small makeshift furnace to convert it into ingots. These ingots, mostly of copper, were then sold off to the brass industry.

Radiowali rented a room for herself, set up her kitchen, and installed a refurbished television and a bed. She missed the well-oiled professional systems of central Delhi but now she had tasted blood. This was her home, her own, not shared with anyone. Once on her own, her identity was that of someone who laughed a lot, was always up for a chat, was hard-working, helpful and caring – unlike at home where she was an ignored, *bechari* – helpless, wretched – woman who always forgot to do one thing or the other.

It was not like people in Karawal Nagar were less judgemental about single women, unmarried, with no kids, living by themselves. But she was now in her mid-thirties, had some money that she had saved in the last few years, and was one of the main supervisors in Kalim's scrapyard. That kept people and their opinions out of her hair.

When Syeda met Radiowali, she had already worked at Kalim's for over four years.

That day she asked Syeda, 'Why don't you eat during the day?' She had noticed that about Syeda.

'I will eat when I get home,' Syeda responded.

Radiowali always ate on time. She said, 'Don't stay hungry for so many hours. Pack two rotis when you come to work.'

Many women did not eat two meals. Either there was not enough food and so the children and the husbands were prioritized or there was no time to cook and pack for themselves. Radiowali used her leverage with Kalim and introduced a mandatory twenty-minute lunch break. That was all it took to ensure the women workers started prioritizing themselves by eating on time.

The last several years of perennial crisis had taken their toll on Syeda. She had lost her zest for life. She had a wooden look, and there was no joy in her laughter.

Radiowali had a spark, a naughty glint in her eye, and warmth.

One day she asked Syeda, 'Don't you sing?'

Syeda was pleasantly surprised. 'I don't sing but there was a time when I loved playing antakshari. I loved filmi songs.'

Antakshari is a traditional Indian game of songs. Each person sings a song that starts with the last letter of the previous participant's song.

'So sing, na? We should all play antakshari,' Radiowali said. 'When lonely, start singing. That's the purpose of songs and music,' she added.

Syeda agreed.

Abke baras bhej bhaiya ko babul
Sawan ne li jo bulaye.
Lautengi jab meri bachpan ki sakhiyan
Deejo sandesaa bhijaye . . .

Radiowali sang this song from *Bandini* which she had picked up from someone in Bhagirath Palace. It was like singing, but it wasn't just singing. In the movie, a female prisoner sings about women who have been abandoned. No one checks on them, no one writes to them or cares for them, and no one is there for them. Except for other women in the same situation, perhaps.

'The song ended with *e*. So you need to sing a song that starts with *e*,' she told Syeda.

So Syeda sang one of her old favourites:

Ek do teen
Chaar paanch chhe saat aath nau
Dus gyarah, barah terah,
Tera karun din gin gin ke intezaar
Aaja piya aayi bahaar . . .

Syeda's friendship with Radiowali grew. It revived her interest in music and films through antakshari and collective TV viewing.

For the first time in twelve years in Delhi, she was part of a community, a collective, a group. She knew women workers in her neighbourhood but everyone there worked in their own pigeonholes, in their own time, with their own employers. So far, there had been no shared space for her, like the one that was taking shape at Radiowali's place.

※

It wasn't like Radiowali was a saint. While she was usually jovial, at times she could be extremely rude, cold, curt.

Roopmati would say, 'Have you asked her why she curses family so early in the morning always?'

Radiowali would rant. Say things like: why should anyone have a family? You earn for them, serve them and then they go their own way. And we sit all our lives nursing those heartbreaks. No one has been there for you or stood up for you or given you a shoulder to cry on or opened doors for you. Or they have criticized you to a point that you never recover from it. There is an unequal space where you are always supposed to give, if you are a woman. And if you aren't meek and don't ask for help, then you are to be detested. They don't like your guts, your survival instincts. As a woman you are supposed to be a permanent victim. Never a hero or survivor. Even when you feel like one, you should never show it. Because how dare you be happy without anyone's help, support, assistance or generosity?

All the women knew her rants were not hers alone. She had broken free and could say those things out loud which the other women couldn't because they were still expending their lives for their family. This would melt something inside Syeda.

Radiowali had lovers. Many women obviously judged her for that. There was a man whose family lived in Moradabad. He was gentle and sensitive, and said sorry when he was late or came after a long gap to visit her.

One day, the women were playing antakshari at her place when someone standing outside pulled her leg: 'Nisha is singing the wrong song!' It was her lover, who had recognized her singing voice across the threshold.

Everyone rushed out to give him and Radiowali some privacy.

This way Radiowali had access to the warmth and intimacy that these women had perhaps lost in their pursuit of survival.

Syeda sometimes felt pangs of jealousy and emptiness. Akmal had long ago stopped narrating his stories of the forests and the rivers. Or paid attention to what she was feeling. She was fed up of this thirty-something layabout, with jet-black dyed hair but the face of a sixty-year-old, who had wanted to become a *baazigar*, someone who dares, but had turned into nothing but a sad drunk.

All the unemployed husbands and fathers sat all day at the *puliya*, the small bridge, in Karawal Nagar, rejecting low-paid work. Instead they burdened their wives with not just running the house but also maintaining the facade of being pure, untouched women.

Like that day, when Syeda arrived at Radiowali's place, and Shalu was crying inconsolably.

'Didn't I ask you to wear old, shabby clothes to work? But you didn't listen,' Roopmati was scolding Shalu.

Ram Kumar, the man who ran the door hinges factory, had hugged her from behind while she was packing the finished products. This had happened in the past too. But that day, Ram Kumar's wife caught them and beat Shalu black and blue, blaming her for seducing him.

'But you should have quit the job the first time he did it,' said Rani.

'It's easy for you to say that. Your husband has a good job, not hers. Who will feed her eleven-month-old son?' replied Urmila.

'But couldn't she have found work in a better place that is more open and has more people?' asked Rani.

Everyone was quiet.

There had been countless such incidents in the past but no one really acknowledged them. Syeda gave a time-tested, rehearsed response: 'Don't do things that make the men pay attention to you. It takes two hands to clap.'

Acknowledging routine sexual harassment by subcontractors meant acknowledging that women who work outside homes are not as 'pure' as the ones who stay at home. It meant letting suspicious husbands stop them from going out to work. It meant not having money to buy groceries or send children to school. It also meant generating hostility in your own neighbourhood, disrupting the ecosystem of Karawal Nagar that sheltered them, employed them, helped them survive.

To be poor is to be guilty of one thing or the other, and this was the last thing any of the women wanted to be guilty of.

Radiowali said, 'Men are not so innocent.'

No one said a thing in response.

The next day, Shalu once again locked up her eleven-month-old child in her rented house after giving him a tablespoon of an anti-spasmodic medicine for stomach ache, as a sedative, to go and apologize to Ram Kumar's wife in the hope of getting her job back.

In January 2009, India launched the Aadhaar card, the world's largest biometric identification system.

'Are you a worker here?' asked Ramesh, a thin, tall young man in an oversized kurta, jeans and a *tote bag* on his shoulder, taking copious notes.

'No,' replied Lalita as she rubbed the almond shell dust from her face with the corner of her saree.

'But you shell almonds? Don't you?' he inquired.

'That's just to cover the milk and vegetable expenses,' she said dismissively.

'But that's still work, na?' asked Ramesh.

'Wo kehte hain na, aadmi kaam karte hain, auratein aaram karti hain. Kaam aur aaram ka matlab hi alag hai yahaan,' Lalita replied in a curt tone as she walked away. Like they say, men work, and women rest. The meanings of work and rest are different here.

On 30 December 2008, the Indian government passed the Unorganised Workers' Social Security Act. Before this, two important labour laws – the Factory Act of 1948 and the Inter-State Migrant Workmen Act – dealt with the safety and well-being of persons at the workplace. But these laws did not recognize home-based workers as 'workers'. The 2008 act was the first Indian law that acknowledged the presence of home-based workers in India.

The act mandated the formation of the National Social Security Board to recommend schemes for the unorganized sector. While the new law recognized the presence of home-based workers, it did not say anything about minimum wages, non-payment of wages, delays in payment, unequal remuneration, special schemes for maternity and childcare benefits, decent work conditions and protection from sexual harassment for such workers.

Activists across the country started identifying workers in various unorganized sectors, to list out their work, and their challenges, to get them registered as workers, and to get their identity cards made to get benefits from social welfare schemes.

That day, Ramesh was attempting the impossible task of getting the home-based workers to admit that they were 'workers'.

Lalita and Syeda walked into Radiowali's place. Roopmati and Rani were napping on the floor. Khushboo and Shalu were also asleep, facing the other side.

All of them had some ailment or the other. Headache, body ache, swelling in their hands and legs, cuts and blisters on the fingers, poor eyesight from working in poorly lit factories for long hours, back problems from sitting in the same posture for too long. You name it and they had it. But the best antidote was voted to be sleep: a nap, or an afternoon siesta which was impossible at home because the children and the husbands wouldn't allow thirty minutes of silent me-time without asking where was this or that.

All of them woke up when Syeda and Lalita got there.

'Uff, ask this one to take a bath before coming here,' Khushboo commented, pointing at Shalu who was packaging naphthalene balls those days and reeked of them.

'Oh! Do you even notice the pungent smell of the incense sticks that you roll day and night,' Shalu retorted, adding to the friendly banter.

They were all watching Ramesh and a woman, in a loose cotton kurta salwar, kajal smeared around her eyes, with some pamphlets in her hand, trying to talk to Suman.

They should issue job slips to all of you!
There should be a written agreement to pay you!
There should be a system to set the piece rate!
You all should get free training from the employers!
You should get minimum wage!

Suman nodded nervously to each of the statements and then ran straight into Radiowali's house, giggling.

'Who are these people?' Roopmati asked.

'They must be here to make Aadhaar cards. The government has announced that they will make one card for everything. Hospital, bank, ration, vote, everything will be connected to it,' Radiowali said.

'She must be a government official or from an NGO to give money or free blankets. Let's go and get our names registered,' said Khushboo.

There was a general distrust of activists and government officials in the area. Their pursuits of identifying illegalities, or regularizing the work chain, had resulted in loss of employment, arrests of subcontractors, raids and sealing of factories. They couldn't risk it. The women were divided and still figuring out what to make of this.

For the next few weeks, everyone tapped into their whisper networks to weave together information about Ramesh and the woman who were going door-to-door to identify home-based workers. They found out that they both had been actively working with home-based workers in north east Delhi for a while since the Unorganised Workers' Social Security Act was passed. They were part of the Bigul Mazdoor Dasta, an organization that was active in trade unions and industrial labour movements. A year back, in 2008, the organization had formed the Badaam Mazdoor Union, Almond Workers' Union, and was actively mobilizing women, who formed the majority of the almond workers in Karawal Nagar, to join it.

The US state of California grows 80 per cent of the world's almonds. Top Bollywood actors like Karisma Kapoor had started promoting California almonds in India. By September 2009, India had emerged as the fourth-largest export market for California almonds after Spain, Germany and China.

Unprocessed almonds and walnuts from the US, Canada and Australia are imported by Indian traders in Khari Baoli in Chandni

Chowk who then hire subcontractors in Karawal Nagar, Sant Nagar, Burari, Narela, Sonia Vihar and other such areas in north east Delhi to process them. The subcontractors employ home-based workers to manually shell and package the almond kernels for peanuts – woefully low wages especially compared to the prices at which the nuts are sold in the export market.

Every day trucks arrived with large gunny bags that were stored at the sixty-odd almond factories in Karawal Nagar. Each factory had twenty to forty women workers who would often arrive with their children and work twelve hours a day, and up to sixteen hours in the winter months. They worked under the strict eye of the supervisors who would ensure that the women and children didn't eat the almonds they were shelling. But some still managed to pop a few into their mouths when the supervisors were not looking.

Syeda had been fired from the pressure cooker factory job for going on leave because she had cholera. She was now working at the almond factory.

Experienced workers like Syeda and Lalita handled two bags a day.

They were paid Rs 50 for processing one bag of 23 kilos but the godown owners made somewhere between Rs 125 and Rs 150 for the same bag for processing. The processed, packaged almonds were then sent back to the merchants of central Delhi who supplied them back to the multinational companies of the West, making around Rs 7,000 per bag.

The Badaam Mazdoor Union had been trying to negotiate better wages for the workers. One day, when Syeda and Lalita visited Radiowali's place after their shift was over, they found sitting there the woman accompanying Ramesh on his inquiry rounds. Radiowali introduced her as Seema, Ramesh's colleague.

She began talking to the women, asking about their families, where they lived and what their children did. The women in turn asked her about her marital status, her caste. Seema patiently answered their questions even as she slipped in remarks about the need to unionize.

There should be safe and hygienic working conditions!
They cannot employ you without providing even a toilet!
They have to provide you with regular employment!

They must take care of medical expenses if there is an accident. Even give compensation!

There should be a crèche inside the factory for young mothers. This will only happen if you become part of a union. If you fight together . . . !

There were many questions. What is a union? Syeda had seen a millworkers' union in an Amitabh Bachchan film but she had never heard of a union with women in it. For decades, labour movements have made demands and successfully negotiated for workers' rights. But most trade unions across the globe unionized, mobilized and strategized for workers in a particular sector, in a defined workspace.

Home-based workers like the women here didn't work in a fixed industry or at a single workspace. All work is seasonal. It comes and goes. Factories opens and shut down. Subcontractors come and go.

After the passing of the Unorganised Workers' Social Security Act, Ramesh and Seema were working hard to form some sort of union for the home-based workers. They had been successful in mobilizing some almond workers in other parts of north east Delhi.

'Have any of you met with an accident in a factory?' Seema asked.

'Many times,' they replied.

'Did any factory owner pay for your medical expense, forget compensation?' she asked.

'No,' they said.

'But it is your right,' she replied.

Lalita turned around to Radiowali. 'What are you nodding for? Didn't Poonam's son burn his fingers with acid while scraping out metal for aluminium wires in your factory? It took him six months to heal.'

Radiowali was quiet.

Roopmati turned around and told her, 'She doesn't *run* the factory. She also works there. Why are you targeting her?'

The others agreed. 'Roopmati is right.'

Lalita was quiet.

Syeda recounted the numerous accidents at a thread ply factory where she had worked as an operator on a twelve-hour shift. There were twenty women like her who worked from 9 a.m. to 9 p.m. and were paid Rs 2,000 per month.

A high-speed machine would wind the thread on to cardboard spools. Their job was to replace the spool when it was full. Almost every week someone's hair, saree, dupatta or fingers would get stuck between the spools or the threads. At least a dozen of them got stitches on their scalp when they were pulled into the machine.

After two years, the factory moved to Shahdara. Syeda only remembered that the factory owner was Punjabi. She switched factories so often that remembering the names of the owners was impossible. It was also considered rude to ask the names of the employers.

'See, if they gave you job slips, we would know whom to ask for compensation,' said Seema. She asked in the same breath, 'Do you have a toilet at work?'

'No, the factory owners sometimes allowed us to use the toilet in their home but that depended on your caste and religion,' replied Syeda.

She was never allowed to use the toilet at Ram Kumar's because of his mother. 'Some of them don't even have a toilet at home,' added Khushboo.

'But they should have one when they employ so many people. That is mandatory,' replied Seema.

They agreed with her but did not believe it was something worth fighting for. There was silence, and even smirks, for things that just seemed too fantastical and impossible.

Seema, Ramesh and many others from their organization kept visiting. But to this day, Syeda cannot hearken back to a time when any of the women were discussing this at home. The men were already disgruntled about their own unemployment. Confiding in them was out of the question.

Lalita was apprehensive and even cynical about Seema and Ramesh's infiltration of Radiowali's place. She told Syeda, 'They are the red flag people. I have seen them a lot, back home in Bhojpur. Forget any of this. We will lose the jobs we have.'

Not that she knew much about politics and political parties, but she was familiar with the cost of rebellion, or revolution as it was called.

Lalita had moved to Karawal Nagar in December 1997, with her husband Bholu Gautam, from Bhojpur district in Bihar. She got married in May 1995, at the age of fifteen. They were from the Musahar community.

Over 70 per cent of Bihar's population works in the agricultural sector. Caste still plays a big role in accessing resources there, just like all over India.

Musahars are classified as Mahadalits, the lowest in the Hindu caste order. For centuries, they have faced deprivation, oppression and structural violence. 'Mus' means mouse and 'ahar' means food. The Musahars were traditionally rat diggers, landless agricultural labourers, also known to eat field rats to ward off starvation.

In parts of Bihar, Musahars form the bulk of agricultural labour. They continue to be socio-economically marginalized because of systemic caste oppression. They continue to be dependent on feudal landlords.

Bholu Gautam's family worked as agricultural workers in the fields of Chunnu Singh Pandey, a dominant Bhumihar caste landowner. Like all feudal landowners, instead of paying fair wages to the agricultural workers, Chunnu Singh would give them a few kilos of rice or dal, some vegetables from the field, permission to set up a shanty on a patch of his land, and a few litres of milk every day for taking care of his cattle and doing farm work.

Bihar was one of the first Indian states after independence to adopt a land reforms act that abolished the zamindari system, a feudal landholding practice. The government was supposed to redistribute land from landholders to landless people for agriculture. But since the ruling party in the state was full of feudal upper-caste landowners, it was never implemented. This is often seen as one of the prime reasons for Bihar being the largest supplier of cheap migrant labour to the country.

Marginalized communities like the Musahars have remained deprived of land that could have bettered their condition, ensured food security and reduced poverty.

Lalita and Bholu Gautam's shanty was in a settlement in the south of the village because the upper castes believed that the winds blow from north to south. 'They didn't want us to pollute the air,' she recalled. Once, when a young lower-caste boy took a dip in a pond close to an upper-caste neighbourhood, he was lynched to death. Untouchability was rampant; their ponds, wells and even walkways were separate. Musahar children were not allowed to go to school.

Lalita was told to never go out alone to collect wood or Chunnu Singh's men would rape her. Often landlords would force them to work as bonded labour in the fields.

There was growing resentment among the oppressed communities in Bhojpur that was channelized by many radical left-wing groups that formed 'red armies' to implement land reforms and provide minimum wages to landless Dalit workers. They punished landlords by holding them hostage, killing them. They even penalized police personnel who ignored the injustices faced by the marginalized communities.

In retaliation, in September 1994, the Brahmins and Bhumihars, the two most dominant caste landowners in the region, founded the Ranvir Sena, a private upper-caste army in Bhojpur with the aim of protecting the privileges of the landowning communities. It spread across various districts to mobilize the landed gentry against various left-wing groups – including the People's War Group (PWG), the Maoist Communist Centre of India (MCCI), and the Communist Party of India (Marxist–Leninist) Liberation (CPI-ML [Liberation]) – aggressively fighting the cause of the landless communities of Bihar. With plenty of resources and the latest ammunition at their disposal, Ranvir Sena members were rewarded for killing those opposing the upper-caste landlords.

In 1995, soon after Lalita's marriage, Pintoo, Chotu and Kalu, three Musahars who worked in Chunnu Singh's fields, were rumoured to have joined the MCC. While working in the fields, Lalita had heard of many secret meetings where they planned to teach the landowners of the village a lesson.

One night, in July 1995, Lalita heard bullet shots. Ranvir Sena leaders, who were known to live in towns and came to the villages only when a massacre of Dalits was to be planned and executed, had arrived. They pulled out Pintoo and five others from the neighbouring shanties, and shot them dead at point-blank range as Chunnu Singh watched.

After the killing, they sloganeered:

Mendhak ko sardi nahin hoti,
Musahar ki baithak nahin hoti.

Like frogs don't catch a cold,
Musahars don't hold councils.

Within a month, in August 1995, the Ranvir Sena was banned. Yet, it was just the beginning of their terrorization of marginalized communities, and several more anti-Dalit massacres would be orchestrated by them. Between 1995 and 1997, they killed almost 150 Dalits in the area, and looted and burned down several Dalit neighbourhoods. They were known to write 'Ranvir Sena' on village entrances with the blood of those they had killed to spread horror and dread. They especially targeted children and pregnant women by killing or raping them to 'check the increase of the Dalit population'. This was all done in the name of 'protecting the rights of landowning farmers'. They claimed that they were waking up the government to the rights of upper-caste Hindus that were being compromised for minorities and lower castes in India.

Gullu, Bholu's younger brother, had already moved to Delhi with Chunnu Singh's son in 1995. The young man, whose education and exposure had made him sympathetic to anti-caste campaigns, had got admission to Delhi University, and Gullu became his full-time domestic servant. As soon as he moved, Gullu changed his name to Pushpraj, King of Flowers. Most children of Dalit agricultural workers tended to be named by upper-caste landowners, who gave them frivolous, thoughtless, meaningless names. A Dalit even having a proper name was seen as offensive to the upper-caste feudal lords.

When Lalita got pregnant in 1997, Pushpraj suggested they move to Delhi as well. They had leverage because of the landlord's son – the ticket out from this system that many did not have. And they took it. For a year or so, they lived in Hakikat Nagar, close to the North Campus of Delhi University, with the landlord's son. When he moved to London for further studies, they moved to Karawal Nagar where both Bholu and Pushpraj found work in a bag factory. Lalita's son was named Raj Bahadur. Bholu and Pushpraj had not just broken away but were determined to establish their respectability through the template designed by the upper-caste feudal lords.

'*Achche ghar ki auratein bahar kaam nahin karti,*' Bholu had told Lalita. Women from good families don't work outside the house.

He was repeating what upper-caste landowners had always said about women back home. They also used this adage to justify the sexual violence they subjected Dalit women workers to, who worked outside their homes, and so were not 'respectable'. After Pushpraj got married, he and his brother decided that the women of their family would not go out to work.

This continued for three or four years. Then, money became tight, more children were born. Bholu was hired and fired several times. One day, after Lalita had to borrow rice from the neighbours to cook a meal for Raj Bahadur, she decided to find work. She started bringing raw materials from subcontractors to work on at home, and when things became even tighter, she began to sneak out for a few hours to work in neighbouring factories, all the while carefully maintaining the facade of a 'respectable family' where men earned and women stayed at home.

She would always dress up in a neatly ironed saree, her head covered with the pallu, when she stepped out. Her hair was always braided, and she was never without vermilion in the parting of her hair, the sign of a married woman. She wore dark maroon lipstick and a dozen bangles on each wrist. The other women would laugh and say, 'Why do you step out like a newlywed bride?'

Lalita would counter, '*Achche ghar ki auratein aisi hi hoti hain.*' Women from respectable families are like this only.

Syeda and Lalita were neighbours. It was Lalita who introduced Syeda to almond shelling work in 2002. Since then, Syeda kept going back to it every once in a while. She often helped Lalita in justifying her absence from home to Bholu.

Breaking almond shells was difficult. They had to be soaked in acid to soften them faster. Since there was no question of any safety gear, most workers used their bare hands, teeth and feet to break the shells. Lalita, Syeda, everyone had disfigured nails, and bruised fingertips. Syeda often found it difficult to eat her meals with her hands, because the chilli and other spices irritated the fingers. There was a joke at Radiowali's place: almond factories teach women to eat with spoons.

Attempting to earn a living and not being entirely truthful to Bholu about it was one thing. But participating in conversations about unionizing meant challenging the status quo. It came with the risks and dangers of the past life – the violence that followed rebellion – that Lalita had escaped twelve years ago. She stopped visiting Radiowali.

༄

On 4 August 2009, the Right to Education Act was enacted to provide free and compulsory education, uniforms and textbooks to all Indian children up to Class 8.

'If you want to work here, you will have to come at 2 a.m.'

'But my husband will not let me,' Lalita replied.

'Then don't come. Has any doctor asked you to work?' replied Balloo, the henchman for Vasu Mishra's almond factories.

Unlike the other petty subcontractors the home-based workers usually worked with, the almond factory owners and associates were either local politicians, or their henchmen, with money and powerful connections. They were often members of mainstream parties like the Congress and BJP, or RSS volunteers.

Vasu Mishra, a Brahmin, was a local leader in Karawal Nagar. He owned several houses, godowns and small-scale factories. In 2008, he had also contested the municipality elections as an independent candidate but lost.

'Anyway, Mishra ji does not like *Bhangi-Chamar.*' Balloo threw a casteist slur at her with a grin.

Casteist language was not new to Lalita but in Delhi; she heard it just a little less compared to Bhojpur.

She kept quiet.

Cases of tuberculosis, asthma, cough and allergies were rising in Karawal Nagar's residential areas. This was attributed to the almond shell dust from the processing factories in the city.

Activists and labour inspectors were prowling too close for comfort to these unlicensed factories. Since the bags were too heavy to take home, the women had to work in the factory premises in the wee hours to escape scrutiny.

It was a December night in 2009 with no visibility. That day, Lalita took Raj Bahadur, now around eleven years old, to the factory as an escort and assistant. The new shift timing was 2 a.m. to 2 p.m. The main door of the factory was locked and the women had to climb in and out of a window in a side alley that was closely guarded at all times. Lalita had told Bholu that she was taking care of Khushboo, who had just had a miscarriage, in the hospital for a few days.

The factory was a 10 foot by 10 foot room with only two light bulbs. Around 8 a.m., the SDM and a few officials raided the area. The windows were locked, the lights were switched off, and everyone was asked to maintain silence.

It was past 3 p.m. The workers had been locked in for seven hours without any ventilation. The brown dust from the almond shells that had been cleaned in the morning had no outlet. It was flying in the air. Everyone's faces and clothes were covered with it.

All of them were coughing. For almond workers, exposed to almond dust for long periods, stepping out every few hours and dusting themselves is essential. Many women like Lalita were accompanied by children to help with the work. There was no toilet. They were growing both restless and hungry. Some had turned red coughing.

Raj Bahadur started hitting the window aggressively, asking the guards to open it. Lalita stopped him but the others joined in. Hungry children started munching on the peeled almond kernels, some stuffed their pockets too. There was total chaos, a breakdown of order.

Half an hour later, Balloo and a few others entered the factory and started slapping the children and yelling at the women. Lalita was horrified when Raj Bahadur started kicking one of the henchmen. She tried to stop him but she was pushed aside. Raj Bahadur was beaten black and blue.

She rushed out of the factory and ran with Raj Bahadur straight to Radiowali's place. She couldn't think what else to do.

At Radiowali's the women were busy making posters for the protest that was being planned. Syeda was painting 'Badam Mazdoor Union' on a chart paper because she was one of the literate few. Most of the others were making effigies, with old clothes and sticks, of the contractors and their invisible Multi National Company employers.

As Radiowali tended to Raj Bahadur's injuries, Lalita looked around.

'What is all this for?' she asked.

'There will be a strike from 15 December. Thousands of almond factory workers will join,' said Syeda.

'This is for our children who are malnourished while we peel almonds for the rich,' added Khushboo.

Lalita was quiet for a long time as she looked at the other women, excitedly readying for the strike. When Raj Bahadur had eaten his fill and calmed down, she got up.

At the door as she was leaving, she said, 'I will come too. But don't tell my husband.'

Ramesh and Seema, in consultation with several workers, had prepared a five-point charter of demands to hand over to the subcontractors to regularize the work.

1. Instead of Rs 50 per 23 kilo bag, they should be paid Rs 70–80 per bag.
2. Wages must be given in the first week of every month.
3. The peeled shells that the workers use as fuel should not be sold to them for more than Rs 20 per kilo.
4. They should be paid double for overtime.
5. They should be given a job card.

Over the next two weeks, a pamphlet listing their demands was handed to several almond factory owners. These people had never seen this kind of rebellion brew in the area. The charter was not well received. The powerful factory owners started identifying the women who were actively involved. Radiowali's place was under constant surveillance.

On the morning of 15 December 2009, Syeda, Lalita and many others from Radiowali's *adda* gathered at the Shaheed Bhagat Singh Nagar intersection in Karawal Nagar, which had the largest concentration of almond factories. Syeda had never seen so many women together in one place in the last thirteen years in Delhi. Nor was she aware that such a large number of women worked in the almond factories in her vicinity. She had crossed paths with many working women in several other factories over the years. At the protest, she met some whom she hadn't seen in a while, and encountered new people too. There were over a thousand of them, forgoing their daily wage, convinced about their fight for something that might improve their lives, even if only marginally.

This was one of the largest unorganized workers' strikes in Delhi in the last twenty years. Leaders from the Bigul Mazdoor Dasta addressed the crowds. Navneet, a member, told them about how their demands were legal under the Minimum Wages Act, the Contract Labour (Prevention and Abolition) Act, and the Trade Union Act.

He shouted:

Hum apna adhikar maangte,
Nahin kisi se bheekh mangte.

We ask for our rights!
Not beg for alms!

Syeda couldn't figure out why but she felt good about this slogan. When the effigies they had made were set on fire, Lalita broke into a parody of a popular Bhojpuri song,

Kashi hille, Patna hille, Kalkatta hille la...
Lachke jab majdoorwa, saari factory hille la...

Ho lachke sab majdoorwa, saari factory hille la . . .
Munsi patwari hille, hille thanedarwa
Malik ki kursi hille, hille re saara jilwa . . .

Kashi moves, Patna moves, Kolkata moves . . .
When workers swing, all factories move . . .
Ho, when the workers swing, all factories move . . .
Clerks, accountants move, police officers move . . .
The owner's chair moves, the entire city moves . . .

Everyone joined in. It was such a fun song. Some broke into an impromptu dance. While they marched around and sang songs, the factory supervisors, the police and everyone else watched. A few hawkers came and started selling moong dal laddoos, bhelpuri and roasted sweet potatoes. The first two days were glorious: the closest similar experience Syeda had had was the annual fairs in Banaras.

It was as though someone had infused new energy in her, she recalls. On the third day, after many years, she ironed her clothes in the morning, applied a besan body scrub before bathing, and combed her hair looking into the mirror, instead of on the go. Like her, many women turned up in their finest clothes, matching sweaters, hair clips, bangles and nail paint. Not having been part of any such march earlier, they thought of it as nothing but a festival they had not celebrated before.

It was the holiday season when dry fruits were in demand in India and abroad. More than 60 per cent of Indians prefer almonds over other dry fruits. Almond milk was also fast emerging as a popular non-dairy alternative prescribed in fancy diets globally. Demand for almonds in the Western world was growing every passing day with Christmas and New Year a mere two weeks away. Factory owners were desperate to end the strike and get the workers back to work.

Some factory owners insisted they would think about wage revision only when the strike was called off and the holiday season was over. That too after 16 January. The striking workers did not agree. Resentment among the owners was growing.

On 17 December, as the workers joined the procession led by Navneet and Ramesh, Vasu Mishra, accompanied by big, burly men, started disrupting the procession by pushing the women around.

When Puttan, his henchman, held Lalita's hand, she slapped him. Vasu Mishra picked up a stick and started digging it into her stomach. Salman and Raj Bahadur tried to save her, and both got roughed up by the goons. Puttan hit Lalita's head on the stone slab of a drain. She started bleeding.

Vasu Mishra roared, 'You chamarin! You and your puppies keep inciting the workers. Have you forgotten your *aukaat*?'

Chamarin, a derogatory, casteist slur again. *Aukaat*. Worth.

Almost immediately, all the women in the vicinity charged at the goons with stones, bricks – anything they could lay their hands on. Puttan and three other men were injured, as were some of the protesters. The police arrived. There was a huge commotion. The children were crying. Salman had scraped his knee, Raj Bahadur had sprained his leg, Roopmati had a torn kurta, and Khushboo had a cut on her forehead.

The police took Vasu Mishra and the three injured henchmen to the hospital. They arrested Navneet and three other members of the union who were also injured but received no medical attention even though they were bleeding profusely.

Five hours passed. It was evening. Many of the women were supposed to return home before their husbands got back but instead they surrounded the Karawal Nagar police station and kept sloganeering. When some of them went inside to talk to the police, the Station House Officer (SHO) said, 'The unionwalas and the strikers need to be taught a lesson. Both by force and by law.'

The police drove away with the union leadership in a vehicle on the pretext of ensuring medical treatment for them at Guru Tegh Bahadur Hospital. But they first took them to the Gokulpuri police station, which was too far away for the strikers to assemble, lodged an FIR against them, and then later presented them at the Karkardooma Court. They were sent to two days of judicial custody.

Vasu Mishra and his henchmen, meanwhile, were released and no cases were filed against them. But he was humiliated because word had spread that he, a Brahmin, had been beaten up by a Dalit woman.

That day when Lalita reached home with Raj Bahadur, Bholu Gautam dragged Raj inside and threw her out of the house. Vasu's men had already informed him of how, for years, she had been violating the boundaries he had drawn. He accused her of dishonouring him and his family. Of compromising her morals, of forgetting her station in life because of her exposure to the city. She pleaded and begged, promising to stop working, but Bholu didn't open the door. She spent the night at Radiowali's place.

That night many husbands had been similarly instigated and there were only a few who stood by their wives who toiled to keep their families afloat. Khushboo's husband told her, 'These English-speaking people from elite universities and colleges will lose nothing. You will. You are not an English ma'am like them.'

Rani's husband accused her of having an affair with one of the 'outsiders'.

Seema tried to convince the women that it was their constitutional right to protest. She said that if they were 'outsiders', so was Gandhi in Champaran and Medha Patkar in the Narmada valley. Nobody knew the historic context of Seema's speech. But they heard her.

It was a long, dreadful night, full of silence and grief, for many.

But Syeda felt as though some part of her that she had hidden away had come alive. In contrast to the other husbands, all Akmal asked was why she was late and why her new clothes were ripped. He served her food to eat, unlike in many homes where the bruised women returned to irate husbands who were waiting for them to cook dinner.

The next day, in the absence of the arrested union leaders, a new interim leadership was elected. Lalita was one of them. The strike continued and, in spite of the hostility of the men the previous night, over 90 per cent of the women workers joined on the fourth day of the strike – compared to 60 per cent on the first three days. Many came along with their families. It was overwhelming.

The godown owners had been provided police protection. The strikers formed groups and raided all the sixty almond processing units in Karawal Nagar and escorted out any worker who was still inside. Union activists paid multiple visits to the office of the deputy labour commissioner of the zone. The charter of demands was presented to them to enforce labour laws at a bare minimum but there was no response.

Lalita, dressed that day in Syeda's salwar kameez and not her usual saree, yelled at one of them, 'Is pollution your only concern? You don't take a minute to shut down the factories then. But you don't care about workers' wages and their health?'

Was this the same Lalita from a *respectable family*, shouting like that? Syeda and Khushboo had a laugh.

By the end of the next day, most of the almond processing industry had come to a standstill.

On the same night, 19 December, the three arrested union leaders were released on bail. Navneet reminded everyone that on the same day in 1927, the freedom fighters Ram Prasad Bismil, Ashfaq Ulla Khan and Roshan Singh were hanged by the British for fighting for the country's independence.

Most of them had not heard of them but they knew the song written by Bismil:

Sarfaroshi ki tamanna ab humare dil mein hain
Dekhna hai zor kitna baazu-e-kaatil mein hain
Waqt aane pe bata denge tujhe ae aasman,
Hum abhi se kya bataayein,
Kya humare dil mein hain.

The desire for revolution is in our hearts
Let's see how much strength the enemy has
When the time comes we'll prove it to the sky,
What can we tell you now,
What is in our hearts.

There was a historic rally the next day, 20 December. Almost 2,000 workers marched from Prakash Vihar and covered the entire area of western Karawal Nagar.

Lalita was leading the march. 'Delhi Police, down, down!' The other women repeated the slogan. Bholu Gautam and Raj Bahadur watched from their terrace. Lalita looked straight ahead.

'Down with this capitalist government!' yelled Seema.

The others shouted, matching her rhythm: *'Poonjiwad pe halla bol! Halla bol!'*

Raise your voice against capitalism! Raise your voice!

Some university students sloganeered and Syeda played the *dafli*, a small hand-held drum-like instrument, they had handed to her. The women workers kept up their sloganeering, though no one understood what capitalism meant, or its relevance to their lives.

The factory owners watched as they stood outside their godowns, where thousands of unprocessed almond bags had been dumped. Due to the strike, the rates of almonds had increased swiftly and supply to international markets been badly hit.

The strike continued for a week, with a large turnout of workers every day. The police stopped openly endorsing the aggression and hostility of the godown owners. But they kept warning the strikers they would have to take action because the strike was threatening the 'law and order' situation of the nation.

On 23 December 2009, roughly 2,000 people came from north east Delhi to protest at Jantar Mantar. This was the first time many of them had travelled to Lutyens' Delhi.

Syeda said, 'This is not Jantar Mantar. I saw on TV that it has a sundial that indicates the time.'

Seema replied, 'That is on the other side. This is the official protest site in Delhi.'

Syeda asked, 'So there is a designated place to protest too? So do ministers come here every day to listen to people?'

Seema laughed. 'No!'

Syeda questioned her again, 'Then why should people come here to protest?'

Seema replied, 'Because this is the centre of Delhi. Parliament is close by and the media pays attention to what happens here.'

This was the time when mainstream news organizations in India started to get heavily corporatized. Profits, not public interest, was increasingly driving journalism. Corporate media houses began to identify the urban rich as their target audience. News organizations across the board instructed journalists to stop doing back-of-beyond, bleeding-heart stories that mess with the 'buying mood' of the viewers in metropolitan cities like Bengaluru, Delhi and Mumbai.

You can't show a story on malnutrition if you have to sell pressure cookers and microwave ovens. The maths was simple.

So no TV media covered the stories of the urban poor or the working classes except when they were suspected of involvement in a crime. Absolutely no one from television covered the demands of the protesting workers in Karawal Nagar. There were some reporters who still came and took a round of Jantar Mantar once in a while, the ones who were still reporting for newspapers and magazines and were not stars in the emerging performative television journalism, the ones who preferred reporting about the people on the ground and not high-ranking politicians, bureaucrats or diplomats in the corridors of power. Some of these reporters took pictures and interviews of the protesting women workers.

After the protest, a dozen women walked over to India Gate. People were lying under the Java plum trees on the green lawns, children ran here and there, and monkeys waited for crumbs from the baskets of picnicking families.

Syeda said, 'See, Salman, those toys we assembled for Rs 35 for 1,000 pieces!'

But Salman, then nineteen years old, was busy looking at the flying spinner toys in the air against the backdrop of India Gate. He and Raj Bahadur roamed around for a bit, eating ice cream from the hawkers on Rajpath, the boulevard near India Gate.

A few pleasant hours were spent there before they took the bus back home. Reshma, fifteen, was upset that Syeda had dumped the Christmas decoration work on her and taken Salman to India Gate instead. Shazeb, twenty, did not come because he had started working part-time at a grocery shop.

The next day, a few newspapers did report on the almond workers' strike. No political party openly extended support to the protest.

In the week that followed, tension was mounting. Some factory owners, in a last-ditch attempt, started mobilizing the petty subcontractors in their support.

Parshuram, who used to run the bindi factory using child labour, asked Syeda, 'Tell me, do you have enough to pay this month's rent after losing wages and participating in this strike?'

Syeda laughed and dismissed the thought. She was in a frenzy. The last few months had been all about understanding that they deserved better because they worked harder than anyone. Something they never valued themselves for before the strike. The protests were an outlet for their collective rage that had accumulated piece by piece, day by day, kilo by kilo, over the years.

Ram Kumar, who had earlier sexually harassed Shalu, told her husband she was having an affair with Ramesh. The union had spoken about sexual harassment at factories and Ram Kumar had been tipped off by Vasu Mishra's henchmen about it. There was rumour-mongering everywhere. But the women kept taking it on the chin. Shalu took Radiowali to her husband to confirm to him that Ram Kumar had indeed sexually harassed her.

The foundations of the international almond processing industry had been chipped. With no solution in sight, some contractors and subcontractors started outsourcing the processing work to other parts of Delhi like Wazirpur in the north and Okhla in the south. They incurred huge losses because the workers there were not skilled at the job and created a lot of wastage due to ruined kernels.

The union had also threatened they would take legal action to get the unauthorized and illegal godowns closed within Karawal Nagar and beyond it. The factory owners were slowly understanding that they were also dependent on the skilled almond workers; it wasn't a one-way street. The employers' unity disintegrated and they split into two groups, one that wanted to negotiate and the other that was more rigid.

On 31 December 2009, Lalita and other union leaders met some factory owners for negotiations. After many hours of discussion, at around 6 p.m., it was decided that the workers would get Rs 60 instead of Rs 50 per bag, the peeled-off shells would be sold to workers for a standard rate of Rs 20 per kilo for fuel, and wages would be paid no later than the first week of the month.

With this compromise, the workers called off their historic strike.

And they agreed to return to work from the first day of the New Year, 1 January 2010.

That day Reshma taunted Syeda, 'After so much violence, such a hue and cry, police action, you managed to increase the rate by only Rs 10.'

'Yes, that's an extra Rs 600 per month, money to buy vegetables for fifteen days,' replied Syeda.

Was the fifteen-day strike worth the petty increment they received? Maybe not. But this was the first time they had collectively asked for something and they were heard, at home or outside. The most basic lesson they learnt was that it was not a crime to ask for fair wages. It was not something to be ashamed of, particularly as women.

'These employers are better than husbands. When we asked for something, they finally budged,' said Suman as Lalita made chai for everyone at Radiowali's place. 'Our families selectively turn deaf on us!'

Everyone laughed.

This was one of the biggest and longest strikes by unorganized workers in Delhi. It created the template of organizing workers where they lived, considering that in the home-based-work economy workers don't have a common factory floor. It also underlined the redundant ways of old trade unions that only focused on male workers of the organized sector.

That evening, Lalita went back home accompanied by Khushboo, Syeda and Radiowali. Bholu Gautam agreed to take her back on the condition that she would never work outside again. She agreed. Her friends were not happy. She sensed this and asked Bholu, 'But you won't stop me from singing once in a while at Radiowali's house?'

He replied, 'Why would I?'

Lalita still had a life of covert work ahead of her then.

After all these years, the women did manage to measure the sky and move the moon. On 31 December 2009, Reshma, Salman and Raj Bahadur stood on the terrace at night and saw the earth's shadow glide past the moon. The yellow full moon turned into dim red. It was a rare sight, a blue moon, and the second full moon in a month. The last blue moon partial eclipse had occurred in December 1982. The next one is predicted in January 2037.

In the new year, almond rates globally shot up by 30 to 40 per cent, increasing the rates of sweets and confectionery because the women of Karawal Nagar had learnt to demand their rights.

6

Soft Toy

I wanna feel the wind in my hair now
Spread the power, everywhere now
Feel the magic just go zip zap zoom
Dhoom machale
Come on all you people
Dhoom machale dhoom machale dhoom

– Song from *Dhoom* (2004)

It was a cold, grey winter evening in December 2012. Shazeb had asked Reshma to buy two dozen glass bangles. Reshma took her own sweet time, carefully selecting the colour and style from Som Bazaar, the weekly Monday market in Karawal Nagar. She assumed Shazeb wanted her help in buying these to gift to a girl and thought he would let her keep at least half for herself. He took them all, which disappointed her.

Reshma was now eighteen and in Class 11. She had started telling everyone she would do BA (Hons) from Delhi University once school was over. Salman was twenty-two and after flunking Class 6 three times, he finally dropped out of school but also had trouble sticking to the jobs that dropouts like him were taking up.

Shazeb had dropped out of school after Class 9, to supplement the family income. He was now twenty-three. Having done odd jobs here and there for three or four years, he had finally been taken in as an apprentice at Bobby's shocker repair shop. He was tall, lanky, clean-shaven, with large, toned biceps after years of lifting heavy loads at shops, factories and construction sites. He had slightly long hair and he would wear a hairband both for style and to prevent it from falling on his face.

Shocker repair shops are commonplace in India. They are present in almost every nook and corner of north east Delhi. Potholes, mud lanes, lack of metalled roads cause motorcycle shock absorbers to go for a toss. A new shock absorber could cost Rs 2,000 or even more. But a roadside shack would repair it for as little as Rs 600.

It was a rolling business in Karawal Nagar. Everyone used bikes in the narrow lanes to carry raw material, finished products, machines, or just to commute.

Shazeb's friends had already started working in factories, as tailor apprentices and construction labourers, or were trying to get into the manufacturing supply chain. Shazeb's job was sought after and considered cool. He was a bike mechanic, after all.

Each day, there was a bike of a new model to repair and ride around Karawal Nagar.

Shazeb had longed to drive bikes all his life. He grew up watching Akmal drag a cart rickshaw day after day. Akmal, tall yet shrivelled, flesh draped around bones, sunken eyes, with dark circles around them, lips red with betel or tobacco. His jet-black hair – which he had never stopped dyeing since moving to Karawal Nagar – now looked like a wig on a scarecrow. Growing up, the boys often had to help him in carrying raw materials, pushing the cart rickshaw with all their strength. Ah, the drudgery of it.

Once, on a hot summer day, Akmal was pulling the loaded cart with all his might over a pothole. But Salman was fooling around, and instead of helping the cart over the pothole, he dragged it back. Akmal came around the cart, drenched in sweat, and beat up Salman so hard with his broken plastic slipper that it left marks on Salman's body for several days. To save Salman, Shazeb pushed Akmal so hard that he half landed in an open drain. Akmal got up and beat up Shazeb too. Both the brothers returned home crying with bruises all over their arms from the beating.

That day, Nabi Ahmed, the namkeen factory owner from Sahapur, took them for a ride on his bike to cheer them up.

That was Shazeb's first bike ride. Akmal's image from that day was etched in Shazeb's mind as what he did not want to be. He wanted to be like Nabi, with money, business and control.

Neither of the boys grew up liking their father or looking up to him. In their minds, it was always Syeda who provided for them both financially and emotionally.

Since that day, Nabi Ahmed started to reward the boys with a bike ride in exchange for wiping down the bike and making it shine. That was when Shazeb learned about bike parts.

Of course, riding a bike had as much of a psychological as a functional value for most boys, including Shazeb. It wasn't just a matter of pleasure.

For most, it was a symbol of attaining manhood. Of having arrived in life. Of course, richer boys like Vikram in Sabhapur arrived way ahead of them.

'You need to dress smart to ride a bike,' Shazeb told Reshma.

Like Salman Khan. And Hrithik Roshan. And John Abraham. Basically, like a Bollywood hunk.

They were symbols of tough men, men who were desired and stood up to bullies, and most of the boys wanted to be like them. The recipe for that included a bike, sunglasses, a pair of jeans, a cell phone and money in your pocket.

So, Shazeb bought two pairs of jeans – with the desired faded, weathered look – from the Gandhinagar wholesale market. Meanwhile, he also saved money to buy a second-hand cell phone.

It took him five months to acquire all the tools of the desirable, tough man kit.

On 15 December 2012, Shazeb's favourite actor Salman Khan was gifted a Hayabusa bike by the automobile company Suzuki. The Hayabusa is one of the fastest bikes in the world. It can reach a top speed upwards of 300 kmph.

Salman Khan has mythic status among north Indian young men. In 1998, he was accused of killing two blackbucks – an endangered species of antelope revered by the Bishnoi community in India. He was sent to prison over this case a few years later, in 2006. The chief judicial magistrate, while announcing the verdict, called the actor a 'habitual offender'. He was also the accused in a 2002 hit-and-run case, tried for culpable homicide because one man was killed and four injured when his car ran over some people who were sleeping on the pavement in front of a suburban bakery in Mumbai. He was later acquitted in both the cases.

He was the bad boy of Bollywood. Yet, also 'bhai', big brother.

Not like his younger brother, Salman, who was named after him but nothing like him, Shazeb thought.

Salman Khan was the big brother who was tough and helped people. Bhai, Robin Hood. About all the accusations against Salman Khan, many like Shazeb would say, 'Bhai is misunderstood.'

If his film flopped, the blame would be on the filmmaker, not Bhai. 'Bhai was made to do the wrong film,' they would say. Shazeb wanted to be like Bhai: revered, looked up to, admired.

'To be good, you have to be bad sometimes,' he told Reshma once.

He was known for possessing a collection of high-end motorbikes, and was often spotted in the media riding fancy cycles.

On 16 December 2012, Shazeb stuck a newspaper cutting with a picture of Salman Khan with the black Hayabusa on the wall of their one-room house, right above the spot where he slept.

The same night, four men gang-raped a twenty-four-year-old student in a moving bus in Delhi. For an entire month following this, the national capital witnessed massive anti-rape protests. Students, common people, everyone collected at India Gate, braving water cannons, police barricades and batons to hold the government accountable. They demanded changes in the Indian rape laws too. It was a spectacle.

The last time one saw such an impromptu gathering at India Gate had been a year back when India won the 2011 Cricket World Cup. Men on bikes, with Indian flags, went in circles around India Gate screaming, some taking off their shirts, some dancing on car roofs and bonnets.

A week after the gang rape, Bobby, the owner of the shocker repair shop, asked Shazeb to join him for a bike rally at India Gate.

That was the day Shazeb asked Reshma to buy the bangles.

Twenty young men left Karawal Nagar at around seven in the evening. When they reached India Gate forty-five minutes later, there were around thirty more bikers waiting for them. Some had posters that read 'Damini deserves justice'.

The rape victim had been given various names in this period. Under Indian law, it is prohibited to use the actual name of a rape survivor/victim. Some called her 'Nirbhaya', Fearless. Others called her 'Damini', inspired by a 1993 Bollywood film where the protagonist's name is Damini and she goes against her family and fights for a rape victim.

They all did several rounds of India Gate, yelling, 'Delhi Police, down, down', 'Damini deserves justice'; on their last round, they threw bangles at the Delhi Police personnel there.

Throwing bangles was a way of saying that Delhi Police were not men enough to protect women. And so they should wear bangles like women. Because for them, being a woman meant being weak.

Shazeb was not bothered by all these deep things. He was riding a Pulsar that had come for repair the same morning. It was a bike that was sold with the tagline 'Definitely Male'.

For him, at this moment, he was as different from his father as possible.

He was riding a bike at India Gate, where he had only been twice in all these years of living in Delhi. The ride on a winter night with a chill in the air made him feel invincible. Top of the world, desirable, tough. The moment when you taste self-worth for the first time in life.

And the chance to humiliate Delhi Police publicly made him feel powerful.

༄

Delhi Police. The words ordinarily made Shazeb tremble with rage. Each time there was a burglary in a house or shop, a bike was stolen, or a dead body was found in the nala, the police would come and pick up a few boys from the neighbourhood.

Four years back, on 19 September 2008, Delhi Police had killed two alleged terrorists in Delhi's Batla House area. The two men killed were from Azamgarh in UP. After the incident, there was a rise in the arrests of young Muslim men as 'terror suspects' all around the country.

In Karawal Nagar, crime was rampant. Everyone fought. Gujjars with Gujjars. Gujjars with Pandits. Rajputs with Gujjars. Gujjars and Pandits with migrants from any community. Gujjars and Pandits with Muslim migrants. Hindu migrants with Muslim migrants. Upper-caste migrants with Dalit migrants. UP Muslims with Bihari Muslims. UP migrants with Bihari migrants.

One day in June 2010, the Thakurs and the Pandits got into a fight over a common Delhi Jal Board tap in Govind Vihar. The fight escalated and both the warring groups swelled. Both opened fire. There were two casualties on the Thakur side. One Ompal was critically injured. Another person called Bhagat Singh was shot dead and his body thrown at Karawal Nagar Chowk at midnight. There were eyewitnesses, evidence.

Yet the police picked up twenty-one-year-old Shazeb who had just started working as an assistant at a grocery shop, Aftab, a worker from Bihar in the pressure cooker factory, and Babloo, the barber next to the grocery shop.

In a few hours, they let off Babloo but Shazeb and Aftab had to stay till night-time, when Syeda came and met the cop. After getting a few tight slaps and a baton on his back from the cops, Shazeb was let go too.

Aftab, barely eighteen, who had come from Samastipur in Bihar, was sent to a police lock-up and later to the overflowing Mandoli prison. Delhi prisons are overcrowded by 75 per cent. They are the most crowded and violent in the country. The undertrial to prisoner population ratio in Delhi jails is 82 per cent. Muslims, with a 13 per cent share in the population of Delhi, account for 22 per cent of undertrials in jail and 19 per cent of convicts. As many as 40 per cent remain incarcerated only because they cannot procure bail.

No one looked for Aftab, nobody tried to get him released. One year later, someone told Shazeb he had been charged for Bhagat Singh's murder.

The police always came to the sweatshops to pick up men, young boys who had recently migrated to find work. They would go missing for weeks, months, years. Very few were fortunate enough to have family members who would come all the way to look for them. Delhi became the city where poor young boys from UP and Bihar came and disappeared.

Shazeb and others were better off because their families did not let them disappear.

The police would specifically target Bihari Muslims because they were so poor. No one came looking for them: not family, not friends or co-workers. The police wanted people to pin the blame on, to 'solve the case' quickly.

The police did this for various reasons. Sometimes, there was pressure to solve a high-profile case; sometimes they were bribed to implicate someone else, or someone specific. At other times they were doing it under political pressure; or to be praised in the media that glorified tough cops; or even to receive rewards, medals and promotions. Justice hurried was justice buried, but it did not matter.

In March 2012, just a day before a BRICS meeting – a multilateral organization comprising Brazil, Russia, India, China and South Africa – a Bihari boy, Dilkash, was apprehended from Karawal Nagar by Delhi Police's elite anti-terror Special Cell.

Assadullah Rehman, also known as Dilkash, was twenty and apprehended from Chandu Nagar in Karawal Nagar. He was accused of running a sleeper cell of a banned organization called Indian Mujahideen (IM) in Delhi.

According to security agencies, the IM aimed to mobilize people committed to 'waging holy war against non-Muslims and the Indian state'.

Between 2003 and 2005, IM operatives were known to use ordinary objects – such as pressure cookers, milk cans, suitcases and tiffin boxes – to pack explosives in for devastating blasts in public places. IM would send emails to media organizations to claim responsibility for the terror attacks. It is believed that the emails cited the Babri demolition of 1992, the Gujarat riots of 2002, and the general 'perceived injustice' to Muslims as instigating their actions.

Based on the IM emails that the National Investigative Agency (NIA) had collected, they were rumoured to use code words. India was 'Innd', Delhi was 'Shaam', Mumbai was 'Gaww', Pune was 'Metro', 'Pistol' was 'chaloo ticket' and AK-47 'reservation'. Explosives were 'Chrnnn' and suicide bombers were 'deposits'.

With so much focus on the IM, the air in Karawal Nagar was thick with rumours and suspicion of young Muslim men. Some said Dilkash was involved in the low-intensity blasts in Pune two months back, others said he was also involved in the Jama Mosque attack.

The rumour mill ran as follows: Dilkash had completed Class 12 and wanted to become an engineer. His parents could not afford further education. That was when he came in contact with Qafeel, an IM operative who convinced him to fight for 'jihad', in return for which they would help him complete his engineering education. Later on, he was trained in an arms factory in Meer Vihar, Nangloi, 30 kilometres from Karawal Nagar, where he manufactured pistols and other arms and ammunition too.

According to the police, he had rented a house in Chandu Nagar in Karawal Nagar from where 1 kilo of explosive powder, a detonator, a timer and a mobile phone were recovered.

After Dilkash's arrest, Inspector Veer Bahadur, of the Karawal Nagar police station, called for Shazeb. Veer Bahadur had received instructions to find out if there were more members of Dilkash's sleeper cell around and if there were more explosives in the area.

Shazeb had just finished dinner and was watching *Agneepath*, with Hrithik Roshan fighting against Rishi Kapoor and Sanjay Dutt.

Hrithik Roshan plays a angsty young man who wants revenge on his father's killer, Sanjay Dutt, and resorts to violence early in life to clean up the web of evil. His righteous mother disowns him. He works for Rishi Kapoor, who plays a Muslim mafia man who sells young girls in the open market. Hrithik's character later kills him too.

Shazeb told Reshma that he could identify with that angst – that sense of being wronged.

The film was about to end when Head Constable Kailash arrived to take Shazeb to the police station.

By the time they reached the station, some other boys had been rounded up too. Veer Bahadur had just finished eating. The buckle of his belt was hardly visible under his big paunch. He said, 'Kailash, why did you get them so soon? I haven't even digested the food yet.'

'So do it now na, sir,' Kailash said as he started clearing the leftovers from Veer Bahadur's table.

Veer Bahadur walked towards Shazeb, held him by his head, and hit his back hard with his elbow.

'What, Mulle? Running a sleeper cell in my area?' he said.

Shazeb was shocked. He had had dinner just an hour back. It all came to his mouth and he puked.

'Saala! All this meat in my police station,' Veer Bahadur exclaimed, looking at the vomit.

He kept hitting his back with his elbow; Shazeb was coughing badly and crying loudly.

Then he moved on to other boys Kailash had rounded up. All Shazeb remembered was Veer Bahadur repeating 'sleeper cell', 'sleeper cell' to all the boys.

None of the boys answered. And no one, including Shazeb, dared to ask what actually was a 'sleeper cell'. He also heard the word 'jihad' as a serious accusation for the first time. *Jihad*. To struggle.

Meanwhile, Syeda and Reshma landed up at the police station with Ramesh, the activist from the almond factory workers' strike.

After the strike, Syeda had learned to uninhibitedly kick up a fuss in police stations. She would use all her contacts from the almond workers' strike to ensure that enough pressure was built for the boys to be released each time they were picked up.

Ramesh asked Veer Bahadur for a warrant.

For Veer Bahadur, the entry of the Special Cell in his territory was a huge humiliation. He did not want to rub salt in the wound by bringing media attention to his interrogation process. And Ramesh was very much capable of that.

Shazeb was let off a day later but they had no idea what happened to Dilkash after he was sent to Tihar.

'Dilkash became one of the trusted aides of top IM people since they were very impressed with the knowledge he had of hardware and his expertise in manufacturing weapons,' Shazeb later heard a police officer say on TV.

The protest at India Gate, in December 2012, was Shazeb's moment to get back at Delhi Police. Raising slogans in protest, throwing bangles at them, changed the power equation.

The thrill of feeling powerful for the first time in his life! That night was great.

The agitation lasted almost two months and then changes were brought into the rape laws.

Men felt good about themselves speaking up for women publicly. But at home, they wanted their clothes clean, meals on time and no complaints. Shazeb too.

Syeda believed that Nirbhaya should not have gone out so late at night. 'Your safety is in your hands,' she would say. And she repeated her rehearsed response to such events.

༄

Babli was nineteen, a year older than Reshma, and a student of Class 11. She had flunked twice in a row at the Girls' Government Senior Secondary School but was still allowed to attend classes which was a rare freedom allowed to a girl of her age in Karawal Nagar. She was the tallest in her class, with long hair, wheatish skin and green eyes. She wore matching hair clips and scrunchies. Her brother, Pillu, a student of Class 8 in the boys' school, would walk ahead of her when they left for school in the morning. He never looked up, was solemn and distant, and always obeyed his father.

When Babli walked, there was a confidence and swagger in her stride that not many girls her age had. Pillu was assigned to escort her everywhere, but with Babli following him, it looked like she was escorting him.

Their father, Ramesh Bainsla, in his early forties, was tall, burly and had a moustache. He mostly wore a white pyjama kurta and an *angocha*, a cotton stole, around his neck. He was solemn, too, but in an authoritative way. Like several people from the Gujjar community in Delhi, he ran a dairy.

In 2008, the Delhi High Court issued an order for all Delhi dairies to be relocated from densely populated residential areas to a planned colony on the outskirts of the city. According to the court, the dairies were leading to sanitation and health problems for both the cattle and the residents.

The majority of the owners refused to relocate, citing distance from consumers, inadequate facilities, including water shortage, lack of veterinary doctors, no supply of potable water, resulting in high morbidity of cattle.

Bainsla did not move either. His was one of the 3,000 illegal dairies that continued to run in Delhi. He owned ten buffaloes and ten cows which were hidden in the dark basement of his three-storey house.

A passer-by in the dark would often find a dozen pairs of shining bright eyes peeping at them from the ventilator of Bainsla's basement. Like fireflies looking for a passage to escape.

The buffaloes and cows hardly ever saw the light of day, except when one of them fell sick and had to be taken to the veterinary hospital. Mostly, they pooped, ate, slept and bathed in that 30 foot by 20 foot basement. They only left when they died.

Pretty much like Babli's mother, Sunita, and aunt, Kamla, who were allowed out of the house for only one additional reason: a family wedding. Babli's mother often said that a Hindu woman arrives at her husband's place in her palanquin when she gets married and must only leave it on a bier when she dies.

Babli was the only girl in the house. She was loved, allowed to study and pair jeans with her kurta once in a while – something that the Gujjar khaps – the clan councils – repeatedly said was a sign of the 'bad character' of a woman. Unlike her aunt and mother, she was allowed to go out, of course with permission from her father and uncle.

Both Kamla and Sunita resented this and piled domestic chores on her as soon as she came home: this was the price she paid for the freedom they didn't have.

Many cattle owners would name their cows and buffaloes after fruits, flowers, vegetables, actors. In Bainsla's house, the older ones were named after Hindi film actresses: Rekha, Juhi, Madhuri. The newer ones would be renamed by the children every once in a while, so a Kareena, named after an actress, would become Virat, the captain of the Indian cricket team. And Katrina would be rechristened Modi. The buffaloes didn't seem to mind it much.

Before the court order, the dairy owners at least kept the buffaloes in a shed, in an open area. But now that it was illegal, in place of the sheds they constructed concrete buildings with basements to hide the buffaloes and leased out the rest of the building to migrant workers.

∽

Over the years, a number of landowning families in NCR, farming and pastoral, had taken up landlordism, in the absence of traditional income-earning avenues.

Government surveys indicate that 33 per cent of Delhi lives in rented houses and over 85 per cent of Delhi's population belong to the low-income group.

According to estimates, in India, 80 per cent of the rented units belong to small landlords.

In the last several years since Syeda and family moved to Karawal Nagar, the living arrangements had changed. In the absence of building regulations, many landlords built multi-storey houses to rent out rooms.

With more people moving in with their families and willing to pay extra rent, the landowners who had the space moved towards a new architecture. They started arranging rooms around a courtyard or in straight lines with a corridor on each floor. Each floor had six to ten rooms.

Sanawur Rehman, a cardboard factory owner, added floors to his existing huge house to rent. He built basic rooms with minimal plaster. Each floor typically consisted of ten rooms. Some other landlords made over twenty rooms on a single floor. Each time a new floor was added, the lower floors would get less and less natural light and ventilation. This led to unhygienic living conditions and breathing problems.

The more recent tenement buildings, like Ramesh Bainsla's, were four or five floors high. They used better-quality construction material like iron and concrete.

The initial idea was to rent them out to single migrant male workers, who often shared rooms. There was only a verbal understanding, and no formal contract, for leasing these places.

While Ramesh Bainsla handled the dairy business, his younger brother, Mahesh Bainsla, who lived with him, handled the tenants. He was clean-shaven, talkative, of medium build, and always dressed in jeans, T-shirt, golden-framed aviator sunglasses, and a cap to hide his balding scalp. He had two sons, Golu in Class 9 and Tinnu in Class 7, who went to the same school as Pillu. Mahesh would be seen driving around his Maruti Alto car through even the narrowest alleys of Karawal Nagar.

Their house had seven or eight rooms on each of the four floors which were rented out for Rs 1,500 each per month. Each room was 8 foot by 10 foot; up to five or six people would sleep next to each other, side by side, in each room. The electricity bill was extra. Even though the electricity company charged Rs 4 per unit, the tenants had to pay Rs 8. That was the norm.

Studies suggest that the urban poor presently occupy less than one-fifth of the total land under residential development in the Delhi urban area. This includes unauthorized colonies, urban villages and slum settlements.

The Bainsla house was in an alley where the sky was not visible because of the balcony extensions in all of the neighbouring houses. There was no space for the air to move around. If you took a deep breath, you could smell the seepage on the walls from the houses all around.

There were three toilets on the ground floor, next to each other. They were shared by over 60 people from all the floors. They were always occupied, dirty and quickly ran out of water. Though Mahesh had engaged a sweeper to clean them once a day, this was not enough for such a large number of users. This was why some tenants continued to use dark corners of the street for defecation.

Cooking was often done inside the rooms, unlike the *slum* dwellers who could cook outdoors with better ventilation.

Mahesh was smart. He had no empathy for the tenants. But he maintained good terms to keep a steady income going. After almost seven years of renting out rooms, he had figured out the circular migratory pattern of his tenants.

Many labourers came to Delhi on a temporary basis to earn money and left as soon as enough was saved. Mahesh came up with flexible arrangements for seasonal migrants to stay for a short time. Some workers who moved locations when they changed jobs temporarily would also be allowed the same privilege. Mahesh would store their belongings, if required, and let them come back in a few months and rent again at his place. There were always four or five rooms reserved for this.

Housing is anyway seen as an individualized problem across classes. So every tenant is always dependent on the negotiations they strike with respective landlords. The expectations are low and it is considered a temporary situation in life. The priority is to earn and save, so substandard conditions are acceptable.

Mahesh had a reputation for being accommodating. But in return he had a few conditions. The tenants had to buy their provisions from the grocery shop owned by him on the ground floor, even though the prices there were higher than in other shops. They also had to pitch in for occasional repairs of the house.

The number of manufacturing units in Karawal Nagar had grown. Workers preferred to live in close proximity to their workplaces since public transport was still poor and they wanted to save on both the commute time and transportation costs. This also meant that all family members had to find jobs in the vicinity and lost out on the chance to explore better opportunities in other parts of Delhi.

Sometimes, people's region of origin also determined the way they lived.

☙

Ghazali was Shazeb's doppelganger: two years younger than him, and of the same height, complexion, hairstyle, except that he also sported a goatee. They were co-workers at the shocker repair shop. Ghazali had come to Delhi at the age of ten; his family was originally from South 24 Parganas district in Bengal. His three elder brothers, two younger sisters and parents were all employed. His brothers worked in garment units in Gandhinagar, his mother and sisters as domestic workers in middle-class households, and his father as a painter. Their collective income was almost three times that of Shazeb's household. Yet, in the past fifteen years they had never thought of moving from the slum close to Shiv Vihar in Karawal Nagar to better concrete accommodation.

The slum where Ghazali and his family lived, unlike other slums known as squatter settlements which were on public land, was on private land, where they had to pay Rs 500 per month as rent for living in a self-made shack.

Over the years, they had extended their shack and also made an enclosure covered with plastic sheets for bathing. The water had to be filled from a public tap in the morning. In the summers when there was a water shortage, the Delhi Water Board tanker would come at ten in the morning. Cooking was also done outside the house, which was a relief, but things got messy during the monsoons because of waterlogging.

The slum had a very high population density which was rising with every passing day.

Ghazali's family were collectively saving money for the following purposes in order of importance: get all the three daughters married, eventually move back to Bengal, buy land and construct a house in the village to be shared by everyone.

For Ghazali, Shazeb was always five steps ahead of him. He set the path that Ghazali always aspired to follow.

Ghazali was obsessed with Shazeb's cell phone, for instance. He knew more about its features than Shazeb, including learning to use WhatsApp and Facebook before Shazeb did.

Shazeb had made friends with the cell phone repair shop owner. He told Ghazali that he could help him get a good-quality refurbished phone under Rs 5,000 from the shop.

But Ghazali refused. 'Bhai, I will do that after the sisters get married.'

Another time, when they planned to go for a meal at the newly opened Delhi 94 restaurant, he refused and said with a smile, 'Bhai, all this expense once the land is bought.' Shazeb insisted that he come and paid for him. He felt an older brother's affection towards Ghazali. Something he had stopped feeling for Salman long ago because of his waywardness and devotion to Islamic puritanism: *I will only eat halal meat*; *Grow a beard but don't have a moustache*; *Don't play Holi, or you will go to hell*. All this but no solid work or focus ever.

One day Ghazali said, 'Bhai, you live in the present, we live in the future. You are so lucky.'

Living in the future meant that neither he nor any of his siblings had ever attended school in Delhi. Till the age of ten, he had gone to school in Bengal, but not since arriving in Delhi. It was an 'unnecessary' expenditure when the children were already earning and adding to the family income.

Like many Bengali families in the slum, Ghazali's father came to Delhi first and stayed with an acquaintance from his village. The first few months were spent at Sarai Kale Khan, an urban village in Delhi, working as a rickshaw driver before he became an apprentice to another acquaintance, a painter in Shahdara in east Delhi. After a year, he brought his family here and settled where the rest of the Bengalis from his village lived. In the last fifteen years, almost fifty families from his village had settled there and helped each other get jobs. They spoke the same language and ate the same food, even looked after each other's children when they went out to work. This was comforting and provided a cushion to all of them.

The thought of reconciling the past his father had left in Bengal with the future they were tasked to build back at the same place troubled Ghazali often. The father desperately needed validation back home through the construction of a house there from his income in Delhi. If things were so bad there that his family had had to leave Bengal, why were they trying to get back to the very place they had escaped from?

At least he was better off than workers like Aftab, who earned a pittance. They had no family or community support. In order to save rent, they lived at their workplaces, including in factories, shops and construction sites. They had to vacate each time there was a labour inspection raid. During those days, they were homeless.

On the other hand, some migrant families from Bihar and UP, like those of Syeda and Lalita, hoped to keep their families in living conditions that at least seemed better than what they thought was the lowest rung. Syeda had been determined to send her children to school and have a rented accommodation that was somewhat private and safe.

'Or else what would we tell people back home? That we left Banaras to live in a Delhi slum? The relocation from the village to a big city should always be an upward movement. Come what may,' Syeda often said. She had contempt for slum dwellers and thought her station in life was superior to theirs.

'And who knows whether they are Bengali or Bangladeshi,' she added disdainfully.

         *

Babli would often sneak out in the evening to meet Salma, her friend from school, who assisted her mother in making rakhis, soft toys, door hangings and similar things. They lived in a single room in a huge, five-storey house with a courtyard. While it was occupied by the same number of people as Babli's house, it had free-flowing air. 'Like the breeze in a jungle with the sweet cacophony of hundreds of small birds,' Babli used to say. The house was owned by Sanawur Rehman.

Most women in the building were engaged in home-based work and would occupy corners in the courtyard to do their work.

Salma's mother Farah and her sister Zeba worked together. They were paid 50 paise per rakhi piece, Re 1 to stuff and sew a soft toy, mostly in the shape of animals – except that a monkey could be blue, a cat could be purple, and a tiger could be pink in this world. The rates hadn't changed in many years.

Every evening, Babli would go and spend an hour at their place. It was a nice break from the cooking, cleaning and cattle-related work at home. It was more creative and enterprising. Coloured threads and pieces of glass, stones, crystals, velvet paper, Fevicol and *laee* – it was so much fun. To Babli, it didn't seem like work at all. 'Because you don't depend on the peanuts this work pays,' Salma told her once, puncturing her enthusiasm.

Since Sanawur's was one of the few houses in the vicinity that had a courtyard, often women from the neighbourhood would come there and work, dry their washed wheat and sometimes even their clothes because they had no sunlight or air circulation in their own homes.

Syeda and Reshma would often join Salma's family in the evenings to work in the courtyard. They were also making the same products that season in 2013.

Around seven every evening, Shazeb would come over, before it was time to hand over a repaired bike, to take the finished products on the bike, from both Syeda and Farah, to the subcontractor and collect their payment.

That was where Babli and Shazeb first met.

༺

Undermining the intelligence of women is a global sport. All kinds of fundamentalists play it all the time. When you mix up this misogyny with religion for political gains, it has great potential to instigate riots, bring down governments and break the hearts of young lovers.

For many decades, Hindu supremacists, who shouted themselves hoarse saying '*Hindu khatre mein hain*', Hindus are in danger, have floated all kinds of theories to justify it.

One such is a theory called 'love jihad'. According to the theory, there is an organized attempt by Muslim men to make Hindu girls 'fall in love' with them. This theory denies all possibility of young Hindu women with functional brains and hearts being in love with a Muslim man of their own free will. Armed with talismans like mobile phones, motorbikes, trendy attire – jeans, T-shirt, sunglasses – Muslim men can make Hindu girls 'fall in love' with them. They then marry them, make them convert to Islam, and use them to have Muslim babies, to out-populate Hindus.

To hide their Muslim identities, young men wear *kalawas*, red threads on their wrists used in Hindu rituals, and give themselves religion-neutral names like Pappu, Raja, Munna, Guddu, Bobby. The theory also identifies beauty parlours, tailoring shops for women, mobile recharging centres, medical clinics and Sufi shrines as possible spots where 'love jihad' is initiated.

Many investigating agencies like the Karnataka Crime Investigation Department (CID) and NIA have probed into 'love jihad' but found no evidence of its existence.

In September 2013, just 80 kilometres from Karawal Nagar, riots broke out in Shamli and Muzaffarnagar districts of UP. This was just six months before the general elections of 2014. The riots started with a rumour that a Hindu girl was harassed by a Muslim man. And soon acquired the 'love jihad' angle.

BJP leaders and Hindu supremacists, swore oaths to the toxic motto: *'Beti bachao, bahu banao.'*

Save your daughters, make Muslim women your daughters-in-law. A sort of Hindu version of 'love jihad'.

Riots broke out in several villages of Muzaffarnagar and Shamli. Houses were burned down, people were killed and maimed, including children, and women were raped. According to some estimates, 100 people lost their lives and over 1,00,000 people were displaced – mostly working-class Muslims.

Babli was in an all-girls school and her brother and cousins were in an all-boys school.

The reason why many girls are even allowed to go to school in India is that those schools are gender segregated. There is no risk of girls mingling with boys and bringing 'dishonour' to the family.

Girls like Babli had no real interaction with boys and men outside their family. Unlike Reshma, who was also in the same girls' school, but met boys outside because of years of shared living quarters with other tenants and no privacy.

Which is why, as promoted by several Hindi films, the only way many boys feel they can express their liking for a girl, talk to her or even just look at one, out of curiosity or raging hormones, is to stalk them. They stand outside their school, their houses, at central points in local markets. And women are supposed to like this kind of attention. Not object to it, but smile and walk past coyly.

For decades, this has been acceptable behaviour for boys. It is a sign of their manhood: *'Ladka jawaan ho gaya.'* The boy has become a man.

Babli had been dealing with this for five or six years already. She hated it.

Pillu, Golu and Tinnu had already been introduced to these ways of manhood. They would stand at the Shiv Vihar square for an hour or two every day. That was where they met Virender Gujjar and Prabhu Gaur, members of the Bajrang Dal, the youth wing of the VHP of the Sangh Parivar. Virender was the elder brother of Adarsh, the boy who whacked Salman in school after the 2002 Gujarat riots.

Like Salman, Virender and Prabhu were school dropouts and unemployed. They grew up in the same locality as the school: Dayalpur. The locality was named after the Gujjar landlord Chaudhary Dayal Singh aka 'Baba Dayala'. It used to be an agricultural village till three decades ago, after which there had been an influx of migrants from Garhwal, Kumaon and 'Purab'.

Gopi Bisht, a five-time BJP MLA, and an active RSS and VHP member, originally from Uttarakhand, lived here. He funded local cricket and wrestling leagues, and engaged young boys in temple feasts and celebration of Hindu festivals like Ramlila during Dussehra, Ganesh Visarjan and Holi.

Many young unemployed Hindu men volunteered for him. They were given designations such as secretary of religious coalitions like the Ganesh Visarjan Society, convenor of Kanwad Yatra, the chairperson of Ramlila Association. This not only gave them a sense of power, authority and political connections but also funds that they could both control and pocket a little.

After the Muzaffarnagar riots, thousands of displaced people had moved to a huge relief camp at a madrasa in Loni in Ghaziabad, just ten minutes from Karawal Nagar. In the next few months, these displaced people started renting houses in Loni and areas of north east Delhi, including Karawal Nagar.

Initially, Syeda was sympathetic. In a way, it brought back memories of the riots in Banaras she had witnessed. But when the subcontractors reduced prices per piece as a result of the surplus labour, she became resentful of the newcomers.

Landlords sensed an opportunity and even tried to increase the rent.

For the first few months, politicians kept coming to distribute relief material to the riot affected. Syeda, Farah, Lalita collectively believed that they needed help more than the riot affected who even owned bikes, almirahs and double beds, and were renting units in the better houses.

An RSS *shakha* is a traditional gathering of the local unit early in the morning for physical and ideological training. The morning *shakhas* in Dayalpur where several men, young and old, came together to sing praises of Bharat Mata, Mother India, and occasionally took out parades in the lanes and alleys of the area, were familiar to everyone in Karawal Nagar.

Since all the riot-displaced people who had moved here were Muslims, it gave new ammunition to local Hindu supremacist groups like the Bajrang Dal of which Prabhu and Virender were members.

Throughout the country, many Sangh Parivar outfits set up associations to stop Hindu–Muslim marriages: 'love jihad' in their eyes. This included organizations like the Hindu Behen Beti Bachao Sangharsh Samiti. Save Hindu Sisters and Daughters Struggle Committee.

Ashok Singhal, the then VHP president, stated in a meeting held by one such organization, 'These godless lust jihadis donning the garb of the Muslim religion as a major weapon have, for the last half a century, been targeting the Hindu girls, women, girl students.'

After the Nirbhaya rape case, the sentiment to protect women was high. Since the Muzaffarnagar riots, the theory of love jihad had become a perfect rallying cry for creating various outfits for mobilizing voters. This activated several radical Hindu outfits in favour of the BJP for the general elections in April and May 2014.

Virender and Prabhu formed the Hindu Kanya Raksha Front (HKRF), a group to rescue Hindu girls in Dayalpur. Their activities included keeping an eye on both young Hindu girls and boys. To increase their informer base, they made a network of volunteers by getting in touch with several boys from the government school through Pillu, Tinnu and Golu.

Golu told Babli one day that young Muslim men were paid for every Hindu woman they converted to Islam. They even came up with a love jihad 'rate list', a sum allegedly paid to Muslim men, based on the caste of the girl who 'falls in love' with them. The remuneration for Rajput girls was supposedly Rs 5 lakh, for Brahmin girls, it was 6 lakh, for other Hindu girls 3 lakh.

'So my rate is 3 lakh.' Babli laughed. 'I will ask Papa to give me 3 lakh so that I don't run away with a Muslim man,' she added in a hushed voice.

Golu was not happy.

⁓

'How does this guy come on a new bike every day?' Babli asked Salma, watching Shazeb loading the bike with strings of ashoka leaves.

She was impressed by his calm expression, the smile on his face, and how good he looked on the bike.

That was the point. For Shazeb, riding a bike wasn't just a matter of pleasure, but also getting noticed.

It was Diwali season. Diwali was on 3 November in 2013. And so fresh marigold garlands and door hangings made of ashoka leaves were much in demand. Subcontractors paid Rs 3 per dozen hangings made by stringing the leaves on a thread. These were made at night so that they could be freshly delivered by the subcontractor to the flower market in the morning. A dozen would take between fifteen and twenty minutes to make. All the women aimed to make at least thirty to forty dozen by the morning, so that they could earn at least Rs 100 in eight hours.

During the day, they would make string lights: add tiny bulbs to long wires. Making a dozen would take less than an hour. For a dozen string lights, they were paid Rs 100. The rates had gone down because of the influx of Chinese lights, but because the Chinese lights would frequently cause a short circuit, there were some who preferred the old Indian handmade lights.

About Rs 200 a day would at least take care of the daily groceries and milk for a family, Syeda had calculated.

The large volume of leaves they strung every day needed space. And so did the bulbs, because they were fragile. At Salma's place there was electricity to work at night and it was clean and dry and spacious. In return, Syeda would sometimes volunteer to cook for Farah or help with household chores.

'I have been cursing myself all these years for working there,' says Syeda.

On 5 November 2013, Mangalyaan, India's first interplanetary mission, was launched – to the planet Mars.

Shazeb was willing to do several rounds of ferrying of raw materials and finished products. It wasn't a chore, it was a pleasure, on a bike. He didn't realize he had become the object of Babli's attention in the process.

Salma told her he was a shocker repair mechanic. 'Too neat and smart for a mechanic. Are you sure?' Babli asked.

Babli knew how to cycle, though she wasn't really allowed to. She would often ride the milk delivery cycle, with cans tied on both sides, during the afternoon, when Ramesh and Mahesh Bainsla were having a siesta. Riding a motorbike was something she wanted to try too.

In Indian movies, many heroes ride a bike: they fight the villain on it, rob banks, woo women, sing songs of friendship, perform stunts, offer help.

By now, the movie *Dhoom* was a franchise. It featured high-end bikes, with its cool robber protagonists whizzing past the fastest cars to conduct sophisticated heists. The franchise dazzled young people across the country. In a way, it increased the craze for street racing, bike stunts on public roads, and even bike-borne thefts.

There was also a new-found interest in bike modification. Bobby had sensed a business opportunity and started training Shazeb,

Ghazali and others in revamping bikes, installing nitrous oxide kits for better horsepower and acceleration, new free-flow exhaust systems, and LED lights.

On 9 December 2013, the Sexual Harassment of Women at Workplace (Prevention, Prohibition, and Redressal) Act was passed.

When Babli heard that Shazeb had seen *Dhoom 3*, at Meenakshi Palace, a rundown single screen in Gokulpuri, she asked him to tell her the story.

He gave himself entirely to the task of narration. Just like the young Akmal. He mimicked, jumped about, contorted his face, flailed his arms like a windmill, all to convey the way Aamir Khan had conducted the heist and his impressions of Abhishek Bachchan. When telling the story he was anxious to preserve the original tempo and effect. He would carefully build up the narrative and would stop Babli from interrupting him.

She sat there, listening to him with fascination.

After that day, their storytelling sessions continued outside Salma's house.

It was not long before he turned to other genres: horror, myth, religion or a mix of everything. 'This very graveyard is made on a waterbody,' he told Babli.

'Why do you laugh? You don't believe me?' he asked her.

Now, the bodies that were buried float in the water beneath it, he added.

What Shazeb claimed was true. Many waterbodies in Delhi had been acquired, flattened and filled in for construction. The Mustafabad graveyard and Eidgah, fifteen minutes from Karawal Nagar, where they had been meeting for their secret dates for several months, was also built over a waterbody.

Similarly, the crematorium in Babarpur near Loni was also a waterbody earlier. In Karawal Nagar too, there had been two waterbodies: one had been encroached on by private builders and the other one had been leased out for ninety-nine years to the DTC to build a bus terminal over it.

In Gokulpur, where the Meenakshi Palace movie theatre was located, the waterbody had been encroached on by twenty-two households that had constructed over it.

'Bodies of old people, small children, young brides, floating in water...' Shazeb would make it as morbid as possible.

That was the reason why ghosts roamed around at night in Karawal Nagar, he said.

'Oh. So there are ghosts too?' she asked teasingly, though she felt a vague uneasiness deep inside her.

'What do you expect? If the body does not disintegrate properly as it should according to Islam, its spirit cannot rest in peace.'

He was so matter-of-fact, she thought.

'But in our religion, you are supposed to immerse the bones in a river to attain salvation,' she replied.

Shazeb was impressed by her quick wit.

A few weeks after their first meeting, Babli couldn't bear to go without seeing him every day. She couldn't explain her restlessness or talk to anyone about it.

Babli recounts that what she liked was that Shazeb would not say those silly sweet nothings to her: 'I love you, you are beautiful.' He told her engrossing stories and they talked. Most men she knew just did not know how to communicate. Her friends had told her that their boyfriends would come to meet them, stand next to them or at a distance, look at them or look at their phones, or exchange side glances, and sometimes leave without saying a word.

Meanwhile, the HKRF had been tasked with preventing the upcoming 2014 Valentine's Day celebrations in the nearby areas. The Bainsla brothers had been told that it was against Indian culture. Unlike love jihad, where they had to keep an eye on Hindu–Muslim couples, this time, they were to target young couples regardless of their religion. 'Western culture of boys and girls shamelessly meeting each other in public needs to be uprooted,' Prabhu told Babli's cousin Tinnu.

Tinnu didn't care much about this. Except that it was an opportunity to roam around in the neighbourhood markets, parks and malls. Mahesh encouraged Tinnu to volunteer, thinking it would help garner some political clout. That might help him with getting municipality permission to build one more floor.

The volunteers were also supposed to encourage young people to instead celebrate Matri Pitru Poojan Diwas, Parents' Worship Day, to save themselves from 'immoral acts' like celebrating love. When Babli's other cousin Golu told his classmates they should put tilak on their parents' foreheads, most boys laughed. 'You become Shravan Kumar, the dutiful son. We will become Shah Rukh Khan,' said one of them, Rahul, extending his arms in the signature style of the *Baazigar* actor, who was now known as King of romance in Hindi cinema.

The day finally came. Babli knew it was a long wait for the bus. Even so, she kept gazing at the road. There was not a single tree along this path. Nearby, there was a wooden shanty with two water pitchers from the Hanuman Temple Trust and an old beggar, his eyes glued to Babli's hands. Beside him was a dog, also eyeing her hands. She was holding a burger that she had made for Shazeb. Often, she would take bus number 324 to Mustafabad Eidgah, where Shazeb would come to meet her at lunchtime, just after her school ended. She had told her mother she had extra classes this whole week because the school year was going to end, so she could meet Shazeb.

As a break from their everyday tiffin of *parantha* and vegetables, Babli had been packing a special tiffin for the three boys and double for herself. She was fond of fast food and made chowmein, momos, fried rice, idlis, paneer sandwiches and now burgers herself. She would give half to Shazeb at Eidgah every day.

Golu had been noticing Babli's sudden interest in cooking. Virender had told him to keep an eye out for local girls who were coming home late after school. On 14 February, volunteers were also assigned to keep an eye on bus stops and restaurants. That day, Golu was to watch the Delhi 94 restaurant, which was just next to the bus stop.

'Apart from the beggar and the dog, he was watching me too,' recalls Babli.

He followed her on a bike with Prabhu. He froze when they saw that she was going to a Muslim graveyard. Prabhu immediately called Virender, 'Love jihad case here. Come quickly.'

Golu requested him to let this one go and promised to see to it that Babli got such a good thrashing at home that she would never dare do such a thing again.

But Virender, who was meanwhile keeping a watch on young people in the local market, alerted other boys and started making phone calls to mobilize a mob. Bobby, who was buying a spare part, overheard the conversation. 'Bike mechanic Shazeb, the one Veer Bahadur caught about the sleeper cell – he is roaming around with a Hindu girl.'

When Bobby called up Shazeb he was explaining to Babli how to remove the tyre and mudguard from a bike to fix the front shocker.

'Shazeb, the HKRF guys are coming for the two of you. Run!' said Bobby.

'Run where? Babli is with me,' he replied.

'If you both want to live, just go,' Bobby said.

Babli had also heard him and told Shazeb they should move fast. There was no time to think.

They quickly got on his bike. Babli asked him to drive towards Majnu ka Tila, the hillock of Majnu, named after Majnu, a lost, desperate lover.

*

'Rescuing one girl is the same as saving 100 cows. One Hindu daughter equals 100 holy cows,' Virender told a few young boys who had gathered at the Mustafabad Eidgah.

Several small teams were formed to look for Shazeb and Babli. Shazeb started getting incessant calls on his phone which he was scared to take. Neither of them had been to Majnu ka Tila before but Babli had heard about it from a friend who had been there and waxed eloquent about the clothes, the food, particularly momos, and the tiny Buddhist places of worship. These had been set up by Tibetan refugees following the 1959 Tibetan uprising, when the Dalai Lama went into exile in north India.

Babli and Shazeb roamed around in the narrow lanes of the Tibetan settlements. Somehow she was not scared at all. That bothered Shazeb.

'Let's go home,' he said.

Babli was reluctant. 'If we go home, they will kill me and perhaps you too. If not, they will get you arrested,' she said.

She had heard Tinnu and Pillu talk about how Virender and Prabhu had earlier 'rescued' girls who had dared to choose their own partners, even if both parties were Hindu.

Tinnu had even told her that they separated the girls who got married to Muslim boys and got them remarried.

'So what do we do now?' asked Shazeb.

'Let's just elope,' Babli replied instantly.

'What does that mean?' Shazeb was shocked.

Babli said, 'They will anyway get me married next year to some dairy owner's son. From taking care of one set of buffaloes, I will take care of another set. How will that change my life?'

'But what about my family? They will go after them,' he replied.

'Call them,' she said.

When Shazeb called Syeda, she was already at the police station. Veer Bahadur had picked up Salman to grill him about Shazeb and Babli. It was a usual tactic. Detain the family members to trace the accused.

The same day, eight girls from a private school in Karawal Nagar had gone missing. There was also an unidentified body found in a sack near the sewer, news of which was flashing on all local news channels. Several parents, local RSS guys, higher-ups, and MLA Gopi Bisht's office, had been putting enormous pressure on the police station and driven Veer Bahadur to the end of his tether.

'Wasn't Shazeb questioned for running a sleeper cell?' Veer Bahadur asked Kailash.

Kailash confirmed it.

'Jihadis, all of them!' Veer Bahadur yelled.

That was when Syeda's phone rang. She went out and told Shazeb to immediately come back. 'They will frame Salman if you don't come. Get the girl back too,' she told him.

Ramesh and Mahesh Bainsla were furious and had vented on Sunita and Kamla, both verbally and physically, for not being able to keep a watch on the girl. Tinnu, Pillu and Golu were also not spared.

Golu was thrashed particularly soundly for not dragging Babli home by her hand, for letting her escape.

Ramesh Bainsla was enraged at the uselessness of the young boys at home but did not make a spectacle of it. Mahesh was seething with rage too but he was also thinking of business. He didn't want to offend the Sangh men but he didn't want to create a scene that scared his tenants either – almost half of them Muslims. He was more interested in keeping this matter private.

He told his brother not to take any calls from the police or the RSS guys, and left with Tinnu and Golu to look for Babli.

Meanwhile, Shazeb was trying to convince Babli to return home. 'We were just sitting and talking. We didn't do anything wrong,' he said, knowing the meaninglessness of this argument if presented to the police and the Sangh men.

They hadn't brought any money with them, nor clothes and documents. It was late and they had to make up their minds fast.

Babli told him, 'I am not going back home to get thrashed by everyone. There is nothing left for me there. I will stay here only.' She later recounts that she didn't think of the future – only that she didn't want to go back and die. It was not fear, it was a resolve to live.

Shazeb was in two minds. What would happen to everyone at home versus the chance, for the first time in his life, to be someone's hero, Babli's hero. A hero who dared to do something out of this world, unthinkable and unimaginable for any boy he had ever known in his family or class. Just like in the movies.

That night, Shazeb and Babli stayed at the Majnu ka Tila gurdwara. Spending a night outside the house with a boy meant that there was no going back for a young woman like Babli.

The next day, Shazeb called Bobby from a public phone. Bobby advised him not to come back as the HKRF people were combing through every tenement and factory to find them. 'Both of you are adults. Get married and finish it off. Then they can't do anything to you legally,' he said.

'Bobby bhaiya is right. Let's get married,' Babli agreed.

Shazeb hadn't thought this moment would come so soon and so unexpectedly. He liked Babli, he loved her too, in the sense that he wanted to be with her. But he hadn't yet thought seriously about spending his life with her, or the technicalities involved in making that happen, considering both of them were from different religions.

He wanted to set up a bike modification shop, and what about Babli? Didn't she want to become a teacher?

'My becoming a teacher is more possible now by marrying you rather than going home. And I love you and want to be with you,' she declared.

Shazeb's reluctance was making her angry. 'You don't love me or what? Then leave. I can take care of myself,' she said.

That was when Shazeb said, 'Let's get married.'

Tis Hazari court was just fifteen minutes from the gurdwara. Babli had seen in the film *Ahista Ahista* that Hindu–Muslim couples could get married in court. They decided to go there the next morning.

They reached at nine the next morning. Several lawyers in black coats were waiting at the gate offering their services: 'Bail. Traffic ticket. Marriage.'

Babli and Shazeb stopped a lawyer and asked about the wedding procedure.

They were informed they could get married under the Special Marriage Act. Any unmarried, sane, consenting adults, where the man was over twenty-one years of age and the woman was over eighteen, and who were unrelated within the degrees of prohibited relationships, irrespective of faith or caste, could get married under this law. It required no ritual. They immediately agreed to do this at a fee of Rs 5,000 to the lawyer. Bobby had agreed to loan them the money.

The lawyer told them that in order to file their application, they needed to provide copies of their permanent addresses, Class 10 certificates to prove their age, and copies of any rent agreement, electricity or water bill, and Aadhaar cards. He informed them that copies of identity proof and photos of three witnesses were also needed but that he could arrange those as part of his fee. Once the complete application was submitted to the SDM's office, a public notice announcing their intention to marry would be pasted outside that office. And the notice would be dispatched to their families.

If no objection was received from anyone in thirty days, they could get married.

'Thirty days!' Shazeb yelped.

'But this was not shown in the film,' Babli said to the lawyer, on the verge of tears for the first time in two days.

They didn't have any of the documents they needed, and where would they go for thirty days! They would be caught and killed for sure, Babli said.

The lawyer then suggested that either one of them could convert and then they could get married under either the Hindu Marriage Act or Islamic law. That could be done in hours.

No notice would be sent to the parents if they took the 'regular' religious marriage route, the lawyer said.

While they were discussing their options near the SDM's office, they saw some young men rigorously scanning the noticeboard that announced the wedding dates of couples planning to marry under the Special Marriage Act. The lawyer told them they were members of the Hindu Kanya Raksha Samiti, a vigilante group, who kept an eye out for such marriages.

Shazeb and Babli left quickly. Shazeb called Bobby once again and told him about the impossibility of a court wedding. Bobby told them to take the night bus to Manali. There were plenty that left from near the Majnu ka Tila gurdwara, as lots of Tibetans regularly travelled from there to meet their families settled in Himachal. He would arrange something for them there. That night they took the bus, both of them going to a hill station for the first time in their lives.

The next morning, they had a choice between a quick Arya Samaj wedding, that requires minimal Hindu rituals, and an Islamic wedding. Since marriage registration of Muslim weddings – for legal documentation – was not mandatory then, they decided to go to the mosque and get married by a qazi known to Bobby. Babli had to convert to Islam and she chose the name Soha after Soha Ali Khan, the actress in the movie *Ahista Ahista*. They were married by the afternoon; by the evening they had done two rounds of the mall road in Manali.

Babli was very happy, Shazeb was too, but he was also thinking of everyone at home and was aching to make a phone call to Syeda. But Bobby had advised against this.

※

It had been a week of Salman being forced to visit the police station every day. The eight schoolgirls who had gone missing had actually gone to Nainital for a picnic! They didn't tell their parents because they would never have been allowed to go. The dead body was also identified. It was a local labourer who had been killed by another labourer because he saw him meeting his wife. So the pressure was off the police for now. But what was to be done with Salman?

Ramesh and Mahesh Bainsla had met MLA Bisht and made a declaration that for them Babli was dead, that they would never accept her even if she were to return. Syeda approached Sanawur. He took the local preachers from twenty mosques in the vicinity to Bisht to promise they would vote for the BJP in the upcoming 2014 general elections. Bisht's office then called Veer Bahadur and asked him to stop summoning Salman to the police station.

Of course, Virender, Prabhu and the local boys were upset with this compromise but their activities got a new impetus thanks to this scandal.

They printed and distributed pamphlets to protect Hindu girls. These said: 'Young girls with mobile phones are the ones who bring dishonour to the family by chatting with boys. Parents should keep a check on that. Once the BJP comes to power, they will push towards a law to stop inter-caste and interreligious marriages.'

They also started taking promises from Hindu landowners not to rent to single Muslim boys, which was followed for some time. But it wasn't a good business prospect in the long run so at some point people again started renting to whoever was interested.

Within three months, in May 2014, the BJP under Narendra Modi won a landslide victory, and Modi was elected as an MP from the Varanasi constituency, Syeda's home district. The BJP formed the government at the Centre, whose credit Virender and Prabhu take till date.

Ramesh and Mahesh Bainsla became Bisht's favourites. They had not only upheld 'Hindu values' by disowning their daughter who had brought 'dishonour' by marrying not just a person of her own choice but also a Muslim man. And they had also provided three men, Tinnu, Pillu and Golu, as full-time volunteers for Hindu fundamentalism.

Babli and Shazeb didn't come back. Shazeb often thought of what Ghazali used to say about him: that he 'lived in the present'. Shazeb had to. There was no choice. He found a job at a garage near the Manali bus stop. Babli was happy to slowly create a new world for herself that included a lot of momos and cool breezes.

'Babli did some black magic on my son,' says Syeda. 'He wouldn't even look at girls. He was only interested in bikes and watching movies,' she continues, not able to come to terms with her son's sexuality and life choices.

Syeda thought Babli needed to tone down the better-than-thou attitude of the youth, which Reshma was acquiring too.

Syeda had hoped to get a dowry for Shazeb's wedding, which could have been used for Reshma's wedding. That was what she had grown up witnessing all her life. Recycling the daughter-in-law's dowry to provide for the daughter. But this wasn't an option now.

The income that Shazeb used to bring home was also gone. She was most hurt by the selfishness of this episode, that Shazeb and Babli had thought only of themselves and not about anyone else, something she was never allowed to do. She cursed Babli under her breath and never forgave her for the spell she had cast on her son.

7

Incense Stick

Bekaar Mabaash, kuch kiya kar,
Kapde hi udhed kar siya kar.

Idle Mabaash, do something at least,
If nothing, unravel the clothes and restitch them.

— Hindustani proverb

Girls would change their route when they saw them. Virender and Prabhu had grown to be the most detested figures by all young women across religions and most young men in Karawal Nagar.

They had built a strong network of informers for the HKRF. Vegetable vendors, cobblers and rickshaw drivers – basically anyone whose work required moving around – were roped in to alert them when a young woman was seen chatting with a man or doing 'unwomanly' things like simply existing in public spaces. Young women who took autos or buses unaccompanied were especially followed.

Any woman found with a man was stopped, even when they were their brothers. They were held hostage and not released till the parents arrived to testify they were siblings or relatives. In return, the informers were promised immunity from the police, political support and freedom from the HKRF's harassment on a daily basis.

Nobody dared to ask HKRF members for payment for the chai, coffee, soft drinks, cigarettes and tobacco they consumed while waiting at roadside shacks.

They checked out women and their clothing, roughed up people, made their presence felt by talking loudly. Many HKRF members would don aviators, jeans, wear a *kalawa* on their wrists, and ride bikes. Just like the boys who were thought to do 'love jihad'. But the HKRF members could be distinguished by a saffron scarf around their neck. Several of them sported a red *tika*, mark, on their forehead, which would give their faces a murderous red tinge after mixing with their sweat throughout the day and spreading all over.

Within three months of Shazeb and Babli leaving, Narendra Modi took oath as prime minister of India. On 28 May 2014, twelve days after taking an oath to 'do right to all manner of people under the Constitution and the law, without fear or favour, affection or ill-will', he became the second prime minister in Indian history to pay tribute to the portrait of V.D. Savarkar since it had been unveiled in the Indian Parliament premises in 2003 by the first BJP prime minister, Atal Bihari Vajpayee.

Savarkar popularized the ideology of 'Hindutva', political Hinduism, that aims to establish a Hindu state in India and the world. He was also accused as a co-conspirator in the assassination of Mahatma Gandhi.

In a 1944 interview, when Tom Treanor, an American journalist, asked Savarkar how Muslims would be treated in independent India, he said, 'As a minority, in the position of negroes in your country.'

A revered figure for the RSS, he resurfaces in the popular national discourse each time the BJP comes to power. His statues and portraits, and the naming of public institutions after him are not just seen as memorials but also celebrated as the triumph of Hindu majoritarianism and the sidelining of Indian religious minorities, particularly Muslims and Christians.

On 29 November 2014, Veer Savarkar Hospital, a fifty-bed hospital under the Municipal Corporation of Delhi, was inaugurated in East Karawal Nagar. It was inaugurated by the Union health minister, Dr Harsh Vardhan, himself a medical practitioner, and a member of the RSS since childhood. Some years later, he would claim that Hindu Vedic theories were superior to Einstein's theory of relativity.

The fact that after the BJP came to power the first public institution named after Veer Savarkar was established in Karawal Nagar provided great impetus to the Sangh Parivar outfits in the area. Virender, Prabhu and other Sangh members saw this as their personal achievement and their morale was boosted no end.

Meanwhile, Syeda couldn't get over the fact that Shazeb chose himself over his family. She would never admit this openly but Shazeb, her firstborn, was her favourite. She was only sixteen when he was born. It was almost as though they grew up together. His support, both monetary and moral, was something she had come to depend on. He knew her faults but never publicly berated her. He would even entertain her while she worked by imitating film actors. He was a breath of fresh air for her.

In Indian families, a mutual obligation, even co-dependence, exists between parents and children. When the child is young, the parents must do their best to raise them, particularly if a boy. When the child is grown up, they are obligated to obey their parents and put them before themselves. This burden of obligation was the only way to be. Except that neither Akmal nor Syeda had followed this template. Yet they were conditioned to embrace the victimhood of being abandoned as parents when Shazeb left with Babli.

Individual needs, ambitions, desires and freedom can exist on the margins and must be pre-approved by the family. The pursuit of self-fulfilment is mostly prohibited.

Akmal's mother, Akbari, never stopped cursing him for abandoning her and living with his family in Delhi. Like Syeda, Akbari too blamed her daughter-in-law for influencing her son. For brainwashing him, for making him take a position, and for becoming a more important figure in his life than his own mother.

'My son was never like this. She is a sorcerer,' Akbari had said about Syeda. Twenty years later, Syeda was repeating the same for Babli.

It was easier to believe that a daughter-in-law had done black magic than recognize a son's desire to break free. Acknowledging the son's agency is harder than blaming the daughter-in-law.

Syeda did not realize how she had started to become like her mother-in-law, her grandmother and all those women who stood on the terrace in Bazardiha when she was humiliated for even looking at a young man. She sounded like the older women in Banaras who detested younger women for being too independent. That was the only way for them to validate the restricted lives they had lived.

She could have left Akmal at one point when she was younger. He was not bringing any money home. He would often lie around drunk for days. She had youth on her side and the affection of Babloo, the supervisor in the walker factory. He used to provide rations whenever she ran short at home, would even sit with the children with their textbooks. She liked the empty space his presence would create in her mind. That space which is created when all responsibilities are swept away. Like a deep, long breath. At one point, he even offered to marry her. But she let that go, pass, slip away, for the sake of her children.

She felt rage at Babli, who had broken the spell of restriction cast on women like her, and escaped. She hated both her and Shazeb's guts in being able to choose happiness over drudgery.

Akmal was silent about the whole thing. Since the boys had hit teenage, there had hardly been any communication between father and sons. He felt small in front of Shazeb, even sidelined. Since Shazeb had started earning, he commanded the respect that Akmal thought was due to him. But in the last fifteen years, Akmal had never got promoted beyond a cart rickshaw driver at the various factories. Of and on, that was all he had done. He had no opinion; if he had one, no one heard it – as always.

Reshma didn't harbour the kind of bitterness Syeda had for Babli and Shazeb. True, Babli was not like Reshma. Babli cared more about her appearance. She was actually bubbly, chatty, and would even sometimes interrupt their work at Salma's courtyard. But she had the kind of softness Reshma never got a chance to nurture.

While Syeda was handling all the mess with the police, maulvis and Bisht's men, Reshma's hands were at work throughout, preparing things by the dozen to keep the house running. All this while she continued to keep up at school. She had crushes on boys too. But even these failed to change her low opinion of men. She didn't know what love was. Or why two people became so crazy about each other.

Crucially, this moment was Salman's chance to shine. To prove everyone, including Syeda, wrong. That he was better than Shazeb, more sincere, reliable, charismatic – the adjectives he had not earned all these twenty-four years of his life.

Salman's antics to please his mother ran parallel with Syeda's rantings about Shazeb's betrayal.

'Look, I have tonsured my head. Now, no girl will look at me to run away with. And I won't go anywhere, okay?' he told Syeda. With his shaved upper lip and the sparse hair on his face that he was trying to grow into a beard, his oversized kurta and a pyjama that ended above the ankles, and his skeletal frame, Salman's sacrifice of shaving his head was not really needed. No woman looked at or talked to him anyway.

Salman had aspirations but did not have the finesse to execute plans. He had started smoking beedis at the age of twelve. He also consumed all kinds of intoxicants like Iodex and whitener, chloroform and different forms of weed. But he never touched beer like the other boys because it was haram in Islam. That's what his madrasa friends had told him. Salman had started hanging out with them after his progressive alienation at school began. He was uninhibited in picking fights with Gujjar boys, Muslim boys and Hindu boys, and would constantly get thrashed in return.

Ever since he had turned sixteen, he would get picked up by the police whenever there were skirmishes, petty thefts, gang fights or robberies in the neighbourhood.

Someone's gold chain is missing. Catch Salman.

Someone's machine part was stolen. Write Salman's name in the FIR.

He had become a 'history-sheeter' in police records, a career criminal with a lengthy criminal record. Someone against whom pre-emptive penalties could be imposed. He was picked up by the police regardless of whether he was involved or not.

This was why Shazeb, who was only detained twice, had maintained a distance from him. He didn't want to be seen with his brother or implicated as a criminal by association. Salman felt isolated and abandoned.

Over the years, even Syeda had started calling him *Dhakkan* Salman. 'He does not even do anything and yet gets caught,' she would say with a laugh.

The more he was bullied, the more he tried to pretend to be tough. Apart from Reshma and some of the madrasa kids, no one else would listen to his boring, convoluted lectures on how to live life and what was Islamic and un-Islamic.

And even Reshma would turn around from time to time and say sarcastically, 'Bhai, have you heard? People take advice only from those whose own lives are sorted?'

With Shazeb gone, additional income was required at home. In the last fifteen years, the monthly house rent had increased from Rs 500 to Rs 2,000. Akmal had only got a Rs 1,500 raise in all these years. From Rs 3,000 when he started in 2001, he was now paid Rs 4,500. Their current house was a *barsati*, a top floor room, so it had some open space in the form of a terrace, but there was still only one small room for the entire family. Syeda barely managed to bring in Rs 6,000–8,000 per month.

Syeda used her contacts to get a job for Salman at a tape factory. She had to literally beg him to take it. Factory-manufactured tape is used for packing and electricity work. The core is made of cardboard and has to be cut with a machine into rings of various sizes, on which tape is wound using another machine. Salman had to manually operate the core-cutting machine. The pay was Rs 4,000 for a nine-hour shift. The supervisor kept telling him to pick up speed, but to no avail. Instead, he would constantly get into arguments with the supervisor. There were three other workers in the factory, all of them women who were better at the work than him. Salman was embarrassed and called the job 'unmanly'.

He was fired in three months.

℮

Salman had no influential friends. His self-confidence was low. He tried to befriend Sukhbir Singh Gujjar's son Vikram, from his Sabhapur days, for some time, hoping distinguished friends would earn him some legitimacy.

Over the years, the 'Sabhapuriya' identity of people from Sabhapur village had become cool, particularly among the young boys of Yamuna Paar.

The 22 kilometre-long Yamuna *pushta* road connecting Sabhapur and Karawal Nagar had now become a four-lane highway. Over the years, in the ever-expanding NCR, with many migrants coming to Delhi and never returning, large patches of land were acquired by real estate developers on the *pushta* road and neighbouring areas. But the road that broke away from the four-lane highway to lead to Sabhapur was still steep and only partially cemented.

In 1996, when Salman and his family moved there, the same road – a mud road then – was used for large processions of buffaloes and cows; the count would go up to a thousand sometimes. Livestock was considered expensive then and a thing to show off. Now, they had been replaced by cars.

Kadam Singh Gujjar, who had earlier operated the jeans factory, now ran a wedding car rental business with his son. Renting high-end cars like Audis, Mercedes and Hummers for wedding processions had become common in Delhi and Haryana. It was a roaring business.

The namkeen factory where Salman and his family first lived was still abandoned, but the bricks continued to have the soot remains from all the gajak they made there year after year. A Veer Gujjar gym had opened up next door. There were more gyms than grocery shops now in Sabhapur. Next to Iftekaar's shanty town now stood a huge gym named Bouncer Factory. Young boys would build muscled bodies there and get hired as bouncers for Delhi high society.

Vikram had also dropped out of school. He still had some affinity with Salman. With his bulging biceps, Vikram regularly participated in the car rallies that had become popular in Jamna Paar.

One day in February 2015, Salman accompanied Vikram to one such car rally. Salman tried to pretend that he knew all about cars. Twenty-six cars passed through the narrow lanes: one Hummer, one Audi, one Mercedes, one Jaguar, two Thars, six Fortuners, one XUV, ten Scorpios, one Creta, one Corolla, one Verna. All the cars had stickers: Veer Gujjar/Gujjar Boy/Being Gujjar/Proud to Be Gujjar; East or West, Government of Gujjar Is the Best.

Haryanvi songs blared loudly from the cars.

Yaar mase milne ko aayo,
Gaadi Fortuner laayo

My guy came to meet me,
In a Fortuner car.

Many young men imagine big cars are the ticket to impress women and find love.

Sitting in an SUV, Salman looked like a skeleton beside the gym-toned, tall, burly Gujjar boys. Young, shirtless boys posed for selfies next to huge cars. It was live-streamed on Facebook.

The next day, someone commented under the Facebook video: *'Mulle ko Pakistan pahunchane ke liye itni badi rally.'* Such a big rally to take a Muslim man to Pakistan.

Vikram did not invite Salman for the next rally. Or the next.

In the first half of 2015, Salman found a job at a construction site in Sector 97, Noida. A housing society was being developed, with tall buildings, a garden, a swimming pool and lifts.

Many such housing societies were being built in Noida. The town expanded to accommodate more residential and industrial complexes, the extension now called Greater Noida. There were skyscrapers after skyscrapers: some under construction, some fully built but unoccupied. Many of them lay vacant for years after construction.

Ghaziabad, Noida, Gurugram and other neighbouring NCR areas have a booming real-estate industry with premium, luxury and middle-income apartments being built every year in large numbers; many have a dedicated gym, club, swimming pool, shopping centre and other amenities. But only the rich or the middle class can afford them. Many of them are second or third houses bought as investments.

In India, almost 60 per cent of poor urban families live in spaces smaller than the size specified for an ideal prison cell.

Land allocation for residential construction by the government is done only for the middle class and above. Real estate private companies have no incentive to create affordable housing for the poor in NCR. This is the reason for the housing shortage in India.

Salman lived on the construction site. This is what real men do, he used to say when he shared pictures of the site on WhatsApp with Reshma.

Within a month, he fell into the under-construction lift shaft and sustained a head injury. His scalp split open, and he had to get several sutures. He broke his leg, too. It took him almost three months to recover at home.

Of course, the building contractor at the construction site didn't help. Nor was it expected, beyond the initial first aid he got.

Syeda was working at the almond factory from 4 a.m. to 11 a.m. She worked at home for the rest of the day, making school bags, threading garments, stuffing soft toys and assembling plastic toys, making Rs 200 to 250 per day. Akmal now had steady work at the bag factory as a rickshaw driver, sometimes doing extra rounds. The monthly household income was Rs 12,000. They didn't have any savings. Syeda took a loan from Parshuram, the bindi subcontractor, for Salman's medical expenses at 5 per cent interest.

Once he had recovered, Salman was too weak to work anywhere. His acute desire to be acknowledged as the new man of the house, a dependable guy, was unfulfilled.

That was when Shazeb re-established contact with Syeda, around September 2015. It took many phone calls to get her to talk to him. In the last year, Shazeb and Babli had moved to Spiti valley in Himachal Pradesh. It was on the preferred route in north India for high-end bikers travelling to Ladakh. Several local garages and expensive bike brands had opened their service stations on the route. Since Shazeb liked his work, he was happy to work hard. He made enough money through his salary and tips to rent a room for Babli and himself. But on the phone, he didn't tell Syeda much. They still had to maintain secrecy. North Indian families are known to wait for years to kill the daughters who brought them 'dishonour'. He was still scared for Babli and himself.

He also didn't want to deal with Syeda's resentment. Even though he felt relieved about no longer being involved in his family's day-to-day affairs, he wanted to stay in touch with them, mostly out of guilt and duty.

When he learnt from Reshma that Salman needed a job, he called Bobby for help. Bobby had started a new transport business and hired Salman as a tempo cleaner-cum-mechanic-cum-substitute driver-cum-guard.

Salman didn't like that he had to get Shazeb's help to find work, but he took the job because it seemed cooler than working in the factories his mother and her friends worked at.

He started spending his free time at the Sayyed Chand Baba shrine, near the Dayalpur police station in Karawal Nagar. This was a forty-year-old Sufi shrine located in a Hindu-majority area, and was visited by people from across religions. In Class 6, Salman would often bunk school and escape there, and the school principal Sudershan Lal would bring him back.

He started taking care of the shrine, doing some repair work here, some sweeping and mopping there. The local maulvis praised him for this. Perhaps he needed that validation. The shrine was becoming his anchor in some ways. Soon, he was a regular at all the mosques within a 2 kilometre radius: Bilal Mosque, Markaj Wali Mosque, Anar Mosque, Dilshad Mosque, Allah Wali Mosque, Bismillah Mosque.

'Soon, Salman became a five-time namazi,' recalls Syeda.

༺

Since the formation of the new government in 2014, Hindu supremacist outfits regularly carried out rallies in Karawal Nagar.

It was the month of Ramzan in mid-June 2015. In the mornings, lathi-wielding RSS men in khaki knickers chanting 'Jai Shri Ram' started doing the rounds of the narrowest lanes in Karawal Nagar. In the evenings, at iftar time, when people pray and break their fast, music was played on loudspeakers that disrupted their prayers.

On 26 June 2015, Salman went to park Bobby's tempo at his house in Sriram Colony, a Muslim-majority area in Karawal Nagar. When he was done, one of Bobby's neighbours yelled at him for parking the tempo in a way that it occupied half of the front of the neighbour's house.

'I will move it first thing in the morning,' Bobby said.

'But this has become a daily affair,' said Mahinder, the neighbour.

The argument escalated. Within ten minutes, several RSS members landed to confront Bobby.

Soon enough, the police arrived and picked up Bobby, his brother Sunny, and Salman. Mahinder recollects, 'I did not call the RSS people or the police. We could have settled it on our own.' It was a quarrel between neighbours but it was turned into a Hindu–Muslim issue.

Within a few years, Bobby had graduated from being a bike mechanic to a bike repair shop owner and now a transport operator. He was influential. Looked up to by the local Muslim boys as an inspiration, Bobby was happy taking many like Shazeb under his wing.

Bobby, Sunny and Salman were let go the same evening. The charges were never made clear, and no FIR was filed. His detention was just a message.

Bobby's detention over such a small quarrel was instrumental in creating an atmosphere of distrust among Hindus and Muslims in the neighbourhood. If Bobby could be mistreated, anyone could be.

In the next few days, an RSS *shakha*, with some eighty volunteers, including Prabhu, Virender, Golu, Pillu and Tinnu, was held in a nearby local park, with police presence.

This further vitiated the atmosphere and created a curfew-like situation. HKRF members even beat up some children found playing gully cricket in the park during the *shakha*. Many people stopped sending their children to school out of fear for a few days. The atmosphere was tense.

The local RSS leaders announced that they would hold an *ekatrikaran shakha*, a consolidation meeting, in the public park of Sriram Colony the following week. They aimed to get over 1,000 volunteers from all over Delhi.

There were hardly any parks in the unplanned Karawal Nagar. This park was used by the local community for recreation and multiple events: weddings, birthdays and any such event that required large gatherings. During Dussehra festival, people staged a Ramlila and burned demon king Ravan's effigy there. During Ramzan and Eid, the local people prayed at the park.

The dates announced by them, 17–19 July 2015, clashed with Eid-ul-Fitr. This move by RSS members was seen as a deliberate, provocative attempt to take over the public park. They had already refused to remove the stage from the previous year's Ramlila.

Anil Trivedi, the local RSS leader and a BJP member, claimed that the Muslims had occupied the park since they had started offering namaz there in 2001. Trivedi had contested the assembly elections from Karawal Nagar at the beginning of 2015 and lost to Kapil Mishra from the then new Aam Aadmi Party (AAP).

Trivedi claimed that the Muslims were trying to grab land.

Since the late 1980s, Hindutva, political Hinduism, has consistently pushed the discourse of and shone the spotlight on Muslim invasion and the destruction of Hindu temples. Trivedi declared that the local Muslims wanted to convert the Ramlila ground into an Eidgah, a prayer ground for Eid. 'Tomorrow, they will say we will do the same with the Kashi Vishwanath temple,' he said.

Mohd Azam, the imam of the Qadri mosque, ran hither and thither, seeking permission from various authorities for people to offer namaz in the park.

Trivedi said, 'This is not Pakistan that they can drive us out of here.'

Even the mahant of the Hanuman temple, Swami Raghavendra ji Maharaj, jumped in to say that the root cause of the problem was that the Muslims of the area wanted to maintain their dominance over the Hindus.

The *ekatrikaran shakha* was held in the morning on Eid, and members dispersed soon after. The namaz was later held under police protection. Syeda was reminded of a similar Eid in 1992 at the Gyanvapi mosque after the demolition of the Babri Mosque.

It was clear to Syeda and many other Muslims that '*Modi aa gaya*'. Modi has come.

In December 2015, Kailash Chaudhary, a cardboard recycling factory owner, set up Hanuman Udyog, a factory that made cow urine products, in his basement in Karawal Nagar. It was also a wholesale shop to buy cow urine and supply it to the refineries.

Many women were hired at the factory. Syeda got a job at Rs 7,500 monthly, working from 8 a.m. to 7 p.m.

Some Hindus believe that cow urine's therapeutic qualities have been mentioned in the Vedas. Since the Modi government came to power, there had been a revival of both cow worship and cow urine and cow dung products. Endorsements from government officials and organized campaigns by Hindu supremacist groups ushered in a new market for cow urine products.

In March 2015, Maneka Gandhi, the then Union minister for women and child development, proposed that Gaunyle, a floor cleaner prepared using cow urine, should be used in all government offices instead of phenyl.

The Sangh Parivar set up a Gau Vigyan Anusandhan Kendra (cow science research centre) near Nagpur and brought out a booklet listing the diseases that cow dung and cow urine can cure. This booklet was widely circulated on WhatsApp. The institute claimed that cow urine could be used in electronic watches and calculators. They even developed a soft drink formula using cow urine.

There was a sudden demand for good-quality cow urine everywhere. Pandits started mandating cow urine in Hindu rituals and wedding ceremonies. It was prescribed to organic farmers as an alternative to pesticides. Ayurvedic doctors began prescribing it to cure skin diseases, asthma, jaundice, anaemia, arthritis, etc. It was also recommended for simpler conditions. 'Administration of 2–4 drops of gau mutra in the nostrils or its consumption twice a day is beneficial for cold,' read one WhatsApp forward.

Many dairy owners in Karawal Nagar sought to supplement their income by selling cow urine and not just cow milk. A litre of cow milk fetched between Rs 22 and Rs 25, but cow urine could be sold for up to Rs 30 per litre. A pregnant cow's urine was considered to contain special hormones and minerals and could bring in up to Rs 230 per litre.

Mahesh tasked Golu, Tinnu and Pillu to take turns staying up at night and ensuring that the cows' urine did not fall on the ground. They had to put a bucket close to the cow to collect it. Sometimes, the cow would move, and they would get sprayed. At other times the cow would pee and poo at the same time. Mahesh would say it was a good omen to get purified by both simultaneously. 'Cow is your mother, so you should have no problem staying awake for her,' he told them.

All three boys detested this work. They knew very well that Mahesh was saying all this only so that the work would get done and he could continue to make money.

At the factory, Syeda had been initially tasked with measuring the cow urine and storing it in jerrycans. The jerrycans were then supplied to several places that manufactured cosmetics.

As a child, Syeda used cow dung to make patties for fuel. In their clay house in Banaras they used a mixture of cow dung and mud to layer the floor. She was not averse to working with cow dung but cow urine was a challenge. The peculiar stench would overwhelm her senses in the claustrophobic basement. 'I would end up not eating or drinking anything for those hours,' she says.

At the factory, they also made various cow urine products. They had to mix herbs, adhesive and cow dung to make dehydrated incense sticks, which were packaged as Nandini Dhoop Sticks. Posters of a white cow adorned with gold ornaments were stuck on cardboard boxes from Kailash's cardboard factory, and then cellophane was wrapped over them.

Some other factories made soap with aloe vera, almond oil and cow urine; skin cream with distilled cow urine and yellow beeswax. They also made a liquid bath soap with cow urine essence and other herbs.

Additionally, cow urine capsules were being sold as laxatives in the market.

In this period, the government announced several projects for scientists to study how cow urine could be used in things as varied as shampoo and cancer drugs.

Several scientists, rationalists and medical practitioners made public statements about the dangers of using various treatments without much scientific study and research. But the political atmosphere did not allow the questioning of any of these products. This was also the year when rationalists like Govind Pansare and M.M. Kalburgi were shot dead by fanatic Hindus.

It was in this factory that Syeda kept bumping into the Bainsla family. Word reached Virender and Prabhu, through Golu, that Muslim women were making cow urine impure and announcements were made forbidding their employment in such factories.

Kailash employed many women of various faiths. He did not fire anyone, because they were skilled and were working for cheap wages. To avoid further confrontation, Syeda and other Muslim women were asked not to leave the factory during work hours so chances of them being spotted were minimized.

The business continued for over a year and a half. Everyone made more money than usual, including Syeda.

༄

Chahiye naan ya roti
Chahiye raan ya boti
Mangaa lo Ram kasam kasht ho jaaye,
Thodi biryani bukhari,
Thodi phir nalli nihari,
Le aao aaj dharam bhrasht ho jaye ...

Want naan or roti,
Want raan ya boti,
Order it, swear on Ram, let it cause trouble,
Some biryani bukhari,
Some nalli nihari,
Bring it on, let us today violate religion ...

– Song from *Bajrangi Bhaijaan* (2015)

In 2014, during the general election campaign, Modi had said that he feared a 'pink revolution', referring to an expansion of the meat export industry. Cows are considered holy in Hinduism. Consumption of beef in some Indian states is prohibited. The BJP promised to cut off subsidies to those export houses that slaughtered cows. This was meant to target Muslims even though, in fact, people across religions are engaged in the meat business in the country. India is, in fact, among the top meat exporting countries in the world.

Within a year of the Modi government, over 200 cow protection groups became operational in north India.

Like many other Hindu women protection groups, Virender and Prabhu's HKRF, morphed into the Gau Raksha Front (GRF), a cow protection group, overnight.

There is a peculiar interchangeability between cows and women for Hindu supremacists. In 2006, Babu Bajrangi, then a prime accused in the 2002 Gujarat riots' Naroda Patiya massacre case, issued a pamphlet on behalf of his trust, Navchetan. It stated, 'If you rescue one girl, it is the same as saving 100 cows. One daughter equals 100 holy cows.' Virender had given his volunteer troops the same conversion rate when they were hunting for Babli and Shazeb.

Temples had mushroomed all over the Karawal Nagar assembly constituency by 2015. The Hanuman temple in Dayalpur was used as the gathering point for GRF activists. Within a 2 kilometre radius, there were clustered a Kali temple, a Durga temple, a Hanuman temple, three Shiv temples including Lal temple and Panchal Shiv temple, a Shyam Bihari temple, a Satya Kabir temple, a Ganesh temple.

The existing network of informers of the HKRF now served the GRF. They were told to sound the alert 'when someone does anything to a cow'. They additionally built another network on highways – the helmet sellers, the coconut water sellers, the soft toy sellers, and even the local ice cream vendor – to tell them about the movement of suspicious trucks and tempos carrying cattle on the highways, particularly on Delhi's Ghazipur border that connected it to UP's Ghaziabad district.

The GRF grew in numbers. The Gujjar community, which ran illegal dairies, was particularly keen to secure political patronage to safeguard its business interests. Mahesh had already pledged Golu's, Pillu's and Tinnu's participation in all Hindutva activists.

Like all such groups, the GRF was strategic. They kept a public distance from the BJP, claimed no association and even threatened to protest against the party if they did not bring a national law against cow slaughter.

Mahesh had bought smartphones for all three Bainsla cousins to bribe them out of their reluctance to spend nights with the GRF and then collect cow urine in the wee hours of the morning. The GRF work was obviously more exciting than the latter.

Babli's brother Pillu was designated the GRF's official videographer. He learned how to edit videos quickly on the phone, adding a racy cow bhajan in the background and cute cow-mother-with-calf pictures in cutaways.

Within minutes, he would start circulating the videos in several WhatsApp groups they had painstakingly created after collecting phone numbers from local mobile shops. They also collaborated with various Sangh units to upload videos of the cow protection raids on different YouTube channels.

On 28 September 2015, India launched its first space observatory, Astrosat.

The same day, Akhlaq, a fifty-year-old man in Bisara, a village in Dadri in NCR, was lynched to death on suspicion of consuming beef. His family had lived in the town for over seventy years.

An announcement had been made on the local temple loudspeaker that a search was to be conducted in their house. A mob of locals seized some meat from their refrigerator. Akhlaq's family claimed it was mutton. Both Akhlaq and his son Danish were hit with bricks, and stabbed. When the police arrived an hour later, Akhlaq was dead, and Danish was severely injured.

After Akhlaq's murder, BJP leader Raja Singh posted on Twitter claiming that the Vedas mandated killing people who slaughter cows, which was found to be untrue.

Akhlaq's lynching was the beginning of the wave of hate crimes against Muslims.

Tinnu and Golu would accompany other young GRF members to the Ghazipur border. They would get on Virender's bike, accompany police patrols on highways at night, and call the other members when they saw a suspicious truck.

Prabhu and Virender would later lead a separate mob to the spot. Armed with sticks, rods and guns, they stopped lorries carrying cattle, extorted money from passengers, and assaulted them on suspicion of cattle smuggling.

They operated on the inherent assumption that if cows were being transported by Muslims, they were breaking the law.

In some places, the assaults resulted in deaths.

There was an incentive to do this. Some BJP leaders felicitated members of mobs who led such hate attacks. The accused in Akhlaq's lynching were even felicitated later in Yogi Adityanath's election campaign in 2017. Participating in hate mobs for all young members of Sangh outfits could be a shortcut to fame and position.

Bobby had been on the HKRF's, and now the GRF's, radar all this time. 'People like him earn money here and then support the Taliban and the ISIS,' said Prabhu. 'They are the most dangerous,' he added. Hindu supremacists tend to accuse all Indian Muslims of aiding Islamic terrorism but they term their own terror-wielding activities as nation building.

The Rashtriya Muslim Manch (RMM) was formed in 2002 by the RSS to open dialogue with Muslims. The RMM is often seen as espousing the RSS's political Hindutva and lending support to BJP election campaigns, insisting that the RSS and the BJP are friends of Muslims. The Gau Raksha Prakostha was formed by the RMM to 'educate Muslims' and 'spread the message of cow protection'. The volunteers of this cow cell moved around to tell Muslims that 'Islam doesn't allow cow slaughter'. Sudershan Lal, the school principal from Dayalpur, had become the chief patron of the RMM in the area.

Many RMM members, with the help of Sudershan Lal, tried to convince Bobby to stop transporting cattle in his tempos. Lal even tried to use his influence as Bobby's former teacher.

Bobby told them that he merely ran a transport business, not a slaughter business. He had many employees, and to pay them, he transported anything that was paid for and legal: cattle, luggage, raw material for the factories in Karawal Nagar, anything.

In February 2016, Bobby got a special order to transport aluminium wires from Palwal district of Haryana to Loni in UP.

The state of Haryana by then provided official government accreditation to members of Hindu supremacist groups as 'cow protection officers'. As a result, several cow protection groups and officers had been stationed on major highways including the ones Bobby was going to be travelling on.

The GRF worked in coordination with Haryana's cow protection officers and other cow protection groups. Pictures of trucks and their locations were shared in real time on their WhatsApp groups for monitoring.

It was late at night, and the winter fog meant visibility was low. Bobby was driving the tempo, and Sunny and another employee, Raja, accompanied him. They were stopped at a checkpoint within Palwal.

'The police stood on the side while the mob attacked the vehicle with rods and batons,' recalls Sunny.

The mob didn't check that the tempo had no cattle. They were focused on Sunny's skullcap and Bobby's beard. They gripped Raja and made him say *'Jai Shri Ram'* repeatedly. Victory to Lord Ram.

The police stopped the attack after about twenty minutes. By then, Bobby had a head wound and Sunny had a broken limb. After the police inspected and found no cattle in the tempo, they asked the three men to leave. 'They did not even stop the *gau rakshak* from fleeing,' says Sunny.

This was the starting point of cow protection raids all over the country moving from targeting Muslims with cattle to attacking any Muslim person showing a marker of their religion – a skullcap, a beard or a burqa – in public spaces.

The next day, a carcass of a dead cow was thrown outside Bobby's garage. Salman had stayed back at the garage that night. Members of the GRF came to the spot. Pillu made a video that was circulated all over WhatsApp. Then they submitted a police complaint at the Dayalpur police station against Bobby, Salman and others for cattle smuggling and slaughter. Of course Pillu and Golu had their own bone to pick with Bobby and Salman.

Bobby paid off the cops to not file an FIR based on the police complaint. The head constable told him how his tempo had been tracked by the GRF and the cow protection group in Palwal was alerted to orchestrate the attack.

Three months later, in May 2016, Bobby left to work in Kuwait after wrapping up his business. Sunny and family followed him a year later. They now run a garment wholesale shop there. 'We were done. There was no space for us to live peacefully,' he says.

Several young Muslim men like Salman were on their own now.

Khoon mein tere mitti,
Mitti mein tera khoon,
Upar Allah neeche dharti,
Beech mein tera junoon,
Aye Sultan . . .

Your blood embodies the earth
Earth embodies your blood
Allah is above, the earth is below
In between is your obsession,
Aye Sultan . . .

– Song from *Sultan*, starring Salman Khan (2016)

Salman would not miss a namaz. In the three months since Bobby's departure, namaz five times a day was his only constant. Sitting idle in the Chand Baba shrine or cleaning different mosques, he would sometimes eat at the mosques; his only companions were the old imams of these various mosques.

Reshma was irritated at him for objecting to her stepping out of the house without a dupatta. Akmal was frustrated at his lectures on why alcohol was harmful. Syeda was annoyed because he just did not try to make a living.

On 1 July 2016, the day of Alvida Jumma, celebrated on the last Friday of Ramzan, Salman got ready to go to the under-construction Bismillah mosque to offer special prayers.

He bathed and put on new clothes: kurta pyjama and a skullcap. After prayers, he had to help the mosque committee distribute food and clothes to the poor and needy, as is the practice on Alvida Jumma. After that, he was supposed to meet Akmal at the Allah Wali mosque in Bhagat Singh Colony of Karawal Nagar.

There was a huge gathering. Alvida Jumma is considered the second holiest day during Ramzan.

As Salman leaned down to touch his forehead to the ground, one of the mosque domes collapsed, falling on him and two other men praying next to him.

Gumbad gir gaya! The dome has fallen.

Once again.

Syeda and Akmal rushed him to Guru Tegh Bahadur Hospital. His neck was broken.

He lay paralysed in the hospital. The mosque committee paid for his treatment. Syeda and Akmal were shaken to the core. They spent the next eight days in the hospital corridor. There was nothing anyone could do for him. He died on 9 July 2016, and was buried within a few hours. The mosque committee did not want to delay the funeral. Shazeb did not take the risk of attending. No one from Akmal or Syeda's family back home made it either.

The mosque committee gave Syeda's family Rs 25,000 as compensation. Akmal's and Syeda did not ask for any action against the mosque administration, nor was any inquiry initiated into how the dome had fallen.

The other two men survived. One had a broken leg, which healed in a month. The other had a head injury. He lived but lost his mental faculties. He could not do anything on his own.

Salman's death affected Syeda and Akmal in different ways. Syeda seemed to have lost some of her purpose. His existence had provided a structure to her days: what to cook, when to sleep, as she sat worrying till he came home in the evenings. She took to tobacco to numb her pain: first with a beedi, and when she couldn't tolerate it, switching to *gutka*, a tobacco mixture, which seemed to take her mind off all thoughts of her second-born who was no longer alive.

Akmal aged ten years in four months. He felt as though he no longer had strength in his body to pull the rickshaw, and so he tried to medicate himself with alcohol.

The house felt empty, hushed.

*

Four months after Salman's death, on 8 November 2016, the Indian government announced the demonetization of all Rs 500 and Rs 1,000 banknotes. Prime Minister Narendra Modi claimed this would 'curtail the shadow economy and reduce the use of illicit and counterfeit cash to fund illegal activity and terrorism'.

The step was a nightmare for the informal economy, the backbone of Karawal Nagar. The factories of Karawal Nagar, which were primarily cash driven, were heavily affected. The entire supply chain of home-based work operated on cash: exporters, wholesalers, distributors, retailers, contractors, subcontractors and home-based workers. With the shortage of cash, there was a huge fall in demand. Everyone involved in the informal economy was badly hit. All the cash had to be deposited in banks. A lot of it was unaccounted. There were strict guidelines for withdrawal and payment methods.

Many factory owners disposed of their cash by clearing pending payments to the workers. Many of the workers did not have bank accounts. Their only savings in cash needed to be deposited in a bank to enable them to exchange the notes. Many people waited in line for days, losing work, to get bank accounts opened, but the banks could not deal with the crowds. As a result, many were still roaming around with unexchanged notes.

Even though the move was projected as a crackdown on black money hoarded by the rich, the poor were the most affected.

Since many of the small factories operated on slim margins, they could not handle the increase in raw material rates. Now, raw materials had to be bought from large establishments, which provided a taxable invoice with every purchase, instead of the small businesses, which were unregistered and so did not charge tax.

Work was just not available.

On 20 November 2016, the Supreme Court of India ordered Indian cinema halls to play the national anthem before film screenings to encourage patriotism.

The garment industry was severely affected. It was the wedding and festival season, but cash-strapped people now had to spend whatever little money they had on essential items instead of non-essentials like new clothes. Syeda managed to get some garments-related work in those days, trimming threads and doing embroidery. But, grief-stricken by the death of her son, she could hardly concentrate and finish the work on time.

Similarly, work plummeted for home-based workers who worked on non-essential goods like stationery, imitation jewellery, festival decorations and hardware material.

Manufacturing units and shops responded to the increase in material costs by extracting them from the piece rates of home-based workers. Their income halved. People were desperate for work, no matter how low-paid or poorly paid. This increased the number of workers, and piece rates decreased further.

Women started queuing outside Parshuram's house at 6 a.m. to pick up bindi materials. The quantity of the material was so small that their work would be completed within two days instead of a week.

Rani could not pay school tuition fees for her daughter for three months and eventually the girl had to drop out.

Shalu was pregnant but had to deliver the baby at home since there was no money to go to the hospital. Radiowali and others assisted her.

Khushboo started looking for a job as a domestic worker in the neighbouring houses.

Lalita's son Raj Bahadur ran away from home because he was not given his daily pocket money of Rs 20. He was found two days later.

Almost everyone cut expenditures and consumption of food. There was little scope to buy protein or fat: dal, meat, milk, ghee. Only a few drops of edible oil were sprinkled over children's meals. People started tempering in water for potato curry that was eaten with rice and roti. To save fuel, the same food was eaten three times a day.

There was no cash to pay rent. Some workers were pushed out by landlords and went back to the village, such as the seasonal migrant workers at Mahesh Bainsla's house.

Since no one had work, they sat unemployed the whole day. Suddenly, they did not know what to do with their time. At Radiowali's place, there were long group therapy sessions: essentially chit-chatting, sleeping or just sitting in the company of friends.

The decrease in demand led to layoffs, so Akmal lost his rickshaw driving job at the plastics factory.

Syeda and Akmal had not bothered to open a bank account all these years. Out of the compensation money from the mosque, Syeda managed to pay off the loan she had taken from Parshuram in 2015 for Salman's treatment for the injuries sustained at his construction job. The rest of the 15,000, and the Rs 6,000 Salman had left behind in notes of Rs 100 in a small box, helped them stay afloat for almost three months.

'People were forced to beg. But we managed quite well because of Salman,' she recalls.

Since there was a limit on the old notes a single bank account holder could exchange, many business owners paid workers to get their share of cash exchanged. They had to stand in bank queues, deposit the old notes from the factory owners in their bank accounts, and withdraw new currency – to return after taking a cut.

Reshma was the only one in the family with a bank account because of her monthly scholarship from the Delhi government. She charged 20 per cent commission from the factory owners, making a total of Rs 10,000 that month, more than Syeda, Akmal, Shazeb or Salman made in their day in Karawal Nagar.

She took charge.

8

Tricolour

Tanne charon khane chitt kar degi
Tere purje fit kar degi
Dat kar degi tere daanv se badh ke
Pench palat kar degi
Chitt kar degi, chitt kar degi
Aisi dhaakad hai . . .

She'll overthrow you, throw you on your back,
She'll assemble all the parts,
She'll give back hard,
She'll answer your moves with even better moves,
She'll overthrow you . . .
She is a strong one . . .

– Song from *Dangal* (2016)

'*Imaandaar ho tum?*' Are you honest?

Reshma did not expect this question in a job interview. It was 10 January 2017.

Nervous, with no suitable response, Reshma handed out her biodata and marksheet to Shyam Tiwari, a stout, forty-something man.

'This is okay, but it does not answer my question,' he replied in a hoarse, authoritative voice as he flipped through the A4 sheets handed to him by Reshma.

Reshma was twenty-two but looked younger. Petite like Syeda but with fiery eyes. Her small face was made of steel. Its glow made it hard to penetrate, to read her thoughts. Once in a while, her razor-sharp tongue would let you know how she felt.

In that sense, she could be honest. But that was not the honesty Tiwari was inquiring about.

In these twenty-two years, she had experienced the world in myriad ways. She had gained emotional maturity much before her time. She honestly thought her mother was heroic in her struggles but also the worst epitome of victimhood. She thought of Syeda somewhat as what Syeda thought of Mehreen: efficient but not much of a mother, less of a nurturer.

Syeda ensured the daily survival of her family but had lost her ability to show warmth, affection, appreciation and encouragement. Syeda made no space for Reshma to be vulnerable, to be herself. In the last three decades, for Syeda, the world had started revolving around her.

'Ammi, I fell from the bicycle. I scraped my knee. It's bleeding!'

'Did you not think what this will do to me?' Syeda would reply.

This had hardened Reshma. Unlike her brothers, she rarely expressed excitement, admiration, joy or pain.

She didn't want to become like her mother, haggard and irritable all the time, caring for the indulged, callous men in her life. She resented the family package she had inherited. People who now only thought of surviving the present day. They didn't care to shape their future or have a vision of it. If they had ever had one, it was long lost. Like many young people, Reshma didn't want to be like that.

Unlike her UPwali 'Banarasi' mother, she was a proud Dilliwali and confident that she couldn't be taken for a ride. She was happy to help in a crisis but was usually protective about her time. When Sanawur Rehman, Salma's landlord, who owned the house where Shazeb had met Babli in the courtyard, asked her to do accounts, she charged him Rs 100 for the day. When Nabi Ahmed, the namkeen factory owner from Sabhapur, asked her to count namkeen packets, eight-year-old Reshma asked for Rs 10 for the job.

Syeda found this embarrassing, but Reshma knew how to neatly administer cocktails of pleasantries and assertion to get her way.

She was also sincere about doing the jobs assigned to her as well as possible.

Reshma's Delhi accent and manner of speaking, which her mother detested, came to her instinctively. '*Tu kar le*' instead of '*Aap kar lijiye*'. Brevity with syllables and familiarity. She would rather intimidate than be taken for granted for her politeness.

Since she was a teenager, she had insisted on wearing jeans, a T-shirt and a stole, instead of a salwar kameez, as worn by her cousins in Banaras. They were all married off when they hit eighteen. Her mamus, her mother's brothers, didn't want them to 'get out of hand'.

Reshma would say aloud that she loved Delhi, many times, just to provoke Syeda. Most migrant families are expected to continue loving their 'homeland' out of nostalgia and guilt. She detested UP the few times they had made visits to the state. Banaras and Chandauli were the only two other cities she had been to in her life. When she went there, she got 'the feeling that someone is wringing your neck' – she would enact her words in front of her mother.

Syeda had warned her to stop rolling her eyes when Salman or her other relatives spoke piously: *Women shouldn't work*; *Wear a hijab*; *Don't talk to boys*; *Jean pant is immodest*. She couldn't bear such 'rustic talk'.

Reshma had always been Syeda's proxy at work.

The garlands are not ready to be delivered in the morning. 'Reshma, don't go to school if they don't get done!'

The crayons are not packaged. They need to be delivered in the morning. 'Reshma, do this first, and then the homework.'

Dinner is not ready. 'Reshma, cook the dinner. You have studied enough for the exam.'

Fifteen kilos of almond kernels have still not been shelled and packaged. 'Reshma, skip school today, do this.'

Not once were her wayward brothers asked to do these things. One was too busy in his *aashiqui*, romance, and the other could not spare time from his *maar-pitai*, getting beaten up.

Yet, they were rewarded. While Syeda and Akmal's sons were bought birthday cakes year after year, not once did Reshma get the same celebration. Daughters didn't need to be pleased, or even expect it.

With the men, Syeda had a filter, sometimes at least. With Reshma, her criticism was uninhibited.

'Ammi, I finished making twelve dozen garlands in half a day!'

'She makes money, not garlands,' Syeda responded. As if Syeda made garlands out of love for the work, Reshma thought.

Reshma was the only one in the family to complete higher secondary education. But Syeda was cruel in her lack of acknowledgement and dismissiveness: 'Got third division and behaves like a governor.'

Reshma would tell herself, 'So what if it is the third division? At least I finished school without help, encouragement, resources and time!'

Reshma began to think that her mother was jealous of her for articulating what she wanted and didn't, for choosing and curating a life for herself – which Syeda never got a chance to do.

But the truth was, the only person Syeda depended on, in her heart, was Reshma. She believed that no matter what, Reshma would stand rock solid by her and resolve any crisis. She was not a quitter. But Syeda's heart was never big or brave enough to acknowledge openly, or even to herself, that her daughter was wiser, more capable and more determined than any of the men in her life.

While Syeda's acknowledgement of Reshma's Class 12 results was lacklustre, Radiowali warmly congratulated her on the achievement. Reshma pined for a mother like Radiowali, who was proud of her. She was also a daughter like Radiowali, doing everything she could for her parents. But Syeda was focused on seeking validation from her entitled sons or lamenting their absence from her life, without an iota of acknowledgement for her daughter's caregiving.

Reshma saw her brothers as an extension of Syeda. Calculating, full of themselves, role-playing 'heroes'. Shazeb never stood up for her like he did for Babli. Salman never cared for anyone in the family but Syeda.

Akmal's role in the lives of the children was to play the bad example.

Study – or do you want to waste your life like Abbu?
Abbu cannot do anything right.
You want to live off other people's money like Abbu?

You want to land up in jail like Abbu?

But even as a bad example, Reshma found more solace in his company than Syeda's, who emanated anxious energy wherever she sat. Akmal would cook and ask the children to sit and eat. He would even serve them a second helping before they asked for one. He would let them be, which Reshma had started valuing more than being provided for.

Unlike Shazeb, Reshma did not cover up Syeda's occasional unscrupulousness or lies.

Kashif, Syeda's brother and other relatives, visited them three months after Salman died. Syeda once again made up a story about Akmal taking good care of them as the primary breadwinner of the house.

Reshma could not take it and yelled, 'Why do you keep lying?'

She turned to them and said, 'Since we came to Delhi, it is mostly Ammi who has been providing for us, not Abbu.'

And then she added what no woman must say, 'And now that Shazeb has eloped and Salman has died, I run the house.'

It was true. But Syeda responded to her honesty with a slap in front of their relatives. It stabbed Syeda's ego to accept that she and Akmal were now dependent on their daughter. Even though she leaned on Reshma all the time, she could not acknowledge her value.

Syeda didn't find her pretty. She would often call her '*Kallo Mai*'. Dark maid.

She also found her demeanour very unladylike.

Now, Syeda and Akmal were the monkeys on Reshma's back. She had a strange mix of revulsion and pity for them. It prevented her from deserting them like Shazeb or Salman, by eloping or dying. Even though she strongly desired both at times. She decided to carry them. But on her own terms.

ℰ

On the interview day, Tiwari's questions firmed up her resolve to be, above all, honest with herself. She was at the right place and time, and she wanted the job at all costs.

Tiwari had started to get impatient.

Reshma gave a to-the-point answer, 'If you want to know if I will steal, I promise I will not.'

Tiwari was impressed. He had a look at his file and told her, 'There was a job to clean the food court. It has just been filled. But a washroom cleaning job is available. You take that one.'

'Washroom cleaning? But I have done Inter,' replied Reshma.

Inter is the old word for Class 12. Before coming for the interview, Reshma had googled jobs in shopping malls. The vacancies listed mentioned that if you had passed Class 12, you could get a job in the shopping mall, and if you had only passed Class 10, you could get a job as a security guard. She didn't think of washroom cleaner as a 'mall job' at all.

'People who have done BA also do cleaning jobs here. When there is another opening, we will move you up,' he said in an authoritative but reassuring manner.

But what would she say at home? They had never been to a mall anyway. Akmal had, but only to the basement with his cart. But cleaning bathrooms?

'Mehtars do this work!' Syeda used to say.

The Mehtar caste is at the lowest rung of the caste system. It is a Scheduled Caste in the Constitution of India. They were traditionally forced to engage in manual scavenging – physically removing human excrement with their hands – and sweeping jobs. Criminal practices like untouchability have long been used to discriminate against them. They continue to live in a separate part of Karawal Nagar. Mostly in *jhuggi jhopri*s, according to Syeda, who even now uses the casteist slur 'Mehtar' for these sanitary workers.

People are still hesitant to have them as next-door neighbours in Karawal Nagar – even the ones who no longer have sanitation jobs.

But this was a mall – not the same thing at all. It had air-conditioned toilets! And Reshma did not have to give details at home at all. She thought she would find a better job once she entered the mall circuit.

Reshma chose to be flexible and took the job offered that day.

Syeda had always looked down upon *cleaning-cooking* work.

She considered domestic work the lowest form of work.

'Cleaning people's dirty utensils, picking up after them, if something breaks then listening to their *rants*, the endless list of things to do and yet the employers are never happy, no weekly offs – a domestic worker has no dignity,' she said. You could be beaten up, assaulted and fired without a salary, and you don't even learn any new skill at the end of the day. Plus the households in Karawal Nagar who could afford a domestic worker paid a pittance for it.

It was *bandhua mazdoori*. Bonded labour.

In these twenty-two years in Delhi, Syeda had faced many spells of unemployment, yet she never took up domestic work, even though it is the most commonly available work for poor women in urban India. But even domestic workers who remain confined in the houses and are paid far less per hour look down upon bathroom cleaners because of the casteist stigma attached to the job.

In India, traditionally, most of this work – cleaning, housekeeping, pantry services and home delivery – has been done by the unorganized sector. In the last two decades, the facility management (FM) industry has started formalizing this kind of work.

It is a fast-growing industry and becoming a significant source of employment. Rapid urbanization and the growth of shopping centres, malls and other large-scale buildings with offices and co-working spaces require fully trained workers to manage these properties.

The guiding principle for EP, the FM company that managed Best City Mall, was 'Managing People & Places to Achieve "Best Value for Money"'.

Most FM supervisors recruit on a regular basis because the turnaround rate for workers is high. These jobs were the most sought after amongst Reshma's friends, classmates and acquaintances her age.

'Who doesn't want a government job, but we don't have the social status to get one. Even when we qualify for lower pay grade jobs, we don't have the money to bribe our way in once we clear the test,' Salma, Reshma's neighbour, often ranted.

Reshma thought that in a mall job, you spend time in an AC space, wear a Western uniform, learn English, learn about big brands, learn etiquette like high-class people, and save money to buy a better phone or whatever you want.

Most importantly, she wanted to spend time in a better environment, away from the one- or two-room dungeons that many like her shared with their families, fetching water, queuing up outside the toilet, fighting for the bare minimum of civic amenities, and listening to the constant cacophony of fights for survival.

The salary for a standard twelve-hour shift was Rs 10,000 per month, far less than the Delhi government minimum rate of Rs 15,500 for an unskilled worker at that time. But that was not an issue for Reshma. She was not given a written contract for the mall job. She was promised the salary in her account, of which Rs 1,000 would be deducted for her gratuity every month. In the first month, she would get nothing: Rs 1,500 would be deducted for the uniform, Rs 1,000 for gratuity, and the remaining would be withheld as a security deposit.

The next evening, when Reshma was about to leave for her first day of training, Syeda stopped her.

'No, it's not a night shift. The training is at night because that's when the mall is empty,' Reshma argued with Syeda, fuming that Shazeb and Salman were never asked these questions or stopped.

Syeda said, 'In that case, I will come with you.'

Reshma had had enough. 'When you said you were going to work in the almond factory at 3 a.m., did we stop you or question you?'

She stormed out.

☙

It was 7 p.m., a chilly winter evening with smog blocking visibility. Delhi doctors had declared a public health emergency. Newspapers reported that Delhi had become the most polluted capital city in the world. The air quality was as bad as smoking fifty cigarettes daily. But Reshma was not bothered by all that. The conversation about pollution in Delhi is what always irritated her. She found it rather elitist.

She put on the flashlight on her phone and walked to the Karawal Nagar bus stop. It took three changes of buses and one and a half hours to reach the Best City Mall, one of the largest malls in Delhi. This part of east Delhi shares a border with the state of UP. It is known for rampant crime: rape, theft, kidnapping.

The mall had been launched in June 2006 with the intent to serve more than 4.5 million urban consumers from the surrounding areas. It was close to the Anand Vihar interstate bus terminal, from which roughly 1,500 buses ply daily, primarily to UP and Uttarakhand. This makes it a hub for all migrant passengers from UP who live in the Trans Yamuna area.

Reshma had seen the mall some years back when they were taking the bus to Chandauli from the Anand Vihar bus terminal.

The mall was visible across the 150-foot wide road: a massive building with shiny reflective glasses, lit at most corners, stretching over a kilometre. She entered the mall from the front and took the escalator to the basement, where she had been asked to come.

Sita, a forty-something trainer, was waiting for the new trainees in a navy blue salwar kameez and lace-up shoes. Reshma had always seen men wear such shoes, but she was happy at the prospect of stepping into them some day.

The average age of mall workers in India is twenty-five. A large proportion of them are women. Reshma noticed that most of them didn't have a gainfully employed husband or father. At least one male member of their family was an alcoholic. FM companies globally attribute their success to the influx into their workforce of women who traditionally receive basic training at home to do this work.

There were fifteen of them in the basement, all of them first-timers. They were made to stand in a queue for inspection. Hands held behind, chin up, legs slightly apart.

Reshma had done this in school. For march-past on Independence Day.

'Standadeeze, Adanshion.' Stand at ease. Attention.

She never understood the 'at ease' part.

Sita roared, 'The first rule of working in the mall. Always use the back door. Customers don't like employees using the front door. The sight is an eyesore.'

Reshma quivered at the thought of involuntarily breaking a rule on the very first day.

It was ten o'clock at night. Most customers had left, except the ones in the restaurants, food court and cinema halls. The new recruits were taken around to be familiarized with the premises.

The mall had a two-level basement parking for over 700 vehicles, and multiple elevators and escalators; employees were prohibited from using any of them except the service lift.

They were tested for their ability to read signs for the exit, washroom, wet floor, food court, basement and lift.

The four floors of the mall had been neatly demarcated into sections for shopping, leisure, food and beverage (F&B), and entertainment. Four multiplex screens ran different movies simultaneously, not unlike the standard 12–3, 3–6, 6–9 and 9–12 timings of a single screen in Indian movie theatres.

Sita had a commanding presence. She told them they were not supposed to access these areas when not at work. 'Once your shift is over, leave the mall premises. Don't hang around to chat and disturb other employees at work,' she said.

There were many spas on the ground floor: Shine Spa, Star Spa, UVin-spa, Moonshine Spa, Smile Spa, Cloud 26 Spa, Spa Life, Day Spa and Spaphoria. Reshma knew of beauty parlours but had never heard of a spa before.

Dolly Balmiki, aged twenty, another new recruit, told her they were massage parlours. She giggled. 'They light candles and give happy endings.' Reshma could not make sense of that either.

Dolly's father had been a street sweeper at the Ghaziabad Municipal Corporation for the past thirty years. He was a permanent employee and earned roughly Rs 20,000 per month.

Her father had made her apply for the contract sweeper job in UP a few months back. In the last decade, many government cleaning jobs have been privatized. In some UP districts, the salary is now as low as Rs 7,000 per month. There have been reports of over 100,000 applications, many applicants with MBA and BTech degrees, for 250 jobs where the literacy requirements are reading and writing abilities of a Class 10 pass.

The mall's FM company preferred not to hire people who had done professional cleaning before because they were likely to be resistant to learning the mall's system.

Dolly did not talk about her family background for the first few months. It was much later that she told Reshma she was happy about getting a job in the mall instead of as a government sweeper. 'Who wants to sweep and clean government buildings or public toilets? People spit, pee, shit anywhere. Is there any point when no one notices?' she said.

Her father would start his day with alcohol. 'He says he can't clean public urinals without getting intoxicated.'

Sita took them to the 'Playzone'. It had trampolines, small rides and a train with panda-shaped carts.

It reminded Reshma of Appu Ghar, the only amusement park she had ever heard of. Located in Pragati Maidan in Delhi, India's first amusement park had been set up in 1984 to mark the 1982 Asian Games. The park closed in 2008 to make way for the Pragati Maidan metro station.

The new Appu Ghar in Gurugram has an exorbitant ticket price of almost Rs 1,500, ensuring that only the wealthy could enter, not everyone – unlike the previous one where the entrance fee had been nominal.

This mall was like Appu Ghar – food and rides – except that people came here primarily to shop in an air-conditioned atmosphere or to sit around pretending to be high class.

'Customers don't like you touching their children. Don't touch their cheeks, pick them up, make them sit on your lap, or take their picture. If you kiss a child, you will be asked to leave immediately. If you love children, love them at home. Not here,' Sita said in one breath.

By now, Reshma was shivering. She had experienced an air conditioned environment only three times before.

The first time was when a McDonald's outlet opened in Shahdara. Everyone was talking about what a cool thing it was to go to McDonald's, and she did not want to be the only one who hadn't been there. She had gone with her classmate. The cheapest burger was the McAloo Tikki burger, which cost Rs 25. A mashed potato and pea cutlet flavoured with Indian spices in a bun, it was far less tasty than the ones available from street vendors, she thought. But it gave the much-needed validation that you are better off than the rest.

She hid it behind the vegetables in the fridge at home and flaunted it in her tiffin box in school the next day. She even saved the wrapper to put around a burger she made for herself at home and took to school.

The other two times she had been in an air-conditioned space were once in a private bank when she had to get a demand draft made and once when she went with Syeda to the office of the pressure cooker factory manager.

But none of her stints in air conditioning were for such an extended duration.

They had had only one ceiling fan at home till three years ago. Then Salman bought a desert cooler, but there was never enough water to fill in the tank to run it for more than half an hour.

According to Delhi Transco, a government-run body, a mall is a power guzzler. The energy it uses daily is enough to light up nearly 2,000 Delhi houses for a day. There were hardly any customers, yet all the lights were on. It was winter, yet the air conditioners were blasting cold air.

But Reshma did not tell anyone she was feeling cold. She had heard from other girls in school that spending time in air conditioning makes your complexion fairer, and she was looking forward to that.

Dolly later told her that the third floor was icy because a *jinniri* named Priya had started living there.

A *jinniri* is a female jinn, a supernatural creature from Islamic mythology. Dolly said jinns and *jinniri*s prefer cold temperatures.

Just a few months back, in September 2016, a seventeen-year-old girl called Priya had jumped from the third floor of the mall and died. She had become friends with a twenty-year-old man on Facebook. After chatting with him for two years and meeting him twice, her parents found out. She could no longer meet him. He was angry at her for avoiding him, and sent her photos to her relatives on WhatsApp. She could not deal with the embarrassment and jumped to her death in the mall. The man was later arrested for abetment of suicide.

Dolly said that Priya, the *jinniri*, now wanted to teach all men a lesson. Reshma was reminded of Begum Samru's ghost, which Radiowali had told her about. She lived without a man. This one died because of one.

⁓

'Grooming, good behaviour and discipline are most important in this job,' said Lajja, the cleaning trainer.

The induction was being held at the training centre in Shahdara. It was equipped with teaching aids and tools for their training.

The new batch was divided into five groups according to their allocated services. First, the housekeepers. Their work included cleaning the premises, maintaining the washrooms, specialized cleaning and facade cleaning. Reshma, Dolly and two other women, around the same age as them, were in this group. The second group was of the office workers. This included pantry workers who were coached about cutlery and other cleaning. Two college students who knew some English were recruited for this. The third group was for property maintenance: plumbers, electricians, carpenters, etc. The fourth was retail support workers: sorting and packing goods, removing magnetic tags, handling customers, etc. Again, college students were hired for this. The fifth group comprised security personnel. Security guards, both men and women, could be armed or unarmed, uniformed or in plain clothes, depending on the facility's needs. There were also trained bouncers for special occasions when celebrities visited and other significant events.

Lajja told them that housekeeping services included everything from dusting to cleaning, scrubbing and polishing floors, cleaning window panels and glass, carpet cleaning, vacuum cleaning, spot cleaning, wall washing and machine cleaning.

FM companies also provide these services to retail shops, supermarkets, department stores, boutique stores, speciality stores, F&B outlets, etc.

'After a few years, many women move inside the shops as saleswomen, etc. That's how you progress and get a promotion. So do your work well if you want to move up,' Lajja said.

She had pictures of the mall, a dirty toilet, clogged drains and overloaded trash bins. She also had a couple of videos demonstrating how to fill a soap dispenser. They had to be filled and nozzles cleaned and checked that they were in working order.

The next video was on how to clean the washbasin, the WC bowl, seat, cover, hinges, underside, rim, tap, jet spray and toilet roll holder.

What is a toilet roll for? Reshma didn't know. 'It is to wipe your bottom,' Lajja said.

'So people don't wash?' Reshma asked. Lajja didn't answer that and moved on. Dolly and Reshma exchanged a look.

There should be no hair, dust, spillages or stains. Everything should be disinfected, paper towels should be fitted neatly, and the air dryers must be clean. There should be no water on the floor; it should be sparkling clean like the rest of the mall. 'If required, mop like we do at home, on your knees,' she added.

She explained the cleaning tools – brushes, mops – and the cleaning chemicals – bathroom cleaner, tile cleaner, WC bowl cleaner and disinfectant. She played a video demoing cleaning techniques and said, 'Learn it by heart!'

After the lunch break, Lajja took a class on grooming. 'No customer wants to see an untidy worker in a mall. They come here to experience the high life, not walk into your mohalla,' they were told.

'Yellow teeth, fuzzy hair, malnourished faces, broken nails. I don't want all that,' she declared.

Lajja listed some daily essentials. It was mandatory to have a bath every day. She added, 'Brush your teeth and apply face cream daily, oil your hair and trim your nails every week, and try not to get burns while cooking. Uniforms should be neat, washed and ironed every day.'

A strict minimal jewellery policy did not allow for any type of flashy or big bracelets, rings, earrings or even watches. Earrings couldn't be dangling ones. Mangalsutras – a necklace worn by some married Hindu women – were to be kept inside the shirt or kurta at all times and could never fall out. Anklets were a strict no-no because they made a sound.

Those with long hair had to always tie it in a bun and cover it with a net for a neat look. Shoes had to be polished at all times.

A strict handwashing schedule had to be followed.

Also, if the name was long or complicated, a modern name had to be chosen in its stead for the identity card. 'No, Dulari Devi or Guddan, please,' she added with disdain. Modern, short, gentrified names were preferred. Identity card had to be worn, at all times, when on duty.

While at work, they couldn't scratch their heads or comb their hair.

When they met the patrons, they were to greet them and smile.

'Show me your smile,' Lajja demanded.

Everyone did.

She told Dolly, 'Don't show your teeth, just smile slightly.'

She told Reshma, 'Buy a light pink lipstick. Your lips are dark.'

Reshma made a mental note. She was thrilled at the thought of telling Syeda that wearing lipstick was a job requirement, and she could not stop her.

Lajja continued with the instructions. Behave so that the customers feel like kings and queens and that you are there to serve them. This will encourage them to keep coming back and feel better about themselves.

'Don't share personal information or your problems: emotions, domestic issues, need for a better job, etc.,' she said. Customers should only see you as a worker. They should feel guilt-free asking for what they want. Their demands should be met at all times without conflict.

Numerous tiny things needed to be done every day. 'But no one should know who did them. Be present but remain invisible,' declared Lajja.

Ameer zaadon se dillee ke mil na ta-maqdoor
Ki ham faqeer hue hain inheen kee daulat se

Maqdoor, don't meet Delhi's rich,
For we have become poor because of their wealth.

– Mir Taqi Mir, eighteenth-century poet

On 22 August 2017, the Supreme Court of India declared instant triple talaq unconstitutional.

Every day, Reshma, like all mall workers, was checked from head to toe by the security at the entrance. They had a register where they would enter all their belongings: earrings, shoes, tiffin box, cash in their purse – everything.

FM companies also regularly tested employees for such proclivities by leaving bait: money, jewellery, purses, shopping bags and even food.

At the exit, they were rechecked to see that their belongings matched the ones they brought in the morning. Tiwari said that was their way of getting rid of dishonest employees.

Theft is the omnipresent undertone, and employees are always seen as potential criminals, the poor ones more than the rest.

Reshma liked cleaning the marble walls and the shiny steel bathroom fittings. At home, she never saw a point in cleaning because it never looked clean.

The first few days were confusing. She would check the toilet each time someone used it. People would leave the WC unflushed, wet the seat with their pee, and leave sanitary pads unwrapped next to the trash bin.

One day, someone got offended by her immediate investigation. She started pacing her checks and waited for the customer to leave the washroom altogether before looking at the cubicle they had used and cleaning it. Some women, only used to Indian-style toilets, would squat on the floor and pee there instead of inside the toilet bowl. One day, the pee flowed from one cubicle into the next. The customer in the other cubicle raised hell.

The cubicles would be wet with the water from the jet spray, which was meant to clean yourself after using the toilet. The water would often not flow into the drain because people's hair would be all over, stuck on the drain cover several times in a day, preventing the water from draining.

Reshma was initially disgusted by the mess people made and left behind them, but then she stopped getting bothered by it. 'Just clean it up because it needs to be done,' she told herself.

Women would often come to the mall only to use the toilet since no public toilets were available. This has been a commonplace practice since malls opened, and it is quite a relief for women who are out and about.

She was fascinated by the women who came to the washrooms and the way they dressed, with their brushes, lip liners, mascara, body shapers, bras that lifted the breasts, sparkle on the cleavage, straight hair that never went out of line, and blue, blonde and red hair streaks.

One day, a middle-aged woman spotted Reshma staring at her. She complained to the supervisor.

'They don't like to be watched. Don't do it,' Rama, her supervisor, warned her.

Rama, in her early thirties, had two schoolgoing children. She had separated from her alcoholic, unemployed husband, who would often accuse her of 'having affairs'. She had worked there for ten years, starting as a cleaner and then moving up to the supervisor's post. She was protective of the other female mall workers. Reshma recalls her telling women workers to support each other.

Another day, Dolly was 'caught' using the toilet by a customer, and they complained.

'They don't want to pee in the same toilet bowl as you. Remember, they have to feel special,' Rama told her.

The cleaners could only use the toilet in the basement and were allowed five minutes for that. Even if their shift was on the fourth floor, their toilet break was five minutes flat. Reshma wondered if there was any rule that mandated the right to adequate bathroom breaks in India.

Customers would send their complaints through email, WhatsApp, tag the mall on social media, or sometimes speak to the customer relations desk on the ground floor. That was the advantage of technology and having an FM service. Customers didn't have to face any embarrassment, discomfort or guilt for being responsible for the firing of a poor worker. They didn't have to know that part.

Reshma and Dolly tried to eat together whenever they could. They got a thirty-minute lunch break. They were allowed to eat in the janitor's room inside the washroom.

There was a canteen for the employees in the mall, but only senior employees were allowed there. If you didn't bring home food, you had to either stay hungry or spend half a day's wages to buy a meal because mall food is that expensive.

Sometimes, they sneaked to the fire exit and ate there.

One day, while Reshma was on her lunch break, a social media influencer clicked pictures of pulled-out tissues, open taps, smudged soap dispensers and overflowing trash bins in the bathroom.

The influencer reviewed Delhi mall toilets as a hook to the Swachh Bharat Abhiyan, or Clean India Mission, a countrywide campaign the Indian government had initiated on Mahatma Gandhi's birth anniversary in 2014. The campaign aims to eliminate open defecation and improve solid waste management in India, but there have been doubts as to its success.

Children tossed things around in malls all the time, and their mothers rarely stopped them. They would unnecessarily squeeze the soap dispensers for the thrill of it, try to put their feet in the washbasin, spill water on the floor, or try to sprinkle water on the hand dryer.

Reshma often observed the behaviour of the women shoppers. At home, they played the role of responsible caregivers and domestic managers. But a visit to the mall was their chance to ignore their screechy children, to not bother about how they misbehaved, touched things and tossed them around. The kids in turn made full use of the opportunity to behave atrociously.

The pictures of the unkempt washroom went viral. The mall's toilet was ranked the lowest among the ten the influencer had reviewed.

Dolly said later, 'Why not review public toilets? Then she will know the situation where the janta urinates! Swachh Bharat is for that, not malls.'

Reshma enjoyed watching TV. But one thing always jumped out at her: all the programmes, advertisements and news were about the wealthy, the mall-going type. Even daily entertainment shows were about the lives of the affluent. Reality shows were full of fashionistas, celebrities and artists.

But then, the rich and the poor no longer coexist. They do not share spaces any more. The Indian poor don't come to a mall. They are not even allowed to, sometimes turned away, because malls want to maintain exclusivity. Reshma wanted to get into this space in her own way.

One day, when Pooja, the security guard, accidentally touched a woman during the security check, she yelled with disgust, 'Don't touch me! How dare you?'

In most parts of Delhi, the rich and the poor may live in the same neighbourhood – but in segregated spaces within that locality. The spaces of the poor are not just invisible to the rich but also have no uninterrupted access to amenities like water, electricity, drainage or toilets that the rich do. No one ever reviews them – the mainstream media or these influencers.

There was a long meeting about the influencer review. The senior management spoke to the team leader, who spoke to the supervisor, who then scolded the cleaners. Reshma quietly apologized. All of them were warned and threatened they would be fired if this was repeated.

※

Dolly lived with her semi-joint family in a one-room house in Balmiki Colony in Ghaziabad.

The house was shared by six people: Dolly, twenty; her brother Rahul, twenty-two; his wife Kiran, nineteen; their one-year-old son Raja; her father Ramesh; and Babloo, her cousin from Hapur, a neighbouring district, who had moved here to look for a job.

Shanti, her mother, had worked as a street sweeper too. Dolly remembers her as a thin woman with a red nose stud. She was dark, with protruding bones, rashes on her fingers, and a constant cough.

With no designated place to dispose of the street trash, workers like her had to set it on fire day after day. The fumes from the volatile matter – leaves, wood, plastic bags and bottles – caused her breathing problems. Continuous exposure to dust, toxins, bacteria, viruses and pollution wrecked her lungs. She was diagnosed with chronic bronchitis and skin disease.

During her ten years of service, Shanti and Ramesh saved up and managed to buy this house. She died when Dolly was eight.

Ghaziabad is the second-largest industrial city in UP. It had been a picnic spot for the Mughal royal family, but those days are long gone. Ghaziabad borders Delhi and is part of the NCR.

With rapid urbanization in the last few decades, morbidity among street sweepers has increased. Most street sweepers have respiratory diseases or eye issues, and regularly suffer accidents, injuries, skin infections, animal bites, etc.

India's annual monsoon season routinely exacerbates the problem, as sweepers must wade through waterlogged streets and unclog the drains.

Dolly's Balmiki community is a Dalit caste believed to be the descendants of sage Valmiki, who wrote the Hindu mythological text, Ramayana. They have traditionally been engaged in sweeping and manual scavenging jobs. They are also referred to as 'bhangi' in a derogatory manner.

Most sweeping and manual scavenging work remains relegated to certain Dalit caste groups. These groups are the pools from which cleaners are drawn, generation after generation. They are subjected to the worst kind of discrimination and untouchability.

The government school teachers where Dolly studied regularly called her 'bhangi' and 'bhangi colony ke bacche', children from the bhangi colony. She remembers not even being allowed to enter the Kesri Mata temple, a Hindu temple in her neighbourhood, because she was from an untouchable community.

Recently, some upper-caste sweepers had been appointed by the Ghaziabad Municipal Corporation (GMC). Her father Ramesh told her they thought cleaning latrines with a toilet brush and picking up trash was against their status. The Dalit sweepers had to do that part of the work.

Laws mandate the provision and use of protective equipment – face masks, goggles, gumboots or gloves – while working but few of these things are provided. Most of these jobs have been privatized, so the workers are afraid to ask. And when they do get some, they are of poor quality.

Dolly's father Ramesh once hurt himself after a rod slipped from his hand because the gloves provided by the corporation were too large and stiff for the nature of his work.

A few years back, the Safari Karamchari Sangh, the union of cleaners, agitated against the GMC for buying substandard soap to wash hands at an exorbitant price. Nothing came of it.

Dolly says, 'No amount of politicians sweeping the roads can create a Swachh Bharat unless the government changes how human solid waste management is done.'

Dolly's brother Rahul became a contract sweeper. When he married Kiran, Dolly was finally relieved of doing all the domestic work.

The house they lived in had been allotted to them, for a price, by the Ghaziabad District Authority as they came under the Economically Weaker Section (EWS) category of the population. Twenty-five years later, they received a notice – and continue to do so every year – from the GMC, asking for immediate repairs because of its dilapidated state. But there was no money to spare. With six members now, the small space was a huge problem.

Even her small one-room house would cost Rs 20 lakh today, even though there was seepage everywhere. So much so that no matter how clean and dry she tried to keep her uniform, it always had a mouldy smell and stains on it. She got several warnings for this until she bought a second uniform the following winter, so she could wash one set at least once a week. Before that, if bathroom cleaner fell on her pants and shoes, she had to wear them all through the day and the rest of the week. Though the uniform did get dirty every day, no matter what.

Mobility was a huge problem. Most women supporting their families did not have a vehicle. Supervisor Rama lamented about her father giving a bike as dowry to her estranged husband, and not her. It would have been of great help to her now.

Ghaziabad's public transport system was not as smooth as Delhi's. Dolly had to walk, take a couple of shared tempos, and then walk some more to the mall. Reporting late for work for two days in a row meant docking of one day's salary.

One day, the tempo guy did not return Dolly's change just to harass her. It was a routine practice to trouble women. With no money to return home, Dolly accepted a few tips from customers by offering extra tissues in the bathroom and pointing them to the most recently cleaned and dried cubicle. The supervisor found out.

In the training, Lajja had told them not to ask for tips and favours from guests.

Dolly said that Priya, the *jinnri*, had asked her to do so to buy a pepper spray and teach the tempo guy a lesson.

As a punishment, she was transferred from Priya's third floor to the basement to clean the bathroom used by the workers.

⁓

On 1 July 2017, the goods and services tax (GST) came into effect. It is a single value-added indirect tax levied throughout the country. It hit the unorganized sector – responsible for 80 per cent job creation in India – the hardest.

Everything that Reshma saw in the mall reminded her of something she or someone she knew had made at some point or another.

The footballs and sports goods reminded her of the World Cup footballs Syeda made, the woven rugs of Syeda's cousin, who was a carpet weaver in Badaun district in UP. The warehouse made her think of her father who plied rickshaws to carry goods, and the lift of Salman's accident.

There were many ethnic clothing stores. Such plain clothes but so expensive, Reshma thought. Syeda could stitch much neater and better fitting clothes than that. Just one hand-embroidered motif and the price of a cotton shirt would escalate by at least Rs 1,000. Syeda was paid Rs 1,000 for an entire embroidered saree.

Reshma liked to read the labels to find out where the clothing was made: Indonesia, Mexico, Sri Lanka, Bangladesh. All of it was identical to what women in Karawal Nagar made for garment contractors.

Weekends at the mall were busy. There were special sales, discounts and offers. Every third or fourth weekend, an emcee was hired to conduct quizzes and programmes on the ground floor for a particular shop or brand. That emcee was always a woman: young, fashionable and wearing Western clothes. Dolly and Reshma were in awe of these women.

'I could do the same, except that I don't know English,' Dolly said.

'There is so much screeching required. I would rather work as a receptionist or a salesgirl,' Reshma said.

Both had decided to save money and join computer and English classes.

One day, there was a big crowd outside McDonald's. It was a kid's birthday party and the nannies accompanying the kids had to wait outside.

Cleaners for FM companies in Delhi are mostly north Indians or north-easterners. Rama said that those from Jharkhand and Chhattisgarh, mostly indigenous areas, were considered too dirty and unfamiliar with the language and so not hired. Many housekeepers, full-time domestic workers and nannies in Delhi NCR are from these regions.

Nannies face a very public kind of exclusion. When families come to eat at the malls, the nanny usually either stands outside, or sometimes plays with the child, as the couple sit inside the restaurant and eat, or is made to sit at a separate table in the food court.

To Reshma, outside McDonald's that day, the nannies looked awkward and out of place. They stood there for almost three hours. No one offered them water, food or cake, even when there was lots of food left on the tables after the party, which was all thrown in the trash. They were fit to raise the children but not to eat with them.

Reshma's shift was in the women's washroom next to the food court that month.

One day, she saw a child lying on the floor and wailing loudly. He wanted a burger. To save themselves from embarrassment, the parents bought him one. The child must have been ten years old. He ate half, left the rest on the tray, and ran to the outlet selling pizza slices for the next tantrum.

After fifteen minutes of pushing his parents around and running around in circles in the middle of the food court, he convinced his parents to buy him a pizza. He ate one out of two slices of pizza while pretending to cry. He finally smiled when his parents bought him an ice cream cone, which he dropped on the floor after licking it a few times.

Reshma regularly observed this pattern. Every celebration of the affluent – the mall visitors in this case – meant food and drinks. It was not restricted to weddings and birthdays, unlike in older times.

The food court had a broad range of cuisines and discount offers. Every weekend, there were attractive schemes: 'Buy three, pay for two', 'Happy hours', 'Ice cream free with the main menu'. This food was often never fully consumed.

Reshma noticed that people tended to order a lot from the menu even if there were just two eaters. 'As if ordering less would affect their honour and respect in society,' said Dolly one day. Hardly any of them would get the leftover food packed. As Dolly said, they found it embarrassing and petty.

During her shift at the washroom near the food court, Reshma befriended Niti, a twenty-three-year-old college student who worked at an Indian food outlet in the mall.

Niti told her about the huge daily food wastage: food left on the plates and unserved food. Items like starters, salad, vegetables, rice and pulao, and chapatis saw more wastage. She said these had a shorter shelf life.

Reports suggest that a Delhi mall generates around 100 kilos of food waste daily from its restaurants and food court. That could roughly feed three meals to fifty people per day. According to Delhi Waste Management Company field supervisors, over 40 per cent of leftover food is thrown in the municipality bins.

Reshma witnessed all of this within a year of demonetization. Even though the Modi government had described the demonetization policy as a 'fight for the poor against the corrupt rich', it had severely impacted the poor in the country – while it seemed to have hardly affected the rich.

Within a year of the demonetization, India slipped three positions to 100 among 119 countries on the Global Hunger Index 2017. This was worse than North Korea, Bangladesh and Iraq, and better only than Pakistan and Afghanistan among Asian countries.

Post-demonetization, home-based workers like Syeda suffered from reduced work, payment in old currency, or non-payment for work done, which meant there was less to spend on food, clothing – and children's education in many households. Reshma had to support her family for almost a year.

But none of that was visible in the mall. Within a few months of demonetization, they were back with cash to shop with and spend in the ways they wanted.

It was December 2017. The festival season: Christmas and the end of the year. The mall decided that, just like in the West, Indian food servers should also break into an impromptu dance, like a flash mob, for the customers – to cheer them up. They rehearsed after work and performed in the evening. No one clapped or paid attention. 'We needed cheering up instead,' recalls Niti.

Apart from serving food, Niti also had to sweep, slice vegetables for the salad, clean the machines and make an inventory for the next day.

One day, when Reshma was helping Niti clean the floor around the food outlet, Rama reminded her of the rule of sticking to one's job, otherwise everyone would be expected to do everything.

⁓

Reshma had to stand all through her twelve-hour shift in the washroom. Once or twice, she was caught sitting on the floor. She was warned not to do this.

Syeda was upset that an exhausted Reshma was not helping her at home to make paper tricolours for the upcoming Republic Day. She complained to whoever was available, 'How can she have pain at such a young age? It is an excuse for not doing housework. She just wants to act superior because she works in a mall.'

All the workers had chronic body and leg pain: Niti at the food court, Dolly on the toilet shift downstairs, Rama the supervisor, and Pooja the security guard. There was no paid medical leave or insurance, and no one could afford to lose even a day's wages. 'We all popped painkillers before our shift started. Everyone had a few tablets in their purse,' reminisces Reshma.

The FM company promised 'Value for money' to its clients. But this optimal cost with maximum efficiency was achieved by squeezing the last second of work from the employees' shift while paying them the bare minimum wage.

During the training, everyone was told clearly to sew their lips shut during their shift. Talking would entail pay cuts.

There was also a code of silence on people's earnings. Rama and Tiwari were both supervisors. While Tiwari was paid Rs 20,000 monthly, Rama was paid Rs 14,000. When Rama asked for equal wages, her team leader, Lajja, told her that if the company made a profit, it would be shared with the workers at the right time.

Demanding better working conditions resulted in job loss. Therefore, Rama was fired two months later for underperformance, a convenient excuse that mostly required no specific explanation.

Rama demanded her gratuity, but she was told the company had lost her form and account details.

Every once in a while, senior managers would come in to inspect the bathrooms. They would prepare long reports on how to clean and how much cleaning liquid to use per task without ever having held a mop or a broom.

One day, the famous singer Mika Singh came to the mall unannounced. Celebrities often visit when a new film or song is released. There was a mob. The mall workers took charge of things: some formed a human chain for the singer's security, and others created a corridor to the fire exit to see him out safely.

Niti kept talking about how useless any of the templates prepared by managers are.

'Managers are paid in lakhs, and we were not even paid Rs 500 per day,' says Dolly.

Reshma's salary remained the same for one and a half years. Pooja, the guard, and many others desperately switched jobs for even a Rs 500 hike in their monthly salaries.

Reshma enrolled for graduation. In July 2018, she decided to learn English and computers to get a job in a 'good company' or at least at a managerial level. She realized if she didn't do this she would remain stuck in the bathroom cleaning–security guard circuit all her life, even if in an air-conditioned mall.

She took two weeks' leave to enrol for a Delhi University distance education course. When she returned to the mall, she had been replaced.

9

Wedding Card

'*Dhukdhuk-dhukdhuk-dhukdhuk,*' Salman shouted, as he shook his arm furiously, pointing a stick at one of the boys as though it was a machine gun.

'Alpha to Charlie, Alpha to Charlie, the rats have entered our area. Over.' He communicated the 'coded' message on a plastic toy phone that was supposed to be a walkie-talkie.

'Charlie to Alpha. Charlie to Alpha. The cat is on its way to devour the rats. Over,' replied Vikram as he emerged from the sugarcane fields and pointed his stick at the same boy.

The boy, with black shoe polish on his face, like the camouflage used by soldiers, pretended to fire back with his stick. '*Dichkyaun-dichkyaun-dichkyaun.*'

More boys appeared from the other side of the sugarcane farm and joined him. They started chasing Vikram and Salman.

Dhukdhukdhuk-dhukdhukdhuk-dhukdhukdhuk.

Dichkyaun-dichkyaun-dichkyaun.

The sound of pretend gunshots pierced the sugarcane fields.

Vikram and Salman ran and climbed to the top of a massive pile of recently cut sugarcane waiting to be loaded on a tractor. Salman took a rubber ball from his pocket and threw it at the boys like a bomb. '*Bhadaaam.*'

Some boys fell to the ground and froze in poses of death. Vikram took out a big plastic pipe he had tucked into his trousers, filled with a bunch of thin arrows he had bought at the Ramlila fair. He sent a hail of arrows towards the other boys. '*Saain. Saain. Saain.*'

The arrows hit the rest of the boys, and they, too, were overcome.

Vikram and Salman shouted in unison as they stood on top of the sugarcane pile, '*Bharat Mata ki jai! Vande Mataram! Jai Hind!*' Victory to Mother India.

The boys got up and joined in. '*Pakistan Murdabad! Hindustan Zindabad!*' Down with Pakistan. Long live India.

Then one of the boys told Vikram, 'Abbe yaar, the army did not kill the Pakistani *ghuspaithiye* with arrows!'

Ghuspaithiye. Intruders.

'It was a rocket launcher, *bhencho!*' Vikram replied, chuffed with his desi invention.

The boys laughed.

Salman added, 'Next time, we will use a real rocket from Diwali. It will end up exactly between your legs!'

'Next time, we will be the Indian army, and you guys will be *ghuspaithiye*,' said one of the boys.

'No!' Both Vikram and Salman were emphatic.

'*Hum toh kisi doosre ki dharti par nazar bhi nahin dalte ... lekin itne nalayak bachche bhi nahin hain ki koi hamari dharti ma par nazar daale aur hum chup chap dekhte rahein,*' said Salman, proudly repeating the Suniel Shetty dialogue from the movie *Border*, released just a year before, in 1998.

We don't even set eyes on someone else's land ... but we are not such useless kids that we will sit quietly if someone eyes our motherland.

'Arre, *Border* was on the 1971 India–Pakistan war, not the Kargil war,' the boy said.

Everyone laughed.

'Whatever, we will not allow *ghuspaithiye* here, nor will we play them,' Salman replied.

This Indo-Pak Kargil war game was well rehearsed, and the boys of Sabhapur played it often.

In May 1999, Pakistani troops disguised as Kashmiri militants had crossed the Line of Control (LOC) between India and Pakistan in Kashmir. They set up base on the Indian side of the LOC in the treacherous high-altitude Kargil district of the then Jammu and Kashmir state.

This happened after the twelfth Lok Sabha had been dissolved. BJP leader Atal Bihari Vajpayee's second term as prime minister had again ended before its full term. The last time, his government had lasted thirteen days; this time, it carried on for thirteen months before it lost a no-confidence motion by one vote in April 1999.

During this war, commonly known as the Kargil war, the BJP remained in charge of the caretaker government. India won the war in July 1999, with the Indian troops eventually taking back control of all the locations captured by the Pakistan army.

Following this victory, fresh elections for the thirteenth Lok Sabha were held in October 1999. The BJP-led National Democratic Alliance, a coalition of twenty political parties, got a majority and formed the government at the Centre.

After the Kargil war, an obsession with identity cards and citizens' lists began. A Kargil review committee was set up that proposed that all citizens in Indian border villages be issued identity cards to keep a check on foreign intruders. A unique identification number for each citizen of India and a centralized database of all Indian citizens were also proposed.

Other commissions were set up to formulate measures to improve national security. Under the chairmanship of L.K. Advani, who was then the deputy prime minister, in 2001, a Group of Ministers (GoM) recommended a 'multi-purpose National Identity Card' for every citizen instead of various cards being used for identity: the income tax-related Permanent Account Number (PAN) card, ration card, driving licence, voter ID card, etc.

This led to the foundation of the Unique Identification Authority of India (UIDAI) and the Aadhaar card project, which was implemented in the following years.

Two years later, in December, Advani introduced the Citizenship Amendment Bill, 2003. It aimed to provide various rights to persons of Indian origin. It included a clause that said, 'The Central Government may compulsorily register every citizen of India and issue a national identity card to him.'

This amendment bill also mandated the Government of India to create and maintain a National Register of Citizens (NRC) and filter out illegal immigrants and their children, for deportation or imprisonment. Since India is not a signatory to the 1951 UN

Refugee Convention and does not have a national policy on refugees, technically, all refugees are considered 'illegal migrants'.

Over the years, many refugees from neighbouring countries have made India their home. Since 1947, many Hindus from both West and East Pakistan regularly moved to India to escape religious persecution. After China invaded Tibet in 1959, lakhs of Tibetans took refuge in India. In Delhi, many lived in Majnu ka Tila, where Shazeb and Babli had taken refuge before leaving for Manali.

After the formation of Bangladesh in 1971, a large number of Hindu and Muslim refugees came to India for a better life. Since many of them moved to the neighbouring Indian state of Assam, it led to decades of resentment, protests and anti-Bangladesh immigrant movements. The creation of a national register of Indian citizens became a popular demand. After Myanmar started committing acts of genocide against Rohingya Muslims in 2016, large numbers of them escaped to India through porous international borders.

Since its first stint at the Centre following the 1996 general elections, the BJP has had 'the detection, deletion and deportation' of illegal migrants on its agenda. It has always made a distinction between Muslim refugees and those of other religions. In its discourse, while the Hindu refugees face religious persecution, the Muslim ones have no valid reason to be in India. Hostility towards them emanates from the Hindutva narrative that Muslims are taking over India and diluting the Hindu majority and thereby threatening a Hindu state.

Bangladeshi Bharat chhodo!
Bangladesh people, quit India!
ABVP ki hai lalkar, ghuspaithiye bhejo seema paar!
ABVP's war cry, intruders must be sent beyond the borders!
The ABVP, or Akhil Bharatiya Vidyarthi Parishad, is a student organization affiliated to the RSS.
Jan-manas ab badla hai, ghuspaith nahin yeh hamla hai!
Demographics are changing; this is not an intrusion but an attack!

These slogans would periodically be painted on Delhi walls by Hindu supremacists, putting every poor Muslim under suspicion of being an 'illegal migrant'.

Syeda had battled the same suspicion when she tried to get the kids admitted to the school in Sabhapur. The school principal, Ratanjot, thought she was Bangladeshi since she did not have adequate identity documents. That was when Sukhbir Gujjar intervened and got them admitted.

Ghazali and his family were not just poor Muslims. They were Bengali, too. Bengal had been divided under British rule in 1905, with West Bengal being predominantly Hindu and East Bengal predominantly Muslim, but significant numbers of each religion were on both sides. It was undone six years later in 1911. East Bengal became East Pakistan in 1947 and then Bangladesh in 1971. Ghazali's family was from South 24 Parganas district in the Indian state of West Bengal, bordering Bangladesh. They lived under the perennial suspicion of being Bangladeshi.

While Hindu supremacists may believe that all Muslims are identical, being from the same religion hardly brought acceptance and assimilation to these Bengali Muslims.

They are dirty. They don't bathe.
They eat raw fish. They don't wash their utensils.
Bengalis only support Bengalis and no one else.

Syeda still believed all these stereotypes about them. She even repeated them first to Shazeb and then to Reshma when she saw Ghazali befriending her children.

Salman, who never liked him, and resented his closeness with Shazeb, started calling him *ghuspaithiya* Ghazali.

Intruder Ghazali.

Reshma modified his name to GG.

⁕

Bataun kya tujhe ai hamnasheen kis se mohabbat hain,
Main jis duniya mein rehta hun vo is duniya ki aurat hain.

How should I tell you who I am in love with, friend,
The world I live in, she is a woman of that world.

– Majaaz Lakhnawi, twentieth-century poet

'Abbe GG, your girlfriend is *bhootiya, saale!*'

GG's friends thought this line from *Stree*, the 2018 Bollywood horror comedy movie, suited Reshma well.

Bhootiya. Ghostly.

Everyone thought that Reshma was GG's girlfriend, except Reshma herself.

Reshma was twenty-four now. Her fiery eyes were made of glass, impenetrable, hard to read. Her tongue had sharpened even further. But unlike in the past, her face had started giving away her feelings, at least when GG was around.

She was in her first year at the Department of Distance and Continuing Education, Delhi University, among the one-third of Indian undergraduates studying for a BA.

Her subjects were political science, history and Hindi. If someone were to ask her how many states there were in India, she wouldn't know. Who was the chief minister of the state of Jharkhand? There would be no answer. Why had she chosen those subjects? Why not BCom or any business-related subject, courses that might have been more familiar to her. Because someone at the admission window had told her that a BA in those subjects is what everyone does. At the time, she could hardly make any sense of the piles of study material she had collected.

She had enrolled for graduate studies because that is the obvious next step for anyone who finishes school. But did it guarantee better chances of getting a job? No. Numerous studies suggest that Indian graduate degrees are worthless. They lack quality and do not make people employable. After her stint at the mall, Reshma was well aware of this. She now knew that what was important was having a job, not the kind of job one had. Choosing what work one did was a luxury her parents had not enjoyed, even when her grandparents had been in the family weaving business, which she had only heard tales of. Yet, she was determined to learn computers because she had convinced herself an office job was not possible without it.

On 31 October 2018, Prime Minister Modi inaugurated the world's tallest statue, the Statue of Unity, in Gujarat.

GG was twenty-eight now. It was 2018. He had filled out a bit in the past four years since Shazeb's departure. He was tall and well turned out, with fitted, ironed clothes over his muscular limbs that were toned by years of hard labour, hair regularly trimmed into a crew cut. The goatee on his face remained. He continued to live in the same slum close to Shiv Vihar in Karawal Nagar while his two elder brothers had moved to the Gandhinagar wholesale market permanently. After Bobby packed up his bike business, GG joined a local car garage. He had graduated from being a bike mechanic to a sought-after car mechanic. Car owners tipped more, and the income was steadier.

His sisters had been married off back in Bengal. His parents had bought a small patch of land in South 24 Parganas. They had moved back after living in Delhi for over two decades. They were still living in a makeshift tent, but this time on their own land. He and his brothers were now saving money for the next thing on the bucket list: to construct a house on that land. Only then could they get married. Since the first two things on the list, getting the girls married and acquiring a bit of land, were checked off the list, GG did buy an old bike and a smartphone of his own. Having never studied beyond primary school, he could only manage basic reading and calculations. Thankfully, he could navigate the smartphone to watch YouTube videos from which he learned how to refurbish old cars for second-hand buyers.

Since both Syeda's eyes – as she called Shazeb and Salman – were gone, she now had to depend on, honestly, her least favourite child, Reshma. This dented Syeda's ego a bit.

Why was Reshma the least favourite? Even Syeda didn't know. She had decided that at some point, even though Reshma ticked the most boxes of being a dutiful child.

With no young men in the family, GG continued to visit them, initially at Shazeb's insistence. Shazeb was torn between the guilt of abandoning them and the need to create his own safe family unit. But later, it was because of Ghazali's own growing attachment to the woman who called him GG.

GG would ferry Syeda's raw materials from the subcontractor and deliver the final products to them. He insisted on dropping Reshma to the metro station on his bike instead of her walking all the way to save money, every time she had to go to Delhi University. He even started taking Akmal to a local drug rehabilitation centre.

When Reshma fought with Syeda, which was often, she would call up GG. And GG would be there in a few minutes. She didn't have to tell him why she was upset.

'You took care of your sisters and got them married. Why could I not have a brother like you?' Reshma said one day. This worried GG: he realized he could be 'bhai-zoned' if he did not say what needed to be said soon.

Bhai-zoned. To be categorized as a brotherly figure instead of a potential romantic partner.

In October 2018, Kerala became the first state to pass the 'Right to Sit' law that mandated shop owners to provide seating arrangements for all workers.

Reshma was determined to take a computer course after quitting her job at the mall and enrolling in distance learning for graduation. Syeda thought it was a waste of time and another excuse for Reshma not to be home. She was hell-bent on getting Reshma to help her prepare her usual per-piece orders. But there was no way Reshma was going back to that life.

That day, when GG picked up Reshma from the metro station, she broke down and cried on the way back, leaning on his shoulder. The memory of the warmth of her tears that penetrated his jacket and touched his skin, the clutch of her hands, kept him awake all night. The next day, he couldn't concentrate while changing oils and lubricants in the car he was servicing. He called her up, and she still sounded sad. This made him even more restless. He couldn't wait to see her and drove straight to her place.

Syeda was sitting outside their room making soft toys. They were now living in a barsati, a big room on the first floor of a house. Syeda preferred barsatis because the terrace came in handy to use as a workspace and keep raw material. The street was visible from the spot where she sat and worked. GG saw her from the street. He called out to Reshma, 'Reshma, that cardboard factory owner is calling you. He has a job for you.'

Reshma came out of the room. Syeda looked at her quizzically. Reshma put on her jacket and walked down. She knew GG was lying but silently hopped on to the bike, and they whizzed off.

He rode the bike to the freshly inaugurated Signature Bridge.

⁕

In 1997, twenty-eight schoolchildren had died after a bus plunged into the Yamuna river from the narrow old Wazirabad bridge. After that, the Delhi government constructed this bridge to connect north east Delhi to the rest of the city and ease traffic. It took fourteen years to build this cable-stayed bridge. It opened in November 2018.

During the fifteen-minute ride, neither of them exchanged words as the crisp November wind touched their faces and bodies, making them move closer to each other on the bike. Halfway across the bridge, GG stopped and asked Reshma to get down. He parked the bike, grabbed her hand and pulled her closer to the railing. Reshma was a bit taken aback. This was the first time he had held her hand, but she did not object.

They both stood there, looking at the Yamuna, lit up by the lights on the shore, with the sound of traffic zipping past them. GG finally mustered the courage to put his arms around her from behind. Reshma broke down once again but did not resist. She held on to his arm as he buried his face in her shoulder. He was tall. She was short. His embrace completely enveloped her. Both of them felt warm yet fuzzy. But again, no words were said. Ten minutes and many deep breaths later, when they both felt calmer, they looked around, noting the young people taking selfies and doing photo shoots on the bridge. Then, they spotted two cranes loading two-wheelers on to a pick-up van and Delhi Traffic Police personnel on patrol bikes. In this first week since its inauguration, the craze for the Signature Bridge was such that it was causing congestion instead of easing traffic.

GG and Reshma ran to their bike when they saw it being loaded on to the pick-up truck. GG knew the drill. He begged the cop to be lenient. The cop replied, 'I am issuing a challan for you. You violated the parking rule, that too to romance a minor!'

'Sir, she is not a minor,' replied GG.

Reshma swiftly pulled out her Aadhaar card to show the cop.

'Rashmi Akmal, wife of Akmal,' the cop read out.

'The ID clearly shows my age is twenty-four,' Reshma pleaded.

'Show me your ID!' The cop took GG's Aadhaar card without acknowledging Reshma's statement.

'Mohd Ghazali! So you are romancing someone else's wife?' he asked GG.

'No. No. I am unmarried. The details on the Aadhaar card are wrong. Also, my name is Reshma, not Rashmi, and I am female, not male. See,' Reshma pointed out.

The situation was surreal but also one that occurred all the time, with some variations. Starting in 2009, ten years after the Kargil review committee's suggestion, most Indians had started using Aadhaar cards as their ID cards in the hope that they would not need any other identity cards to function in India. But it was also well known that most Aadhaar cards had wrong personal information and the most distorted photos ever.

'But who gave you permission to take selfies in the middle of the bridge and block traffic?' the cop asked.

'We didn't take any photos,' Reshma replied.

'Show me your phones,' the cop ordered.

Both of them handed their phones to him. There were no pictures. GG slipped the cop Rs 500, and in exchange, the cop returned their phones and ordered the crane operator to put the bike back on the road.

GG drove Reshma straight to her place. Reshma held his shoulder tight and sat even closer than usual. When they reached Reshma's house, she asked him if they could drive around a bit more. GG didn't say anything, simply accelerated and took off. They drove around till midnight. When they reached home, Syeda was waiting for Reshma on the terrace, furious. Reshma had crossed all limits, according to her. She had called them many times, but neither answered their phone.

As Reshma got off the bike, GG told her he knew where she could learn computers and later get a job. He left.

As Syeda harangued her for her immoral, disobedient and shameful behaviour, Reshma was lost in thought about GG. She didn't even retort that Syeda never questioned her sons when they were out at night. For the first time, Reshma realized that GG always noticed everything she was feeling or going through. He knew even when she didn't tell him. She felt an affinity with him that surpassed anything she felt for anyone. She felt safe, understood and taken care of, special – something she had never experienced in her own family or outside. Was it love? She didn't know. But after having someone like that in her life, she never wanted to be without him.

⁂

Since the 1990s, cybercafes have been places to surf the internet, check emails, apply for jobs, play video games, get printouts and hang out with friends for as little as Rs 10 per hour. Around 2010, cybercafes started going out of business because of the increased use of cheap smartphones and mobile data. Many cybercafes started reinventing themselves as Digital Seva Centres: one-stop shops for all things online.

In 2015, twenty years after the internet became available in India, the Indian government launched the Digital India programme to make its services electronically available to everyone. This was based on the contested idea that internet technology is the country's key mover of economic, social and political change.

Even though many Indians, even in the socio-economically marginalized sections, had been accessing the internet on smartphones for a long time, their online activity remained confined to using Facebook, WhatsApp, YouTube and email, at best. However, the government interpreted this widespread access to the internet as universal digital literacy. Without imparting appropriate skills, the government expected people to do everything online. Online access to government documents helped those who were literate or from privileged classes, but the others were left at the mercy of Digital Seva Centres.

In Karawal Nagar, Buddy Cyber Cafe had now not only become Hare Rama Digital Seva Centre but also started training people in the basic use of computers: managing files and folders, using the internet and common software like MS Word, PowerPoint, Excel, etc. Like Reshma, there were a lot of takers for these courses because everyone believed that learning computers made you more employable than a school certificate or a degree. The monthly fee of Rs 900 was nominal. GG knew the owner, as he serviced his car and used the centre to access the Regional Transport Office (RTO) website to complete sales-related paperwork for his second-hand cars.

In August 2019, Reshma completed her computer course and was hired as a Digital Seva Centre operator at GG's request, of which she was unaware. The owner could meet the request easily because Reshma was an efficient, uncomplaining worker. She was paid Rs 6,000 per month.

Earlier, there used to be some human interface – a person or an office – for making labour cards, ration cards, national pension scheme cards, life insurance policies, caste certificates, farmers' scheme cards and suchlike. Now, the Digital Seva Centre operators do that for people. They pay electricity and water bills; book train tickets; generate marriage, birth and death certificates, income certificates and bank statements; initiate online money transfers, share investments or bank loans; apply for and download a domicile certificate, Ayushman Bharat card and, most importantly, your vital identification papers: Income tax card, Aadhaar card, passport, voter card and driving licence.

For these services, the customers have to pay much more than the nominal government fees since they have no choice but to depend on these private centres run by agents and operators.

The Aadhaar card is now the most often used ID card. It is issued as a free-of-cost voluntary identification card.

Many petitions have challenged the legality of the Aadhaar programme, which collected citizens' biometric data without adequate security and legitimacy on the grounds of the 'right to privacy'. But since 2015, the central government has insisted that the Indian Constitution does not grant a 'right to privacy', and mandating Aadhaar for welfare schemes and other government services does not violate the Constitution.

On many occasions, the Supreme Court of India has ordered that the Aadhaar card is not mandatory to access essential services, yet in practice the state continues to make it compulsory.

In some states, Aadhaar is not only mandatory to avail liquefied petroleum gas (LPG), used as cooking gas, subsidy and food grains from local Public Distribution System shops, it is also demanded for jobs in the National Rural Employment Guarantee Act (NREGA), railways, state services, for employees' pensions, and sometimes even for state board exams, engineering exams and more.

According to the National Food Security Act passed in 2013, the government is supposed to provide 5 kilos of subsidized foodgrains to over 75 per cent of the Indian rural population. Several starvation deaths linked to Aadhaar have been reported from all over the country due to not receiving rations because of the failure of biometric identification and people's inability to prove their identity.

The fingerprints of people who do hard labour often wear off and fade. Their fingerprints must be updated in the Aadhaar system, which is not easy even though the Aadhaar identification system is designed to be regularly updated.

The government rates are Rs 50 for each service. But the Digital Seva Centres charged at least Rs 100 for each job – updating a photograph, fingerprint, iris scan, mobile number, gender, address, or email in the system – even though most errors are introduced by the Aadhaar officials themselves when making the cards.

The government website often throws tantrums, with system errors, too little time to read the captcha code, or failure to send or receive the OTP. The last is a huge problem for the poor nationwide because the OTP comes on mobile phones, and many people do not have phones or would have given phone numbers at the time of registration that were now redundant or had changed. All this leads to a roaring business for Digital Seva Centres that have mushroomed all over the country.

Reshma had started learning the tricks of the job and spent more than her designated hours there.

The older cybercafes had cubicles, places for young couples to hang out on the pretext of surfing the internet. But, after the government made it mandatory for cybercafe owners to keep a record of the photo ID of users, many young people who could afford it started to use, instead, online apps, which allowed the booking of budget hotel rooms for a few hours. Others, who didn't have the money, were back to parks and old monuments in Delhi.

Reshma had been assigned one such cubicle as her workstation. GG would spend an hour with her here before dropping her home each evening.

The embrace at the Signature Bridge, almost ten months earlier, was not repeated or discussed. This hour at the Digital Seva Centre, when their fingers and hands touched and brushed against each other's while scrolling up and down with the mouse as Reshma attempted to teach GG some computer skills, was what GG woke up for each morning. These were the moments when GG often saw Reshma's big smile, which no one had seen in years. GG's friends had dubbed her Bhootiya because she had acquired the reputation for scolding any client who came with incomplete information or missing documents. She had mastered the system and would still complete their job at breakneck speed. But since no one recognized any merit of a woman with a bad temper, she was Bhootiya Reshma.

Reshma looked forward to meeting GG because he was the only person in the world with whom she could let her guard down. Since she had left the mall, she had had no friends. She simply didn't get along with Syeda and was tired of Akmal's way of life. She couldn't go without seeing GG for even a day. She craved that embrace of long ago. It had sent such a current through her body that she often tried to recreate it in her mind. GG was her confidant, caretaker and nurturer and slowly became her soulmate – except that she never consciously thought of him as that, never admitted to herself or anyone else that he was her boyfriend.

Chehre pe saare shehar ke gard-e-malaal hai,
Jo dil ka haal hai wahi dilli ka haal hai.

The face is full of sorrow of the entire city,
The condition of the heart is the condition of Delhi.

> – Malikzada Manzoor Ahmed, twentieth-century poet

A Nation is formed by a majority living therein. What did the Jews do in Germany? They being in the minority were driven out from Germany.

> – V.D. Savarkar, 14 October 1938, suggesting Hitler's anti-Jewish pogroms as a solution for Indian Muslims

During the 2019 general election campaign, Home Minister Amit Shah, Modi's key commander, declared, *'BJP sarkar ek-ek ghuspaithiye ko chun-chun kar matdata suchi se hatane ka kaam karegi.'*

The BJP government will pick out each and every infiltrator and remove their name from the voters' list.

He also referred to illegal immigrants, mainly from Bangladesh, as 'termites' multiple times in his campaign, holding them responsible for poverty and unemployment in India.

In global history, whenever terms like 'termites', 'vermin', 'mad dogs' and 'cockroaches' have been used for communities, a genocide has followed.

It was during the general elections in Delhi in 1996, a year after Syeda and her family moved to Delhi, that the BJP had first come to power on a four-point agenda: ban cow slaughter, remove Article 370 of the Indian Constitution that gave special status to Kashmir, introduce a uniform civil code, construct a Ram temple in Ayodhya. This would transform India into a Hindu state.

Twenty-three years later, when the BJP was re-elected in the 2019 general elections for a second consecutive term, it had already banned cow slaughter in most Indian states. In August 2019, when Reshma started working at the Digital Seva Centre, the BJP government revoked the special status of the state of Jammu and Kashmir and split it into two union territories. In the following days, they went on to work on the remaining items on the list.

It was past 8 p.m. on an October evening in 2019. The 10 Futa Road of Karawal Nagar was blocked. GG was stuck on his way to the cybercafe to pick up Reshma. A crowd had gathered to catch a glimpse of Manoj Tiwari, a Bhojpuri singer turned Member of Parliament from the North East Delhi constituency for two consecutive terms, 2014 and 2019. He had arrived to carry out the 'Gandhi Sankalp Yatra', a government initiative to celebrate Gandhi's 150th birth anniversary and spread the message of cleanliness.

'Gandhiji wanted to establish Ram Rajya in India!' claimed Manoj Tiwari.

Ram Rajya. The rule of the Hindu god Ram.

Mahatma Gandhi popularized the concept of Ram Rajya. In 1929, he wrote in *Young India*, a journal, 'by Ram Rajya, I mean divine raj, the kingdom of God'. He also wrote, 'I acknowledge no other god but the one god of truth and righteousness.' According to him, Ram Rajya is this kingdom on earth, a kingdom of right and righteousness, that has a utopian rule. It was not meant to follow a certain religion.

North east Delhi has a large migrant population from the Bhojpuri belt of UP and Bihar. That was the key reason for Tiwari's electoral win there. Since he had sung particularly raunchy numbers in the initial days of his singing career, each time he came to Karawal Nagar and neighbouring areas for a public meeting, the crowds went berserk, singing his songs and shouting his film titles while he spoke.

'Daroga Babu, I love you!' someone yelled from the crowd, referring to one of this popular films.

Police Officer, I love you!

Tiwari continued, 'Under Prime Minister Modi's leadership, we are realizing Gandhi's dream of Ram Rajya.'

As he spoke, a loudspeaker in the vicinity started blaring another Manoj Tiwari number.

Hothwa mein madham laali,
kajrari nainwali,

Chal chaleli matwali,
bagalwali jaan mareli ho,
bagalwali jaan mareli!

Light lipstick on the lips,
The one with kohl-lined eyes,
She sways when she walks,
Oh, the next-door woman is killing me,
Oh, the next-door woman is killing me!

The organizers tried to remove some boys who broke out into a dance in the audience, which caused a scuffle.

At one point, Manoj and Gopi Bisht, the local BJP leader and former MLA, who were sharing the stage, began to talk about the evils of single-use plastic.

Many who heard him that day, including GG who was stuck in traffic nearby, were amused at the irony of this being brought up in a constituency filled with single-use plastic factories that provided considerable employment and supplied the wholesale market.

Boom!

Suddenly, someone threw a cracker on the stage. It fell next to Gopi Bisht, and some sparks flew on his kurta, singeing it in places. There was panic. The crowds dispersed.

The next day, Anil Trivedi, the local BJP member, urged the cops at the Khajoori Khas police station to investigate the incident. Trivedi was the same local BJP member who had claimed in 2015 that Muslims were taking over the parks in Sriram Colony by offering namaz in large numbers there.

The police were zealous in following up on Trivedi's complaint about the Sankalp Yatra incident. They started analysing the CCTV footage. GG was summoned the very next day for questioning.

'Sir, why me again? I was stuck in traffic,' GG told Santosh Yadav, the SI at the police station.

'But you were standing in the direction from where the *oon* bomb was thrown on the stage,' replied Santosh.

Oon bomb. Wool bomb. Cracker.

'I don't know anything. The organizers pushed out the boys who were dancing to Bhojpuri songs. It must have been one of those boys,' said GG.

'Why? You were not dancing? Haan, why will you? You are Bangladeshi.'

'Sir, I am a Bengali from South 24 Parganas in India, not Bangladesh. I have lived longer in Delhi than I have in Bengal. I understand Bhojpuri!' GG tried to explain.

'You g*huspaithiye* are termites, always causing trouble,' replied Santosh.

Amit Shah's term for so-called intruders was now part of common parlance.

When GG recounted this to Reshma, she asked, 'But all your ID documents say you are Indian. How dare he?' Reshma, as usual, was ready to pick a fight with the cop for his offensive talk, but GG stopped her. Her reaction intensified GG's feelings for her as no one had ever stood up for him. Especially not a woman. That too with a cop.

GG had a ration card, an Aadhaar card and a driving licence, but they all had mismatched demographic details. This nationwide problem was normalized to the point that most people did not bother to correct them until there was a serious requirement. Reshma herself was dealing with a similar problem.

Bhoore Lal, a garment subcontractor from Gandhinagar, had told Syeda he had a contact in the DTC recruitment system and could help Reshma get a job. The DTC started hiring female bus conductors in 2010. Over sixty years after its formation in 1948, DTC had finally found it acceptable to open up these jobs for women. The job requirements were as basic as passing Class 10, handling cash, doing accurate calculations, greeting passengers and assisting those with special needs – most of which women across centuries had been trained to do all their lives, and were better qualified for than men in many ways.

Bhoore Lal had informed them that a bribe of Rs 70,000 by January 2020 would be sufficient – just that much to get a government job that promised health insurance and retirement benefits. Reshma was convinced it was worth a try.

Reshma needed to submit an Aadhaar card, her Class 10 certificate, her caste or category certificate, her PAN card and a self-declaration certificate.

On her Class 10 certificate, her name was 'Reshma Akmal'. On her Aadhaar card, her name was 'Rashmi Akmal', the wife of Akmal, as the traffic cop had seen on Signature Bridge. On her PAN card, her name was 'Reshmi Akmal'. Thankfully, the date of birth was the same in all the documents.

Most people did not notice these discrepancies in their cards because they were illiterate; some did not know the English spelling of their names – which could, anyway, be spelt in many different ways. Shalu could be Saaloo, Saalu, Shaloo. Mohammed Arif could be Mohd Aarif, M. Arif or Mohammed Aarif.

Some people like Syeda and Akmal did not even know their dates of birth, so they carelessly provided a different one in each document.

The previous year, in July 2018, the final draft of the National Register of Citizens in Assam was published. This was the only state where this exercise had been carried out so far in India. Over 40 lakh people across religions were left out of this draft because of mismatched government documents and a lack of legacy data to prove that they were Indian citizens. They were declared 'descendants of foreigners'.

Going by the NRC process conducted in Assam the previous year, people had to submit many documents issued before 24 March 1971 that had either their names or ancestors' names to prove their citizenship. They also needed to provide some papers from a list of acceptable documents. These included electoral rolls, land and tenancy records, citizenship certificates, permanent residential certificates, refugee registration certificates, passports, insurance policies, other government-issued licences, employment certificates, bank accounts, birth certificates, educational certificates and court records. If the person did not have any of these documents in their name, they could submit the same in the name of their grandparents or parents with an additional document establishing their relationship with them.

Many people in India do not have these documents.

It took Reshma over a month to fix all the details in her documents. While doing that, she decided to put Syeda's and Akmal's papers in order, which they considered a useless exercise. They only had Aadhaar cards and ration cards, each with wrong information, including name spelling, gender, and date of birth. She fixed that, too. While at it, she applied for a PAN card for them. For GG, too, she initiated the process of standardizing the spelling and details in all his documents.

❦

It had been five years since Shazeb and Babli had left. Tinnu and Pillu had been packed off to a private engineering college in Greater Noida. Golu had flunked Class 12 twice, so Mahesh and Ramesh Bainsla were training him to take over the dairy business. He remained in touch with Virender and Prabhu, who, after converting the Hindu Kanya Raksha Front, HKRF, into the Gau Raksha Front, GRF, had now changed it into United Hindu Front (UHF). Golu was fast emerging as the employer of many UHF volunteers in his dairy.

All these years, the Bainslas never tried to directly attack or contact Syeda's family. Neither did they attempt to find out where Babli was. Once they had decided that Babli was dead for them, she was treated as dead and, if remembered, never talked about. Babli never called them, not even when her first child was born early in 2019. Syeda and family were happy but detached on hearing the news.

One day in November 2019, Syeda returned home after her shift at the almond factory. It was back to odd hours: 2 a.m. till 2 p.m., late payments, wages as low as Rs 80 per bag, an increase of only Rs 20 in ten years. But that was the only consistent work available for home-based workers like her in the winter season. Akmal was once again not working. His legs and body ached day and night, and he dozed on the terrace all day, making no attempt to find a new job.

Syeda walked past a rally led by the UHF.

'*Hum Hindu jagane aaye hain, hum Hindu jaga ke jayenge!*' they sloganeered.

We have come to awaken the Hindus. We will not leave till we awaken them!

A group of twenty boys on bikes and on foot repeated the slogans after them.

'Ram Lalla hum aayenge, Mandir wahin banayenge!'

Ram Lalla, we will come, and construct the temple at the same spot!

In the last two months, Syeda had been so caught up collecting her dues and taking loans from subcontractors to put together Rs 70,000, the bribe for Reshma's DTC bus conductor job, that she had not paid attention to the Supreme Court verdict on the event that had changed her life twenty-seven years ago. Not that it made any difference to her daily life now; she and Akmal were already displaced from Banaras, distanced from their families, and transposed to an entirely new galaxy called Delhi, which was now what may be considered home.

On 9 November 2019, the Supreme Court of India passed a judgment allowing the construction of a Ram temple in Ayodhya at the site where Hindu supremacists had demolished the Babri Mosque on 6 December 1992.

Ram Lalla, the infant Hindu god Ram, was a petitioner in this court case and claimed ownership of the disputed land. In this several decades-long case, the deity was treated as a juristic person, a non-human legal entity recognized by Indian law and entitled to rights and remedies like a human being. Because Ram Lalla was a minor, he was represented by a senior VHP leader who was considered Ram Lalla's closest 'human' friend'.

The apex court handed over the land to a trust to construct the Ram temple.

No one was punished for demolishing the mosque.

An alternative plot of land was given to the Uttar Pradesh Sunni Central Waqf Board, a body overseeing the affairs of Sunni Muslim charity properties and institutions, to build a mosque to replace the demolished Babri mosque.

Like many Hindu political groups all over India, the UHF was taking out a victory march after the Supreme Court verdict.

That day, for the first time in many months, Syeda voluntarily took the rest of the day off to do nothing and napped beside Akmal in the sun.

Reshma and GG were not so affected. It was just a mosque they had heard of. Yes, the Hindu supremacists were happy. 'But let them be. Ignore them. It is not like any mosque allows me to pray there,' Reshma would say.

Within a month, on 11 December, the Indian Parliament passed the Citizenship Amendment Act (CAA), 2019. It amended the Citizenship Act of 1955 to accelerate the citizenship of 'persons belonging to minority communities, namely, Hindus, Sikhs, Buddhists, Jains, Parsis and Christians from Afghanistan, Bangladesh and Pakistan, who entered India on or before December 31 2014'. According to the Act, they would not be treated as illegal migrants. Under this law, Muslims from these countries were not eligible for the same treatment. The government also proposed a simultaneous nationwide preparation of the NRC to determine the number of 'illegal immigrants' in the country. Many have interpreted the government's strategy to use the CAA along with the NRC to render the Muslims, who cannot show these documents, stateless.

Internationally, many found parallels between the CAA and the Reich Citizenship Law, which reconceived German citizenship to exclude certain people. It led to the Holocaust under Hitler's regime. Observers also noted similarities with Myanmar's 1982 Citizenship Law, which stripped the Rohingya Muslims of their citizenship.

This was the first time since India's independence that a law had been passed where religion was used as a criterion for citizenship in the country.

There was a nationwide uproar over the passing of the CAA and the proposed NRC. Both of them together were seen as a two-step mechanism to weed out Muslims from India.

That week, Reshma witnessed a deluge of people, missing out on factory work and daily wages, lining up at the Digital Seva Centre to get their documents in order.

There was no time to eat, and GG waited till late at night to drop her home; the owner of the centre promised Rs 2,000 extra that month for overtime. Many neighbours had started pointing out how Reshma would come home late at night with a man, complaining it was a bad influence on the rest of the young girls in the neighbourhood.

Syeda just couldn't understand why Reshma was doing twelve-hour shifts for a mere Rs 8,000 per month while working overtime, when earning Rs 12,000 to work in any factory for the same amount of time was possible. Tensions were brewing both at home and outside. There were widespread protests all over the country.

Syeda watched a lot of TV news on the anti-CAA–NRC protests as she dressed up Santa dolls for Christmas. On 15 December, police and paramilitary personnel entered the premises of Jamia Millia Islamia University in south Delhi, without the permission of the university administration, to stop a protest by students. They were beaten up, and the library and other buildings were tear-gassed and hit with rubber pellets. The students sent SOS messages pleading to be rescued. They were flushed out late at night and paraded with their hands in the air like criminals. Over 200 people were injured that night.

Similar police action was observed in Aligarh Muslim University and other parts of the country.

A few days before Christmas, the UHF patrolled many parts of Karawal Nagar. Reshma was anxious. GG had not answered his phone all day. He hadn't even come to pick her up in the evening. So she went to look for him. When she reached his place, she saw him sitting in the middle of the debris of his shack. He was fixing his bike. It was dark and foggy. There was no light except from the torch on his smartphone.

'What is all this? What happened?' she asked.

GG looked at her and turned away. He carried on mending his bike.

'Who did this?' she asked again.

GG still did not reply.

The UHF had vandalized some shacks in this slum in Shiv Vihar because they were the homes of Bengali Muslims.

'*Bangladeshi, waapis jao! Ghuspaithiye, waapis jao!*' yelled an adolescent boy, a new UHF member Bangladeshi, intruders, go back.

'*Kaagaz nahin dikhayenge! Kaagaz nahin dikhayenge!* Here!' yelled Virender as he smacked the tarpaulin, the bamboo props, the makeshift bathroom, the bike and anything in sight. He identified

GG as the one involved in throwing a cracker at Manoj Tiwari in October. GG stood and watched as they broke his bike.

Kaagaz nahin dikhayenge.

We won't show our documents.

This became a famous slogan against the CAA and NRC in protests that had mushroomed all over India.

Reshma took a cardboard box and gathered all of GG's intact belongings: clothes, utensils and pictures of his sisters and parents. Then she told him, 'Let's go home.'

GG was not sure what she meant.

'You earn enough. You don't need to live in a shack. Your house in Bengal can get constructed even if you live in a proper room,' she said.

GG knew Reshma was being Reshma, who couldn't express love and care without scolding. He smiled and did as he was told. They tied the cardboard box on the bike and headed for Reshma's house.

Syeda was shocked. How could she allow GG to live with them when people were already talking about Reshma and this man?

She scolded Reshma as GG waited on his bike downstairs. Akmal calmly stepped in, escorted GG upstairs and made him at home. He offered his cot to him to sleep on that night. Reshma's faith in Akmal's warmth was reaffirmed.

Syeda and Akmal entered the new year with no enthusiasm. GG and Reshma entered 2020 with the hope of a better life.

༄

Shehar kare talab agar, tumse ilaaj-e-teergi
Sahib-e-ikhtiyaar ho, aag laga diya karo!

If people ask you for a cure for darkness,
If you are in power, set the city on fire.

— Peerzada Qasim, twentieth-century poet

'Women are organizing melas everywhere,' Khushboo told all the others gathered for Radiowali's farewell.

Melas. Fairs. Khushboo was referring to the protest gatherings and sit-ins organized by Muslim women against the CAA–NRC.

Radiowali had decided to move to Moradabad permanently with her lover. He had been a constant in her life for many years. He lived alone, was a widower, and all his children had moved out. This was the lover who had pulled her leg while the women were playing antakshari when he came to visit once.

Most of the women were happy for Radiowali. Syeda was too, except that she felt the urge to protect Radiowali from the flames of marriage.

Radiowali said, 'What did Seema from the union used to say? *"Shaheedon ki mazaron par lagenge har baras mele. Watan par mitne walo ka yahin baaqi nishan hoga!"*

Fairs will be organized every year at the tombs of martyrs. This will be the only remaining mark of those who died for the country!

Radiowali was referring to the protesters as martyrs, ones who were penalized for fighting for human rights.

'Of course, they are martyrs. Doing Hindu–Muslim. *Kaagaz nahin dikhayenge*. Arre, show them the papers,' said Roopmati.

Khushboo responded, 'Yes, they are Muslim women like me. But you are Hindu. Do you have a birth certificate, own land or have a school certificate? Did your mother and grandmother have these documents? Where will you bring them from?'

Radiowali jumped in. 'Don't worry. Roopmati has a lot of money to pay the Seva Centre to make her papers while she loses out on her daily wages!'

'But what about land records? Roopmati, did you or anyone in the family in Bihar own land?' Khushboo persisted.

Roopmati was silent.

Apart from being discriminatory towards Muslims, the proposed CAA–NRC also involved a tedious, time-consuming, resource-intensive process to get the official papers in place, putting everyone, including women, Dalits, Adivasis and most working-class people from the unorganized sector, at risk. There were already reports of many Hindus in Assam also being declared 'foreign nationals' who were selling their land to pay the legal fees to appeal in tribunals and courts.

By January 2020, many women-led anti-CAA–NRC protests had mushroomed nationwide. It started with the Shaheen Bagh protest in Delhi on 15 December 2019, a spontaneous women-led protest in solidarity with the Jamia Millia Islamia students who had been attacked by police and paramilitary personnel. Soon, there were similar sit-in protests in various parts of India. There were multiple sites in Delhi, too: at Hauz Rani in South Delhi district, Sadar Baazar in North Delhi district, and Inderlok in North West Delhi district. But the maximum number of protest sites in Delhi were in North East Delhi district: at Jaffrabad, Chand Bagh, Khajoori Khas, Old Mustafabad, Seelampur, Turkman Gate, Kardam Puri, Sundar Nagari and Lal Bagh.

The protests were no longer just against the CAA and NRC. They were also against poverty, unemployment, gender-based violence, gender- and caste-based discrimination, and to demand equality and justice.

The women would complete their household chores in the morning, join the sit-in protests early evening, and stay till late night or sometimes all night. The men would let them go and sit on the road with other people, which was unprecedented access to public spaces for many of these women. Performers, artists, students and other social groups joined them in the evenings. There were songs of protest and solidarity. They did turn out to be melas, as Khushboo described them.

Reshma was sad that Radiowali was leaving. For a long time, she had been the only source of warmth and empathy in her life. She was the only woman Reshma looked up to and secretly aspired to be like. She gave Radiowali a pair of headphones as a farewell gift. Many other *akash napnewali* women, those who measured the sky, in Karawal Nagar also lost their measuring scales with Radiowali's departure.

Around the same time, in early January, political campaigns for the upcoming Delhi assembly elections, to be held on 8 February 2020, began.

During the election campaign, many BJP leaders tried to channelize confusion about the CAA–NRC into hate and bigotry against the protesters. Many from the privileged classes and landowning Hindu castes could not empathize with the protesters because they had access to old government records that established their citizenship.

On 20 January 2020, Anurag Thakur, an MP and a central government minister, shouted out a notorious slogan at an election rally in Delhi – *'Desh ke gaddaron ko'* – prompting the attendees to follow up with the more incendiary half: *'goli maaron saalon ko.'*

The traitors to the country,
These rascals should be shot down.

Even though the Election Commission of India sent a notice to Thakur, no case was lodged against him.

In the past six years in power, the Hindu supremacists had popularized the notion that anyone critiquing the government was betraying the country. Anyone who protested, disagreed, asked questions or debated was 'anti-national'. By that logic, everyone who was part of these protests was labelled 'anti-India', 'anti-national', 'traitor', part of the *'tukde-tukde* gang'.

Tukde-tukde gang. Divisive gang.

This narrative was frequently repeated by many office-bearers of the BJP and the government.

On 27 January, Amit Shah, the home minister, addressed an election rally, asking people to press the EVM button in the Delhi election with such aggression that the protesters in Shaheen Bagh should 'feel the current'. He said, 'Your vote for the BJP candidate will make Delhi and the country safe and prevent thousands of incidents like Shaheen Bagh.'

On 30 January, Tarun Chugh, the national secretary of the BJP, wrote on social media, *'Aaj yeh tukde-tukde gang ka head office ban chuka hai shaitanibagh, aur ye log Bharat ko, Delhi ko, Syria banaana chahte hain, hum banne nahin denge.'*

This Satan bagh has become the head office of the divisive gang. They want to turn India and Delhi into Syria. We won't let that happen.

These posts and speeches were circulated on WhatsApp non-stop. Tejinder Pal Bagga, another BJP candidate in the Delhi assembly elections, declared on 30 January, 'And on February 11, after the results, a surgical strike will be done on this *adda.*'

These speeches continued fuelling sectarian sentiments and emboldened groups like the UHF. Even though the Bainsla family was not interested in Syeda's family, Virender and Prabhu kept a watchful eye on Reshma and GG. How could they forget that the loss of one Hindu daughter meant the loss of 100 holy cows? Reshma was not only helping people get their documents in place round the clock, making it complicated to weed out *ghuspaithiye* through the NRC, but she was also befriending GG, a *ghuspaithiya* himself.

The continuous inflow of sectarian poison helped instigate young people against the protesters.

On 30 January 2020, a young man named Rambhakt Gopal fired his gun at the gates of Jamia Millia Islamia University in the presence of Delhi Police and injured one student. Just two days later, Kapil Gurjar, another young man, entered the Shaheen Bagh protests and opened fire, wounding one student.

UP Chief Minister Yogi Adityanath spewed further vitriol in an election rally in Delhi on 2 February: *'Boli nahi, goli se samjhaya jaayega.'*

Bullets, not words, will be used to shut up the protesters.

The same day, Hindu Sena, a Hindu supremacist group, mobilized a large group to 'remove' all protesters from Shaheen Bagh forcefully. This was called off after the intervention of Delhi Police.

Syeda saw many young men in the area with Golu during this period. She could not recognize any of them, so she dismissed them as outsiders who had come to participate in the election campaign.

The election results were declared on 11 February. The AAP won a comfortable majority and formed the government in Delhi once again. But in Karawal Nagar, it was BJP candidate Gopi Bisht who was elected MLA.

Though Syeda felt the simmering heat of sectarian tensions, she did not want to attend any of the protests now that the BJP had won in their constituency. BJP leader Bisht had played a prominent role in hushing up the Shazeb–Babli incident after he was promised votes. Anyway she could not take any time off from her current job: stationery packing for the upcoming academic semester. She was working sixteen hours daily to pay off the loan taken to pay Bhoore Lal the bribe for Reshma's job.

On the evening of 23 February 2020, GG insisted that Reshma leave work at the Seva Centre early and come home with him. She made an excuse at work – that she had a fever – and took off with him. When they got home, GG told Syeda and Reshma, 'People are saying there might be riots in the area.'

He showed them a video that had gone viral the same evening. In the video, Kapil Mishra, a former AAP MLA from Karawal Nagar who had now joined the BJP, had led a rally in Maujpur, just a kilometre away from the Jaffrabad protest site.

Since 15 January, hundreds of women had been sitting in protest near the Jaffrabad metro station in north east Delhi. There was a similar protest in Kardam Puri near Maujpur Chowk.

In the video, Kapil Mishra is standing next to Ved Prakash Surya, the deputy commissioner of police for North East district, in full riot gear. Kapil Mishra makes a speech, 'On behalf of all of you, I am saying that till the time Trump goes back, we are going to go forward peacefully. But after that, we will not listen to the police if roads are not cleared after three days. By the time Trump goes, we request the police to clear out Jaffrabad and Chand Bagh. After that, we will have to go on the roads. *Bharat Mata ki jai! Vande Mataram!*'

US President Donald Trump was on a two-day India tour over 24–25 February. Prime Minister Modi had organized a 'Namaste Trump' event for him in Ahmedabad in response to a similar event, 'Howdy Modi!', hosted for Modi in September 2019 in Texas, US.

In the wee hours of 24 February, around 4 a.m., the neighbourhood was awakened by loud sloganeering.

'*Jai Shri Ram! Jai Shri Ram!*' Victory to Lord Ram.

'*Har Har Modi!*' Hail Modi.

'*Modi ji, kaat do in mullon ko!*' Modi, cut these Muslims into pieces!

'*Aaj tumhe azadi denge!*' Today, we will give you freedom!

By 10 a.m., the slogans had intensified. Through news and phone calls, Syeda and her family heard that apart from Karawal Nagar, many areas of north east Delhi, including Khajuri Khas, Chand Bagh, Gokulpuri, Maujpur, Jaffrabad, Mustafabad, Ashok Nagar,

Bhagirathi Vihar, Bhajanpura and Kardam Puri, were affected. When GG looked out from the terrace, mobs with saffron flags had filled up all the alleys of Shiv Vihar, Karawal Nagar.

Usee ka shahr, wahee muddaee, wahee munsif,
Hamein yaqeen tha, hamaara qusoor niklega.

It's his city; he himself is the petitioner, and himself the judge;
I was sure I'd be held guilty.

— Ameer Qazalbash, twentieth-century poet

There was a loud banging on the main door on the ground floor of Syeda's barsati in the Shiv Vihar area of Karawal Nagar. Someone was trying to break it open with a baton. It was 10 a.m. on 25 February. Syeda, Akmal, GG and Reshma had remained locked inside for over a day.

The mob shouted, *'Shiv Vihar jayenge, burqewaali laayenge.'*
We will go to Shiv Vihar,
And bring back burqa-clad women.
'Bahut see Sakeenaayein aaj pakdi jaayengi.'
Today, many Sakeenas will be captured.
This was a reference to the female Muslim protagonist of the movie *Gadar: Ek Prem Katha*, released in 2001, where a Sikh man manages to get his Muslim wife released from Pakistan. But essentially, these were threats of sexual violence against women.

GG asked everyone to pack their belongings. Reshma had dialled many times to call the police, but no one arrived.

Golu led the mob, which kept coming back every hour. A month back, Syeda had seen him actually helping outsiders identify Muslim houses in the vicinity. Around 2 p.m., the four of them jumped from their terrace to the one next door. Syeda sprained her leg, and Akmal bruised his face. GG hid them behind the water tank.

In the markets, a Muslim shop between two Hindu shops was vandalized. In the various neighbourhoods of Karawal Nagar and adjacent areas, petrol bombs were thrown inside only Muslim houses. The violence was not spontaneous. It was planned and targeted at Muslims.

Syeda could hear gunshots everywhere. A mob of fifty to sixty people was downstairs with sticks in their hands. They were pelting stones from all sides. A petrol bomb fell next to her, which she tried to extinguish by hand. When she couldn't, all four of them ran downstairs into a house. The ground floor was full of wooden material. It was a factory for doors and windows. It had already caught fire, and the hall was full of smoke. The occupants of the house were hiding in the toilet. Upon seeing Syeda and the others, they came out. All of them ran to the terrace and jumped to the next building.

When Syeda peeped downstairs, she felt the mob was made up of outsiders, people who did not live in Karawal Nagar. Smoke was pouring from the houses; the lanes were full of lathi- and gun-wielding men sloganeering *Jai Shri Ram! Jai Shri Ram!* There were gunshots, loud sounds of doors and houses being broken, children wailing, and people pleading for mercy and help. She saw one man fall to the ground after being shot. She saw an old woman jumping from the fifth floor of a building, injuring her skull and lying in a pool of blood. All she could do was watch silently, trying to control her fear.

On this terrace, one of the women was going hysterical, shrieking for her children. During the escape attempt, they had gone missing. She was calling out their names. GG asked her to be quiet. She, in turn, started slapping GG. She was in a frenzy. Reshma calmed her down while GG jumped back to the previous house, found the children who were hiding behind piles of wood, and brought them over.

There were reports of mobs throwing acid. Several people had been shot dead. Someone was using a loudspeaker, asking all the Hindus in the area to come out and join them in driving out the Muslims.

In the adjacent lane, some Muslim elders had stacked up chairs as a barricade to prevent the mob from entering from both sides, and to stop the Muslim young men from retaliating. There were loud cries and commotion.

Reshma was still calling up the police, to no avail. Syeda stopped her. By now, news had spread that the police were hand in glove with the rioters. The police were deliberately staying away, avoding rescue efforts. At some places, they had even hauled up Muslims, beaten them up and made them sing 'Jana Gana Mana', the national anthem, to prove their loyalty to India.

There was CRPF deployed in some areas, but they claimed to have no orders to act. Syeda was distrustful of these forces because of her previous experience in Banaras when they had vandalized their home and the loom and looted them.

By 6 p.m., it was clear they could not escape during the day. They stayed hidden behind water tanks in silence, and jumped from one house to the next, one by one, when possible.

It was only as late as 9 p.m. that a combined force of CRPF, armed forces and police entered the area and, for the first time, threw tear gas shells at the Hindu mob and gradually started rescuing people.

Syeda walked ahead, asking Reshma to walk behind her. She was trying to save Reshma from the sexual violence many women had reportedly faced in these riots. Akmal walked behind them, his leg bleeding profusely. GG walked in the rear, holding a bag of their belongings, mostly documents and some money.

In the morning, many people left for their ancestral places or to live with relatives in other parts of Delhi for shelter. Sabhapur was also burning, so she couldn't have gone to Raziya. Syeda decided they should leave for Moradabad to stay at Radiowali's new place. She could not think of any other place where she would be welcomed in such a crisis.

Radiowali took them in without questions. News was coming in from all over about the targeted violence, deaths and vandalized buildings.

All the mosques and shrines Salman had been attached to had been vandalized.

Allah Wali Mosque in Bhagat Singh Colony, where Salman was to meet Akmal the day he was fatally injured, had been destroyed. The four-storey structure was attacked on the evening of 24 February by

200–250 people. They not only burned the mosque but also several copies of the Quran inside the structure. Some climbed the minaret and planted a saffron flag, chanting *'Jai Shri Ram'*. And the police watched as it happened. The video went viral.

The Auliya mosque in Shiv Vihar, where Salman had his madrasa friends, was set ablaze on 25 February evening. Mobs wearing police uniforms and helmets broke the lock of the mosque and the madrasa next to it. They chanted *'Jai Shri Ram'* and blasted LPG cylinders to demolish the structure.

Chand Baba shrine was forty years old and located in a Hindu-majority area; both communities would visit it. On 25 February, around noon, when the shrine was empty, a mob surrounded it from all sides. They said, 'This is a Hindu locality!' Young boys shouted, 'This belongs to Muslims, break it!' *'Har Har Mahadev!' 'Jai Shri Ram!'*

Once again, a Sufi shrine that was visited by people of all religions was declared Muslim and attacked. They used iron rods, hammers and petrol bombs. Petrol was poured inside the tomb, and it was burned down.

They even attacked and looted some Hindu shops to put the blame on Muslims.

When she heard all this, Syeda finally came to the realization that the demolition of the Babri mosque in 1992 was only the precursor, the beginning. The Hindu supremacists were not after one Muslim mosque. They were after all of them, every single one of them. The warp and weft that was undone almost thirty years back could never be woven back again.

༄

Dilli hui hai veeraan, soone khandar pade hain,
Veeraan hain mohalle, sunsaan ghar pade hain.

Delhi has become desolate and lies in ruins,
The neighbourhoods are deserted, the houses are abandoned.

– Mushafi Ghulam Hamdani, eighteenth-century poet

Everyone in Karawal Nagar knew one of the most important rules in gully cricket: if the ball falls in a drain, pull it out and bounce it three times for the germs to die before resuming the game. If it falls in a filthier drain, you must beat it till it returns to its original colour.

Both cricket balls and dead people were regularly found in these drains. The minuscule proportion of people who live in gated colonies in developed India may find this horrifying, but it was part of daily life here.

Decomposed dead bodies were regularly fished out of drains near Karawal Nagar. A four-year-old boy who went missing after an election rally, a seven-year-old girl bitten by an animal, an adult man killed by his wife and her lover, a dead labourer from a factory – it could be anyone. If someone was missing for too long, you had to search for them in the nala.

In 2006, when the remains of sixteen children were found in Nithari village in Noida, where two men were accused of kidnapping poor children, sexually assaulting them, killing them and eating them, they were recovered from a nearby drain – an obvious place to look, according to most Karawal Nagar residents.

Delhi has more than 697 drains that are deeper than 4 feet. The city does not segregate stormwater and sewage, though technically, they are managed by different departments. Practically all drains bleed into each other. All the waste from the kitchen to the toilet goes into the same drain.

Between 23 and 29 February, during the Delhi riots, several people went missing.

After about a week in Moradabad, Syeda and her family decided to come back to Delhi. Several relief camps were set up in north east Delhi, and the Delhi government announced schemes to rehabilitate and compensate riot-affected people.

Syeda's family decided to go to the Eidgah relief camp in Mustafabad, one of the largest relief camps set up by the Waqf Board with the help of the Delhi government.

Over 1,000 people took shelter there.

Many in the relief camps were still looking for their family members who had gone missing during the riots. After many appeals to find missing persons were voiced, Delhi Police responded to the High Court that they were constantly looking for dead bodies in the drains of north Delhi.

At least eleven bodies were retrieved from the big drain that lined north east Delhi, bordering Shiv Vihar in Karawal Nagar and flowing downstream via Johripur and the Bhagirathi Vihar *puliya* and towards Loni in UP.

During this period, the UHF and many other small Hindu supremacist groups took out rallies in the riot-affected areas, including Karawal Nagar, warning all Muslims to vacate the area before Holi on 9 March 2020. As a result, more and more people were flooding into the relief camps.

By now, officially, fifty-three had died and over 500 were injured. The Delhi government had announced various slabs of compensation for the dead, wounded and those who lost their houses and commercial units. The state government also announced that each household that lost their home and household items would get immediate relief of Rs 25,000.

But since Syeda and her family had missed out on applying for compensation in the first week, they were far behind in the queue.

⁂

Fifteen days after the riots, on 11 March 2020, the World Health Organization declared the coronavirus outbreak a pandemic. They recommended social distancing of 6 feet, which was simply not possible in the relief camp where at least fifty people slept in each 6 foot by 10 foot tent.

Within two weeks, on 24 March, Prime Minister Narendra Modi declared a twenty-one-day nationwide lockdown to prevent the spread of COVID-19. Barely four hours' notice was hardly adequate preparation time for those who lived a hand-to-mouth existence.

Nobody really understood what this virus was and what was happening.

'Some people in China drank a bat's blood, ate its raw meat, contracted coronavirus and spread it across the world to finish humanity,' said Najma at the camp.

Syeda wondered if that was worse than humans killing each other.

Many Indians even believed the mainstream media's Hindu supremacist propaganda that COVID-19 was an Islamic conspiracy to end the world. Not American because the Indian government had so recently hosted US President Donald Trump with 125,000 people in attendance in a super spreader event at a stadium in Ahmedabad. But Islamic, because the Tablighi Jamaat, an Islamic congregation, was held in Delhi and two other places in India in March with thousands of attendees.

After Modi's lockdown announcement, the Delhi government promised the camp dwellers Rs 3,000, 20 kilos of wheat, and 10 kilos of potatoes, and asked them to vacate the camp to prevent the spread of the virus.

Khushboo and her husband decided to leave for their village. Many workers like her across Delhi did not have enough savings to even buy food to survive for the next three days, let alone pay rent to extortionist landlords who declared that rent needed to be paid – lockdown or no lockdown. Some who had no savings stayed in the factories shut due to the lockdown. Many workers who had a homeland and family to go to, decided to pack up and return to them. The train and bus stations were clogged. With no means of transport, many walked thousands of kilometres and died on the way in their quest for the security and warmth of their homes and families. Syeda and Akmal did not even have that.

While thousands trudged home on foot, Indian ministers posted social media posts of them playing ludo and watching reruns of the serial *Ramayana* on TV. People were making banana bread, gardening and making art. Celebrities posted videos of them cleaning their own houses in the absence of house help, some for the first time in their lives.

Walking from the Mustafabad relief camp to Karawal Nagar took over an hour. No rickshaws or vehicles were available.

Syeda went to her barsati, still full of soot, debris and haunting memories. She could still smell the ash in the air. For a few seconds, she was overcome by déjà vu: was she in Banaras looking at their burned-down loom or in Karawal Nagar? The similarities were nauseating. The house was in utter disarray. Her TV was broken, as were the second-hand washing machine and fridge, and her trunk, which she called her CV, had been vandalized. The other trunk that had her jewellery – one pair of gold plated earrings, two pairs of silver anklets and Rs 20,000 that she had collected to pay the bribe for Reshma's job – were obviously missing. The bed was badly damaged, and the mattress had been set ablaze. The mob had blasted the LPG cylinder, as in all houses. Someone had even broken and twisted the blades of the fan.

She salvaged whatever she could – mostly clothes, kitchen utensils, her old cooler and some bed sheets – and brought them back to the camp.

When Akmal went looking for a place to rent in Karawal Nagar, some Hindu Gujjar landlords stated that they would not rent out to Muslims. Others, scared by the spread of the pandemic, refused to take in any tenants at all.

After the almond factory strike, Lalita's husband, Bholu Gautam, had bought a plot of land in Sriram Colony. They had constructed two rooms on the ground floor and one on the first floor. The plastering was yet to be done, but the place was theirs to improve upon whenever possible. Syeda and her family went there. When they arrived, Bholu asked Syeda to leave. Lalita did not even come to talk to her.

The riots were not about Aadhaar cards, land records or any identity proof or documents to establish Indianness or their citizenship. They were about who could be killed, maimed and looted to create New India. A Hindu India.

౿

If this exists, that exists;
If this ceases to exist,
That also ceases to exist.

– Dependent Origination, Buddhist doctrine

Rehmat was outside the house that morning, trying to deal with the seepage. Like most houses in Nasbandi Colony, his house had also been constructed without any pillars, and the walls were just four inches thick. The seepage had weakened the structure of the house, and bits and pieces of it kept falling from here and there.

He had bought the two-storey house from Sadaqat, who was given this small patch of land by the government for undergoing a vasectomy. Thousands of people were given about 50 square yards of land under the Indira Gandhi government's mass sterilization programme in the 1970s during the Emergency. That was the government's way of controlling India's population for the progress and growth of the country.

This area in Loni, Ghaziabad, in UP, was earlier named after Gautam Buddha: Buddha Nagar, 'the land of the awakened'.

Now it is called Nasbandi Colony, 'the colony of the sterilized'.

Nasbandi Colony is a ten-minute drive and a half-hour walk from Karawal Nagar. Though the name indicated sterilization, it is in no way sterilized. Since it is close to north east Delhi, it is overpopulated with people who keep NCR running but lack affordable accommodation closer to their areas of work. Many of them work in the factories on either side of the Delhi–UP border.

Even though it was carved out by the government, the colony was never developed. In the last forty years, the civic bodies have neither laid sewer lines and stormwater drains nor provided piped water. People walk in stagnant water and scum in the narrow lanes to reach their seepage-addled houses.

When Rehmat bought it from Sadaqat, it was only two rooms, 5 foot by 8 foot, one above the other, with a narrow staircase. He installed a toilet on the landing between the two floors with a plastic sheet curtain. Though this gave tenants a private toilet, privacy was a big question mark. 'Only a man can think of such a toilet,' said Reshma when she saw the house.

Prabhu of the UHF had announced that the group's aim was to get North East Delhi district declared the first Hindu Rashtra district, so no riot-affected person could rent a room in Karawal Nagar for the longest time. GG therefore found this house in Nasbandi Colony and rented it for Syeda, Akmal, Reshma and himself.

The neighbourhood was the filthiest Syeda had ever lived in. There was muck and water all over the lanes to the house. The lanes were narrow and people had made stairs on the road to enter their homes. Flies, plastic bags, human shit and mosquitoes were everywhere. But the rent was just Rs 1,200 and they had no other option.

Syeda made several calls to Bhoore Lal about Reshma's job. But he had gone back to Barabanki and switched off his phone. In some places, the government started offering the poor free rations, but Syeda's ration card was a Delhi one. She was denied rations in the Ghaziabad ration shop.

GG's brothers asked him to move to Gandhinagar, but he refused. All this while, GG kept Reshma and her family fed. The money he had saved to construct his family's home in Bengal came in handy. Syeda was still distant from him, but he was completely at home with Akmal, and Reshma, of course.

After the two-month lockdown, Akmal started working as a rickshaw driver in a nearby steel almirah factory. His wages had dropped by a thousand rupees: he was to be paid Rs 7,000 monthly. A month later, Syeda found a job in the wedding card factory in Tronica City for Rs 8,000 per month. GG also started working in a garage in Loni on reduced wages. After some effort, Reshma finally found an instructor's job at a Digital Seva Centre close to GG's garage.

On 26 November 2020, the largest and longest farmers' protest in modern India began in Delhi against three farm laws passed by the central government.

By the end of 2020, GG asked Reshma what she thought of marriage. Reshma told him impulsively that she never wanted to get married and did not have a good opinion of men. GG was heartbroken.

Within a week, he announced he would return to South 24 Parganas and may not return. Syeda was surprised but encouraged him to do this. Of course, sons should meet their parents. Not like Shazeb, who had not come to see them in the last six years. Akmal was sad but didn't say much.

That was when Reshma became convinced she could not live without him – something GG had felt about her for the past few years.

Three days later, Reshma asked him to stay. Not go back.

'Only if you marry me,' he said.

'If that's what it takes,' she replied.

Within a month, they were married in the presence of GG's brothers, Akmal and Syeda, Reshma's friend Dolly and GG's friends from the garage.

Syeda was still unconvinced about this union, but which union in the world had she known to be perfect? She could not have, anyway, been able to get Reshma married because she had no money, savings, jewellery or the ability to find a groom who would accept the untamed Reshma.

Reshma and GG rented a house just next to Syeda's.

A few days after Reshma's wedding, Syeda walked to the bus stop early one morning to go to Tronica City, carrying her tiffin containing the gajar ka halwa Akmal had cooked that day.

Author's Note

I have worked on this book for almost nine years. This is a product of interacting with roughly 900 people. These interactions were a combination of hundreds of hours of unstructured interviews, group discussions, informal chats and structured questionnaires.

All the names of people living in Banaras, Chandni Chowk, Sabhapur, Karawal Nagar and Nasbandi Colony have been changed. This is to protect their privacy and identity. None of the characters are composite. None of the events are conflated.

Everything that is written is with the consent of the characters. They were aware that I am a journalist and that the interactions with them would be part of my book.

The majority of my fieldwork took place in 'factories', sweatshops, homes of the home-based workers, police stations, relief camps, markets, highways, courts, hospitals, malls, industrial areas, urban villages, unauthorized colonies, slums, *jhuggi jhopri* clusters and other public places.

I am not a historian, economist or a political scientist. I have used no disciplinary boundaries. As a reporter, the only training I have is to dig out information, corroborate it, analyse it, find the story and tell it. That is what I have done here.

I have witnessed a number of events in the lives of those depicted in the book since the end of 2014. All the events narrated in this book are based on the memories of the people I interviewed, and were later corroborated through further interviews, and documents such as government and newspaper reports, legal and police records, and also academic papers and industry-specific reports.

Many of the events recounted have no public records like the frequent detention of the poor in police stations for questioning, the incidents that took place inside factories, the records of disparate wages that are paid to people in the informal sector, the number of abortions conducted at a private clinic, and violence and crime within neighbourhoods.

Documentation requires influence, importance, and resources which the poor don't have. The state also does not document the lives of the poor to avoid accountability. The only records that exist are oral histories.

It was hard for most people to recall their age or exact birthday or that of their family members. This is fairly common among a large majority of the poor and the old. The same was true for other numbers like their wages or the per-piece rate they got for jobs.

In all my reporting years, including for this book, when I have asked women about facing a certain type of violence, they always deny having faced it personally but give detailed accounts of someone they know who had faced such violence. This is because the shame of the victim or the survivor is greater than that of the perpetrator. Uncomfortable questions beget uncomfortable questions. When you ask, you are asked too, and you are duty-bound to answer. That's when partial trust is developed. Once enough time was spent with them, I would find out that all the while they were talking about themselves.

Initially, all stories unravelled, bit by bit, randomly without any pattern. Once I started putting them together chronologically, in an attempt to look at the complete picture, I went back with more questions.

But memory is never chronological and acts of remembering and forgetting are complex.

Recounting the sequence of some events over and over again is not a pleasant exercise. And when the events recalled are steeped in trauma, the sequences are fragmented, the episodes incomplete, the narratives selective, and the people often inarticulate.

Like when I asked Syeda to recount all the fifty-plus jobs she had done in the past thirty years, she was irritated, 'Would you ask a construction labourer how many houses he constructed in these years? Would he remember all addresses, contractors or owners?'

These details were not of any significance in a life where the employer and the job are so fast changing. Working in a factory where incense sticks are made of cow urine was no different from making doorknobs. What was important to me as a storyteller was a mundane detail for Syeda.

When people have rehabilitated themselves over and over again and chosen a narrative about themselves, there are silences and erasures too. Till 2018, four years after I first met her, I did not know that Syeda had another son, Shazeb. Then one day she told me why he left in 2014. He had fallen in love with a Hindu girl which had put all their lives at risk. After that I thought I knew all that there was to know about him but then, one year later, I found out about how he was tortured by the state, in the name of national security, in 2010.

Some scenes from the past are reconstructed from people's memories and direct quotes have been put in according to recollected experiences and exchanges through overlapping primary and secondary interviews.

In some places where people have 'thought' or 'believed', those feelings and experiences have been recounted to me by those people.

While many events in the book took place before I met Syeda, Salman's death in 2016 and the Delhi riots in 2020 which took place while I was working on the book were heartbreaking.

Soon after the Delhi riots in 2020, my visits to Karawal Nagar increased. This is when I began to be stalked for over five months, and received incessant acid-attack and gang-rape threats for my reporting. The stalkers menacingly told me over hundreds of phone calls which vegetables I had bought recently, which part of my balcony I was sitting on and where my partner was headed. One day, there was a break-in attempt at my house after another warning to stop reporting on the riots and Hindu supremacist organizations. The attempt was unsuccessful. The police did not do any investigation and told me that 'I was imagining it'.

When I told Syeda this, she said dismissively, 'Ignore it. *Kutta bhaunkta rehta hai. Haathi apni chaal chalta rehta hai.*'

The dog keeps barking but the elephant keeps following its path.

Her response not only underlined my privilege and the luxury of dwelling on my fears but also her ceaseless use of hope as a tool of resistance.

My sincere thanks to those journalists who continue to do shoe-leather journalism and consistently report on the areas mentioned in the book. Their work may be unacknowledged in their own newsrooms but it is definitely shaping the first draft of the history of those on the margins.

I have also benefited immensely from the following books: *The Warp and the Weft: Community and Gender Identity Among Banaras Weavers* by Vasanthi Raman, *Nickel and Dimed* by Barbara Ehrenreich, *Gulab Bai: The Queen of Nautanki Theatre* by Deepti Priya Mehrotra, *Women Workers and Globalization: Emergent Contradictions in India* by Indrani Mazumdar, *The Other Side of Silence: Voices from the Partition of India* by Urvashi Butalia. In many ways, these works validated the events and stories I gathered for the book.

I don't intend to be a voice of any community. I have told this story in the way I have understood it, in the hope that it honours the struggles, journey and memories of Syeda and her family and friends; in the hope that India never forgets its diversity of voices.

The flaws and shortcomings are entirely mine.

Acknowledgements

This book is a result of hundreds of invisible contributors. People who spoke to me, who gave me knowledge, their time and trust. I am particularly indebted to Syeda, her family and everyone in Karawal Nagar who opened their lives – good, bad, grey, complex – to me, knowing full well that that may make its way to the book. To them I am forever indebted.

I had never read a non-syllabus full-length English book till I attended college. From that to this, my first book is a journey that has thrived on the kindness and generosity of countless known and unknown people. My gratitude to the following in no particular order:

Rajan Johri, for helping me find my initial path in Delhi.

Two public universities that made exceptional and affordable education accessible to people like me: Delhi University, Miranda House – I owe my life to the three years there; and Jamia Millia Islamia University, AJK Mass Communication Research Centre – it taught me that journalism must always question power.

I am grateful to the numerous feminists who have shaped me through their work and shaped my worldview.

All my editors, colleagues and mentors in the last seventeen years of my work life, including Harinder Baweja, Geeta Seshu, Siddharth Varadarajan, Kalpana Sharma, Krishna Prasad, Abhinandan Sekhri, Vinod Jose, Ammu Joseph, Laxmi Murthy, Arunava Sinha.

The Network of Women in Media India (NWMI), for being my sounding board and providing endless solidarity. Committee to Protect Journalists (CPJ), for always extending support. Santanu

Borthakur, Rebecca John and Kunal Majumder, for ensuring my freedom, every now and then.

Simar Puneet, for planting the thought that I could write a book too. Neyaz Farooquee, for his friendship, and for prodding me to put together a book proposal – without him there wouldn't have been a book at all.

The Appan Menon Memorial Grant, for kickstarting my research.

Ramachandra Guha, for his generosity. For opening doors to those who have no access and experience. For inspiring, mentoring and watching my back all along, when he didn't have to.

Everyone at the New India Fellowship: Rivka Israel, for patiently reading and editing early drafts and holding me accountable to deadlines; Yauvanika Chopra, for existing and for indulging me in discussing trash TV and vain thoughts in the middle of a workday.

Manoj Mitta, for his stellar journalism that has inspired me for decades. For offering to read my manuscript and giving crucial, sharp feedback.

Josy Joseph, for all his work and his kind support. For hand-holding my entry into the publishing world. For reading my manuscript at short notice and encouraging me.

Nivedita Menon, whose work has influenced all of my adulthood. For her kind words about the book.

Pratap Bhanu Mehta, for his bigheartedness, always. For getting the book and how.

Kanishka Gupta, my agent and guide, for helping me navigate a new world with confidence. At Footnote, Vidisha Biswas for her thoughtfulness and for championing the book. Natasha Drewett and Djinn von Noorden, for astute reading and making the book legible for readers outside India.

At Juggernaut, my publisher Chiki Sarkar, for accepting the book. Nishtha Kapil, Rimli Borooah, Shyama Warner and Devangana Ojha for their patience, and sharp eyes to make the book better.

Parth Mehrotra is the best editor one can have. For being straightforward but gentle. For pushing and believing in me and the book, in moments when I didn't. For teaching me so much through his words and actions.

The friends who helped in the last few years of total seclusion. Who allow me to be vulnerable, nurture me with love and warmth, and fill my cup that runs empty so very often: Mallika Taneja, Shipra Nigam, Rakhi Sehgal, Aastha Dang, Bhanu Pratap, Ajoy Ashirwad, Manjusha Madhu, Aswathy Senan, Ashley NP, Shashank Shekhar, Padma Priya, Sana Fazili, Anita Cheria and Bhavna Kumar.

My family: Achla Sawhney for being there; Eera and Ishan, for bringing joy.

Mayank Dixit, my elder brother, for the countless pocket monies, and for introducing me to books, newspapers and magazines. Devi Dixit, my mother, for motivating me to write, and for passing on her love of films and literature to us. But most importantly to both of them for standing by my life choices at crucial moments and helping me do my thing, in my own way. Not many get this invaluable backing.

Mirchi – my cat – my home, companion, co-writer, protector-in-chief.

Nakul Singh Sawhney, my enabler, my love, my world, whose *ishq* brings me *barqat*.

Index

Aadhaar cards 149, 151, 259, 266, 268–9, 274–6
AAP (Aam Aadmi Party) 216, 284
abortion 94, 125
  sex-selective 127
ABVP (Akhil Bharatiya Vidyarthi Parishad) 260
Adityanath, Yogi 222, 284, 284
Advani, L. K. 20–3, 26, 259
Aggarwal, J.P. 61
agricultural workers 155, 157
Ahmad Shah mausoleum, Banaras 29–31
air pollution 64–5, 66, 160
Allah Wali mosque, Karawal Nagar 225–6, 288–9
almond processing 151–2, 159–62
almond workers' strike 161–71
Almond Workers' Union (Badaam Mazdoor Union) 151–4
Ansari, Dr Anees 25
antakshari 146
Arjun Sengupta Committee 127
Arvind Mills 87

attachment of property (*kurki*) 34
Auliya mosque, Shiv Vihar 289
Ayodhya 20–1, 277 *see also* Babri mosque; Ram temple

Babri mosque, Ayodhya 20, 28–9, 33, 62, 178, 277, 289
Bachchan, Amitabh 6, 13, 23, 153
Badaam Mazdoor Union (Almond Workers' Union) 151–4
Bagga, Tajinder Pal 283
Bajrangi, Babu 220
Balmiki community 249
Banaras (Kashi, Varanasi) 1–3, 20
Bangladesh 67, 260–1 *see also* refugees
Begum Samru 141–2
Bengal 261
Best City Mall, Delhi 236–54
Bhagirath Palace, Chandni Chowk 138, 140, 143
Bharti, Uma 28
Bhojpur district, Bihar 155–6
Bhumihars 156
Bigul Mazdoor Dasta 151

biometric identification cards *see* Aadhaar cards
Bisht, Gopi 191, 199, 203–4, 273, 284
BJP (Bharatiya Janata Party) 20, 22–3, 27, 61–3, 203–4, 206, 220–2, 259–60, 271–2, 282–5
Brahmins 21, 80–1, 91, 156

CAA (Citizenship Amendment Act) (2019) 278
   protests against 279, 281–3
cancer 92
cash economy 226–7
Chandni Chowk, Delhi 51, 61–2, 138
Chandra Shekhar 26
Chauhanpatti, Delhi 75
child labour 104, 107–10
cholera 106–7
Chugh, Tarun 283
cinema 6, 8, 17–18, 36
Citizenship Amendment Bill (2003) 259
Clean India Mission 247
Congress party 23, 28, 61–2, 159
construction sites 212–13
COVID-19 291–2
cows
   urine products 217–19
   protection 220, 223 *see also* GRF (Gau Raksha Front)
CRPF (Central Reserve Police Force) 25, 288

cybercafes 267 *see also* internet access

dairies 182–3, 221
Dalits (Scheduled Caste) 19, 33, 156–8, 249
dargahs *see* mausoleums
Delhi
   assembly elections (2020) 282–4
   floods 91
   languages 60
   migration to 70
   slum clearance 67
Delhi Master Plan 65, 96
Delimitation Act (1972) 97
demonetization 226–8, 253–4
dengue fever 64, 92
Digital India programme 267
Digital Seva Centres 267–9
Dixit, S. C. 24
DTC (Delhi Transport Corporation) 130, 195, 274

East Bengal 261
East Pakistan 67, 260–1
Election Commission 142–3
elections *see* general elections *and under* Delhi
electoral fraud 143
electronic voting machines (EVM) 142–4
electronics industry 137, 140, 142
e-waste 144–5

facility management (FM) industry 236–7, 240–2, 245–6, 252, 255–6
factories 64–5, 68, 72–3, 86, 93, 114, 116–22, 131–3, 161–2, 210, 217–18, 227
Factories Act 140
Factory Act (1948) 149
factory closures 64, 67
FIFA World Cup 2002 104

Gadodia Market, Delhi 54–5
Gandhi, Indira 28, 294
Gandhi, Mahatma 206, 272
Gandhi, Maneka 217
garment industry 86–90, 128–9, 227
Gau Raksha Prakostha 222
general elections
    1984 20
    1989 20
    1991 22–4
    1996 61–3, 271
    2004 142–3
    2014 203–4
Ghaziabad 68, 133, 212, 249–50
Global March Against Child Labour 104
Godowlia 18, 23
GRF (Gau Raksha Front) 220–4, 276
Gujarat riots 112, 178, 220
Gujjarpatti, Delhi 75
Gujjars 75, 78, 80, 91, 221
Gulab Bai 5, 8

Gyanvapi mosque, Banaras 24, 32, 38, 216

haemophilia 84
healthcare work 125
Hindu Kanya Raksha Samiti 202
Hindu Sena 284
Hindu supremacism 19–20, 112, 189, 214, 260–1, 283, 291
Hindutva 20, 62, 206, 216, 260
HKRF (Hindu Kanya Raksha Front) 192–3, 196–200, 205–6, 215, 220
Holi 81–2
home-based workers 96–7, 102–5, 108, 123–6, 128–9, 134, 150–3, 227 *see also* piece work
housing societies 212

IM (Indian Mujahideen) 178–9
immigrants
    from Bangladesh 260, 271
        see also refugees
    illegal 259, 271, 278
industrial action *see* strikes
informal economy 226
internet access 54, 267–8
Inter-State Migrant Workmen Act 149
Islam 29, 94, 126, 196, 209, 222, 241

Jain, J.P. 61–2
Jain Studios 61

Jamia Millia Islamia University 279, 282, 284
Jamna Paar, Delhi *see* Yamuna Paar
jeans *see* garment manufacturing
Joshi, Murli Manohar 28

Karawal Nagar, Delhi 95–8, 108, 123, 160
   temples 220
Kargil war 258–9
Kashi *see* Banaras
Kashi Vishvanath Mandir Mukti Samiti (Committee for the Liberation of the Kashi Vishwanath temple) 37–8
Kashi Vishwanath temple, Banaras 24, 28
Kashmir 271–2
   separatism 21, 62
Khan, Salman 18, 174–5
Khan, Ustad Bismillah 3
Khari Baoli, Delhi 54
Kumar, Akshay 87
kurki (attachment of property) 34

land reform 155–6
landlordism 183–5, 192
left-wing groups 156
Lohta 9–10, 19, 25, 27, 33–4
Lohta riots 30
Loni, Ghaziabad 130, 191, 294
'love jihad' 189, 192–3, 196–8

Madanpura 9, 25, 37
Madanpura riots 23–5

Mahadalits 155
Mandal Commission 21
marriage, inter-faith 201–3
Mathura 20
mausoleums (dargahs), Sufi 10–11 *see also* Ahmad Shah mausoleum
Mehtar caste 235
migrants 10–11, 65, 70, 87–8, 91, 95, 97, 125, 155, 177–8, 184–5, 188, 191, 211, 228, 232, 238, 272 *see also* immigrants
Mishra, Kapil 285
Modi, Narendra 203, 205, 216–17, 220, 226, 285, 291
Momin Ansaris 4, 19
multinational companies 96, 102, 105, 109
Musahars 155–7
Muslim League 4
Muslims *see also* Rohingya Muslims
   discrimination against 278, 293
   hate crimes against 221–4
   hostility to/attacks on 91, 178, 285–91 *see also* riots, Hindu–Muslim
Mustafabad, Delhi 97
Muzaffarnagar riots 190–2
Myanmar 278

Narasimha Rao, P. V. 26
Nasbandi Colony, Ghaziabad 294

National Capital Region 137
National Food Security Act (2013) 269
National Social Security Board 150
nautanki 3–4, 6, 63
NIA (National Investigative Agency) 179
Noida (New Okhla Industrial Development Area) 137
North East Delhi constituency 133–4
NRC (National Register of Citizens) 62, 259–60, 278–82, 284
    in Assam 275
    protests against 279, 281–3

Other Backward Classes (OBCs) 19, 21–2, 75

PAC (Provincial Armed Constabulary) 25, 30–3, 36
Paharganj, Delhi, explosion 62–3
Pakistan 20, 258–9
partition of India 4, 20
Personal laws 19
Phoolan Devi 63
piece work 89, 92, 95–7, 101–2, 128, 134
police bribery 53, 178
police brutality 31–3, 176–8, 180
police searches 25
pollution *see* air pollution; water pollution
pollution controls 89, 93
porters 52, 55–7
Pre-Conception and Pre-Natal Diagnostic Techniques (PCPNDT) Act (1994) 127
prisons 177

raisins, cleaning 58–60
Ram Janmabhoomi campaign 20–3, 58, 61
Ram Lalla 277
Ram Rajya 272
Ram temple, Ayodhya 58, 61–2, 271, 277
Ranvir Sena 156–7
rape *see* sexual violence
RMM (Rashtriya Muslim Manch) 222
'red armies' 156
refugees 67, 198, 260
    from Bangladesh 74, 260
    Muslim 260
    from Myanmar 260
    Tibetan 198
relief camps, Delhi 290, 292
riots, Hindu–Muslim 22–3, 28, 30, 190 *see also* Gujarat riots; Lohta riots; Madanpura riots; Muzaffarnagar riots; Shamli riots
Rohingya Muslims 260, 278
RSS (Rashtriya Swayamsevak Sangh) 20–1, 112, 192, 206, 214–16, 222, 260
Ruf N Tuf 87

Sabhapur, Delhi 68, 75, 77, 87, 123, 211
Sangh Parivar 20–1, 24, 28, 58, 61, 74, 217
Sarva Shiksha Abhiyan 123
Savarkar, V.D. 206–7
Scheduled Castes *see* Dalits
sexual harassment 139, 148, 150, 169
sexual violence 157–8, 175–6, 190, 192
    protests against 175–6, 181
Shah, Amit 271, 274, 283
Shamli riots 190
shocker repair shops 173
Signature Bridge, Delhi 265
Sikhs 2, 19, 28–9
Singh, Kalyan 22
Singh, Manmohan 26
Singh, Raja 221
Singh, V. P. 21, 26
slums 67, 117, 184, 186
Special Marriage Act 201–2
spices, cleaning 60–1
Sriram Colony, Delhi 215–16
sterilization programme 294
street sweepers 249
strikes 161–71
Subhash Pandit 80–2, 92
Sufism 10, 29
Sukhbir Singh Gujjar 75–6, 78, 80–5, 92
sweatshops 108, 116, 178

technology industry 137–8
Thakur, Anurag 283
Thakurs 33, 75
Tiwari, Manoj 272–3
trade unions 152–4 *see also* strikes
Trans Yamuna, Delhi *see* Yamuna Paar
Trivedi, Anil 216, 273
Tronica City, Delhi 130–3
Trump, Donald 285, 292

UHF (United Hindu Front) 276–7, 279, 291, 294
Unorganised Workers' Social Security Act (2008) 149–51
unorganized workers 127–8, 149–50, 236
Uttar Pradesh (UP) 1, 22, 30, 65, 68, 91, 238–9

Vajpayee, Atal Bihari 62–3, 258–9
Varanasi *see* Banaras
Vardhan, Dr Harsh 206
VHP (Vishwa Hindu Parishad) 20, 24, 191

water pollution *see* Delhi
weaving industry 2, 9, 26–7
West Bengal 261
West Pakistan 260

Yamuna Paar (Jamna Paar, Trans Yamuna), Delhi 67–8, 70, 75, 117